HEALTHWISE®
HANDBOOK

A SELF-CARE MANUAL FOR YOU

Canadian Edition

■ Donald W. Kemper
The Healthwise Staff
Diana Stilwell, Editor

A Healthwise® Publication
Healthwise, Incorporated, Boise, Idaho
(A not-for-profit organization)
Twelfth Edition

Standard Healthwise cover design by Beth Workman

Illustrations by Consuelo Udave, June Perry, and Mac Browning

Healthwise Handbook, Twelfth Edition, 1995

Copyright © 1976, 1991, 1995 by Healthwise, Incorporated, P.O. Box 1989, Boise, Idaho 83701.

First Edition, 1976
Second Edition, 1978
Third Edition, 1979
Fourth Edition, 1983
Fifth Edition, 1985
Sixth Edition, 1986
Seventh Edition, 1987
Eighth Edition, 1989
Ninth Edition, 1990
Tenth Edition, 1991
Eleventh Edition, 1994
Twelfth Edition, 1995

12hwhb-Canada-8-97

ISBN:1-877930-33-4

Printed in the United States of America.

Table of Contents

Part III: Staying Healthy

Part IV: Self-Care Resources

To Our Readers

No book can replace the need for doctors — and no doctor can replace the need for people to care for themselves. The purpose of this book is to help you and your doctors work together to manage your health problems.

The *Healthwise Handbook* includes basic guidelines on how to recognize and cope with over 180 of the most common health problems. These guidelines are based on sound medical information from leading medical and consumer publications, with review and input from doctors, nurses, pharmacists, physical therapists, and other health professionals. We have worked to present the information in a straightforward way that is free from medical jargon. We hope you find it easy to read and easy to use.

While this book does not eliminate the need for professional medical help, it does provide a better basis for you to work with your doctors to prevent and jointly care for health problems. If you receive professional advice in conflict with this book, look first to your health professional. Because your doctor is able to take your specific history and needs into consideration, his or her recommendations may prove to be the best.

You will notice that, throughout the book, references are made to brand names for a variety of medications and preparations. The use of brand names is strictly for educational purposes and should not be interpreted as an official endorsement of these products. The decision about what product to purchase resides entirely with you, your health care provider, and your pharmacist.

We have made our best effort to create a publication that uses the most up-to-date information available and is in accordance with current standards of practice.

We are continually adding to and improving the book. If you have a suggestion that will make this book better, please send it to *Healthwise Handbook*, P.O. Box 1989, Boise, ID 83701

We wish you the best of health!

Disclaimer

This book is intended to provide you with a wide range of medical and health information to assist you in making appropriate health care decisions. Readers should be aware that this publication does not in any way replace consultation with a medical practitioner, nor is it intended to act as a substitute for any treatment prescribed by your doctor. The authors or publishers are not responsible for any problems that may develop from use or misuse of the information provided in this book. If you suspect that you have a medical condition or problem, or if any self-care recommendations fail to provide positive results within a reasonable period, please consult a competent health care professional.

About Healthwise

Healthwise is a nonprofit organization working to help people do a better job of staying healthy and taking care of their health problems. Since its founding in 1975, Healthwise has won awards of excellence and recognition from the Centers for Disease Control, the U.S. Department of Health and Human Services, the American Society on Aging, and the World Health Organization.

Our clients range from volunteer organizations and church groups to Fortune 500 companies, major unions, state and provincial governments, hospitals, insurers, and health maintenance organizations.

For more information on the programs or publications below please contact Healthwise at P.O. Box 1989, Boise, ID 83701, (208) 345-1161.

Healthwise Program - This nationally replicated program gives consumers the resources and skills to improve the quality of care provided at home, and helps them decide when to call a health professional. Program components include the *Healthwise Handbook* and self-care workshop (live or video-based).

The *Healthwise Handbook* has been translated into Spanish and German (for Switzerland). A South African edition is also available, as well as this edition adapted for Canadian content.

Healthwise for Life - Meets the self-care and medical consumerism needs of older adults, retirees, and MediCare participants. Program components include the award-winning *Healthwise for Life: Medical Self-Care for Healthy Aging* handbook and Healthwise for Life workshop (live or video-based).

It's About Time: Better Health Care in a Minute (or two) - This 32-page booklet offers quick, easy-to-use action steps that promote good doctor-patient relationships.

Partnership Program - This training and orientation program helps health professionals learn how they can better support their patients' self-care efforts (CME credit).

Pathways - A guilt-free approach to healthy changes in ten areas, including stress, nutrition, fitness, smoking, alcohol and drugs, and relationships. The handbook, *Pathways: A Success Guide to a Healthy Life,* is the cornerstone of the interactive Pathways workshop.

Growing Wiser - The book, *Growing Wiser: The Older Person's Guide to Mental Wellness,* and Growing Wiser workshops focus on memory improvement, mental vitality, coping with loss and life change, maintaining independence, and self-esteem for older adults.

Healthwise Knowledgebase™ - This electronic health information system is used by managed care organizations, health clinics, nurse call centres, and as part of online services. The *Knowledgebase* compiles health information from medical resources, is written in consumer-friendly language, and is organized around medical decision points.

Acknowledgements

This 12th Edition of the *Healthwise Handbook* combines the best of old and new. The 1st Edition, published in 1976, was written and edited with major contributions from Kathleen McIntosh and Toni Roberts. Since then, scores of people have helped to improve and update the book.

The current edition reflects an extensive review by the physicians of Kaiser Permanente, Northern California Region, which was coordinated by Steven Freedman, MD. Their many helpful comments and suggestions have contributed greatly to the quality of the entire book.

Special thanks go to Diana Stilwell, Editor, and to Molly Mettler, who was a major contributor to the writing and editing. The proofreading and editing assistance of Jean Miller and Jane Woychick, Associate Editors, and the layout and production work of Andrea Blum, Terrie Britton, and Cindy Hovland are greatly appreciated. Carrie Wiss, Viki Smith, and Nancy Van Dinter also provided invaluable assistance.

This book would not be possible without extensive help and guidance from health professionals. In particular, thanks go to Steven Schneider, MD, who was the principal medical reviewer for this edition, and to David Sobel, MD, MPH, whose role in the Kaiser Permanente review was greatly appreciated. In addition, the following health professionals were particularly helpful.

Physicians

Janet Aguilar, MD

Richard Aptaker, DO

Paul H. Baehr, MD

Timothy Batchelder, MD

Richard Blickenstaff, MD

William S. Bourquard, MD

Wayne Coleman, MD

Thomas M. Cornwall, MD

Bruce Davis, MD

Gail Eberharter, MD

Patricia G. Engasser, MD

Michael Felder, MD

Ira Fielding, MD

Andrew Fox, MD

William Fuchs, MD

Marty Gabica, MD

Michael P. Gibson, MD

Ira Golditch, MD

Matthew Handley, MD

C. Dan Henderson, MD

Raymond Hilsinger, MD

J. Chris Kantarian, MD

Elisabeth Kelley, MD

Robert Klein, MD

Craig Koch, MD

Roger F. Lake, MD

Robert LaPerriere, MD

Spenser Larsen, MD

Felicity McNichol, MD

Edwin Matthes, DDS

Marti W. Nelson, MD

Dennis Mills, MD

W. Christian Oakley, MD

Albert M. Palitz, MD

James T. Pozniakas, MD

Vincent Quintana, MD

Peter Roan, MD

Physicians - continued

T. Steven Roosevelt, MD, PhD,
    FCLM, CDE
Cajsa Schumacher, MD
Warren Scott, MD
Stanford Shoor, MD
Gary Stein, MD
William Sueksdorf, MD

William Teubl, MD
Stanley Tillinghast, MD, MPA
Carol Weed, MD
Madelyn Weiss, MD
Michael Weiss, MD, MPH
Carl F. Wurster, MD, FACS

Nurses and Nurse Practitioners

Andrea Bickert, NP
Marian Broida, RN
Gene Drabinski, RN
Judy Dundas, RN
Jayne Hanich, RN
Randi Holland, RN

Sheri Rickman, RN
Margo Sturgis, RN, GNP
Kristine Theis, FNP
Susan Van Houten, RN, BSN
Susie Whittinghill, RN
The staff of Employee Managed
Care Corporation

Physical Therapist

Lynn Johnson, PT, ATR

Health Educators

Frances D. Alves, MPH
Joyce O. Arango, DrPH
Patricia M. Forman, MPH
Bob Gorsky, PhD
Joan Greathouse, MED
Jim Giuffré, MPH
Pamela J. Larson, MPH

Nutritionists

Susan Kayman, DrPH, RD
Ruth Schneider, RD, MPH

Physician's Assistant

Rebecca A. Goldsmith, PA-C

We also wish to thank those health professionals and consumers whose review, suggestions, and input on previous editions were the foundation for the current book.

Most of all, we would like to thank the millions of medical consumers who use the *Healthwise Handbook*. It is your actions that reward us the most and inspire us to constantly look for ways to improve this handbook.

Funding for the development of the original *Healthwise Handbook* was provided by the W.K. Kellogg Foundation of Battle Creek, Michigan.

Donald W. Kemper, President
Healthwise, Incorporated
August, 1997

Canadian Acknowledgements

The Canadian edition of the *Healthwise Handbook* reflects an extensive review by health professionals and others, not all of whom can be listed here. Their many helpful comments and suggestions have contributed to a successful adaptation of this book for a Canadian audience. This book would not be possible without the extensive help and guidance of health professionals.

In particular, thanks go to Brian Winsby, MD, the principal reviewer for the British Columbia Medical Services Commission; Andrew Larder, MD, the principal reviewer for the Calgary Regional Health Authority; and Golda Goldman, the principal reviewer for Health Alliance. Special thanks also to Ernest Higgs, MD, and Laurel Brunke, MSN, for their respective contributions to the British Columbia review.

Acknowledgement and gratitude are extended to the following individuals for their role in the review and revision of the book:

Darlene Abbott, MSc
Vicki Anderson, RN
Richard Backus, MD
Mary Bates, BScN
Tom Bailey, MD
June Bergman, MD
B.C. Ministry of Health
  library staff
Linda Campbell, BSR
Linda Carswell
Barbara Clough, MA
Mark Collison, MPA
Cliff Cornish, MLS
Shiela Early, BScN
John Forster-Coull, PharmD
Cory Gurevitz, MBA
Sharon Harold, MA
Rick Hudson, MD
Andrew Hume
Patricia Kaatz, RN
Dianne Kirkpatrick
Pearl Lo, BNS

Bob Mackie, BEd
Colleen Maloney, BSN
Lorraine McMillen, BN
Esther Moghadam, MEd
Eileen Moritz, MEd
Val Munroe, RN
Richard Musto, MD
Karen Pielak, BSN
Howard Platt, MD
Doris Schuh, RD
Martin Serediak, PhD
Janice Sorested, BSN
Heather Thomas, RN
Lois Toms, LLB
Cathy Ulrich, BSN
Malcolm Williamson, BDS

Introduction

The *Healthwise Handbook* can help improve your health and lower costs associated with your health care. We hope it is a book you will turn to time and again as health problems arise.

The book is divided into four sections:

Self-Care Basics. What you need to know to be a wise medical consumer.

Health Problems. Prevention, treatment, and when to call a doctor for over 180 common illnesses and injuries.

Staying Healthy. Tips and techniques for dental health, fitness, nutrition, stress management, and mental wellness.

Self-Care Resources. How to manage medications and what you need to have on hand in your home to cope with health problems.

Most people will not read through the book from cover to cover in one sitting. It is more of a topic-by-topic book that you can use to look up what you need when a problem or interest develops.

We do recommend that you read pages 1 and 2 and three special chapters right away:

Page 1, **The Healthwise Approach,** is a process to follow every time a health problem arises. Page 2, the **Ask-the-Doctor Checklist,** will help you get the most out of every doctor visit.

Chapter 1, **The Wise Medical Consumer,** offers important information you can use to improve the quality of your health and reduce costs to the health care system.

Chapter 2, **Prevention and Early Detection,** lists the immunizations and screening tests that are important to staying healthy and detecting health problems early.

Chapter 19, **Your Home Health Center,** lists medications, supplies, equipment, and resources you may wish to keep on hand.

The rest of the information in the book is there when you need it. We have enjoyed writing this book and keeping it up to date. We hope it will help you succeed in better managing your health problems.

The Healthwise Approach

Step 1. Observe the problem.

- When did it start? What are the symptoms? _____
_____
_____
_____
_____

- Where is the pain? Dull ache or stabbing pain? Comes and goes?
Constant?_____
_____

- Measure your vital signs:

  Temperature:_____   Blood pressure:_____ / _____

  Pulse:_____ / minute   Breaths:_____ / minute

- Think back:

  Have you had this problem before?   Yes _____   No _____

  What did you do for it:? _____
  _____

  Any changes in your life (stress, medications, food, exercise, etc.)?
  _____
  _____

  Does anyone else at home or work have these symptoms?_____

Step 2. Learn more about it.

- *Healthwise Handbook* (note page number): _____
- Other books or articles: _____
- Advice from others (lay or professional): _____

Step 3. Make an action plan.

- Your "tentative" diagnosis: _____
- Home care plan: _____
- _____
- When to call your doctor: _____

Step 4. Evaluate your progress.

- Are your actions working? _____

Ask-the-Doctor Checklist

Before the visit:

- Complete the Healthwise Approach on page 1 and take it with you.
- Take a list of medications and record of last visit for similar problems.

During the visit:

- State your main problem first.
- Describe your symptoms (use page 1).
- Describe past experiences with the same problem.

Write down:

- Temperature: _____ Blood pressure: _____ / _____
- The diagnosis (what's wrong). _____
- The prognosis (what might happen next)._____
- Your self-care plan (what you can do at home). _____
  _____
  _____

For drugs, tests, and treatments, ask: (See pages 8 to 10.)

- What's its name?_____
- Why is it needed? _____
- What are the costs and risks? _____
- Are there alternatives? _____
- What if I do nothing? _____
- (For drugs) How do I take this? _____
- (For tests) How do I prepare? _____

At the end of the visit, ask:

- Am I to return for another visit?_____
- Am I to phone in for test results? _____
- What danger signs should I look for?_____
- When do I need to report back? _____
- What else do I need to know?_____
  _____
  _____
  _____

*You, the individual, can do more for your health and
well-being than any doctor, any hospital, any drug,
and any exotic medical device.*
Joseph Califano

Chapter 1

The Wise Medical Consumer

The quality of your medical care depends more on you than on your doctor.

To become a wise medical consumer, start with three basic principles:

- Work in partnership with your health care provider.

- Share in every medical decision.

- Become skilled at obtaining medical care.

By following these three principles, you will gain more control over the quality of your health care as well as play an active role in helping better manage costs to our health care system.

Work in Partnership With Your Health Care Provider

Good partnerships are based on **a common goal, shared effort, and good communication.** If you and

your health care provider can make these things happen, you will both gain from the partnership. You will get better care and your health care provider will practise good medicine.

Five Ways to Be a Good Partner

1. Take good care of yourself. Both you and your health care provider would prefer that you don't get sick in the first place. And if problems arise, you both want a return to good health as soon as possible.

2. At the first sign of a health problem, observe and record your symptoms. Your record of symptoms will help both you and your health care provider make an accurate diagnosis. And the better job you do recording early symptoms, the better you and your health care provider can manage the problem later.

- Keep written notes on the symptoms. Record when, how long, how painful, etc., for each symptom.

- Note anything unusual that might be related to the problem.

- Measure and record vital signs. See page 22.

- Add regular updates and watch your progress. Are your symptoms getting better or worse?

3. Practise medical self-care at home. As the front-line partner, you can manage a lot of minor health problems on your own. Use this book, your own experience, and help from others to create a self-care plan.

- Learn all you can about the problem.

- Keep notes on your self-care plan and what you do.

- Note whether home treatment seems to help.

- Set a time to visit a health professional if the problem continues.

4. Prepare for office visits. Most medical appointments are scheduled for 10 to 15 minutes to deal with one problem. The better organized you are, the more valuable the visit.

- Prepare an Ask-the-Doctor Checklist like the one on page 2.

- Update and bring a list of symptoms and your self-care plan.

- Write down your main concern (chief complaint) and practise describing it. Your health care provider will want to hear that first.

- Write down your hunches or fears about what is wrong. These are often helpful to your health care provider.

- Write down three questions you want answered the most. (There may not be time to ask a long list of questions.)

- Bring along a list of the medications you are taking.

5. Play an active role in the medical visit.

- State your main concern, describe your symptoms, and share your hunches and fears.

- Be honest and straightforward. Don't hold anything back because of embarrassment. If you don't intend to fill a prescription, say so. If you are getting alternative treatment such as acupuncture or chiropractic treatments, let your doctor know. To be a good partner, your doctor or health care provider has to know what's going on.

- If your doctor prescribes a drug, test, or treatment, get more information. See page 7.

- Take notes. Write down the diagnosis, the treatment and follow-up plan, and what you can do at home. Then read it back to your health care provider to be sure you have it right.

Finding the Right Health Care Provider

If you don't have a family doctor (primary care physician), now is the time to get one. Everyone needs a regular doctor. Over time, your regular doctor becomes familiar with your personal health care needs and can ensure continuity in providing the care you may require. A variety of physicians working on separate health problems may not see the whole picture. When choosing a family doctor there are lots of questions to ask, but these three matter most:

- Is this doctor well-trained and experienced?
- Will this doctor be available when needed?
- Will this doctor work in partnership with me?

Training and Experience

For most people, a good choice for a family doctor is a college-certified family practice doctor. In choosing a family doctor, you have every right to ask about their training and how much experience they have had as a practising, licensed physician. You might also consider asking if they have areas of special interest that relate to your own circumstances, such as working with the elderly, young families, or children. It is also important to know the views of your family doctor regarding how they work with other medical specialists. See page 11 for a brief description of medical specialists.

Availability

Because health problems rarely develop when it's convenient, ask your health care provider what their office hours are and how they manage after-hour inquiries.

- What are the office hours?
- If I called right now for an office visit, how soon could I be seen?
- How much time is allowed for an office visit?

- Will the doctor discuss health problems over the phone?
- Does this doctor work with other health care providers? If so, ask who they are, what their area of expertise or speciality is, and why he/she chose them for referrals. A physician's relationship with other health professionals is important.

Partner Potential

During your first visit, tell your doctor that you would like to share in making treatment decisions.

Pay attention to how you feel during the visit.

- Does the doctor listen well?
- Do you think you could build a good working partnership with this doctor?
- If the answer is "no," consider looking for another doctor.

But I Want a Take-Charge Doctor

Not everyone wants to be a partner with their doctor. Maybe you don't like to ask questions and you don't want to share in any decisions.

Would you rather just let your doctor tell you what is best for you? If that's what you prefer, tell your doctor. Most physicians have a lot of patients who do not want to be a partner. Let the doctor know what you expect.

Is It Time for a Change?

If you are unhappy with how your doctor treats you, it may be time for a change. Before you start looking for a new health care provider, tell your current doctor how you would like to

Other Health Care Providers

There are many kinds of health care professionals, in addition to medical doctors, that can assist you with a health condition. Here is a description of some health professions:

Chiropractic: Diagnosis and treatment, mainly of back and neck pain, based on the relationship between the spine and the nervous system.

Massage Therapy: The practice of working by hand on painful or injured muscles, connective tissue, and joints.

Naturopathy: A drugless system of therapy, making use of natural substances and treatments.

Optometry: The diagnosis and treatment of the eyes, including vision care and the prescription of corrective lenses.

Physical Therapy: Therapy directed towards prevention and alleviation of movement dysfunction.

Podiatry: The diagnosis and treatment (surgical and nonsurgical) of foot problems.

Psychology: Therapy for mental and emotional problems.

be treated. Your doctor would probably be pleased to work with you as a partner—if only you would say that's what you want. Otherwise, your doctor may think that you, like many other patients, want your health care provider to do all the work.

Share in Every Medical Decision

Except in an emergency, you cannot be given a treatment or test without your "informed consent." You must be informed of the risks and agree to the treatment. In a partnership, however, informed consent may not be enough. The real goal is **shared decision-making,** where you actively participate in medical decisions.

Why should you help make decisions with your doctor? Isn't the doctor paid for knowing what to do? Well, the choices aren't always black and white. With many health problems, there is more than one option. Consider these examples:

You have moderately high blood pressure (160/95). Your doctor says that exercise and diet might bring it down, but most people don't succeed that way. Your doctor recommends you start on medication to control it. You would rather try exercise and lose weight than take pills for the rest of your life. The best decision depends on your values.

Your three-year-old has a headache and a fever. The doctor says it's probably nothing to worry about, but you say your hunch is that it might be meningitis. Some testing may be appropriate.

You have been suffering from carpal tunnel syndrome for several months. Your doctor is now recommending a wrist splint and a steroid injection. You would prefer trying just the splint with aspirin first. If that doesn't work, you will consider other medication. Your doctor agrees that this is a good plan.

In each case, the treatment you choose will have an effect on your life. Therefore, the best medicine for you combines your doctor's medical expertise with your personal values.

Eight Ways to Share in Medical Decisions

1. Let your doctor know what you want. Tell your doctor that you want to help make decisions about what to do for your health problems.

2. Do your own research. Sometimes you need to learn things on your own before you can fully understand what your doctor is saying. See "Do Your Own Research" on page 14 for some ways to get the information you need.

3. Ask "why?" Always ask "why?" before agreeing to any medical test, medication, or treatment. Asking why may help you discover another option that better meets your needs.

4. Ask about alternatives. Learn enough to understand the options your doctor thinks are feasible.

5. Consider watchful waiting. Ask your doctor if it would be risky to wait a while (day, week, month) before treatment.

6. State your preferences. Tell your doctor if you prefer one option over another based on your personal desires and values.

7. Compare expectations. Tell your doctor what you are expecting from the treatment and ask if that is realistic. If appropriate, discuss side effects, pain, recovery time, long-term limitations, etc.

8. Accept responsibility. When you make shared decisions with your doctor, both of you must accept the responsibility for the outcomes.

Shared Decisions About Medical Tests

Medical tests are important tools, but they have limits. Some people think that the more tests they have, the better off they'll be. Wise consumers know medical tests have costs and risks as well as benefits. To help your doctor make good choices about tests for you, *you* need to:

Learn the basics.

- What is the name of the test and why do I need it?

- If the test is positive, what will the doctor do differently?

- What could happen if I don't have the test?

Consider the risks and benefits.

- How accurate is the test? How often does it indicate a problem exists when there is none (false positive)? How often does it say there is no problem when there is one (false negative)?

- Is the test painful? What can go wrong?

- How will I feel afterward?

- Are there less risky alternatives?

Let your doctor know:

• Your concerns about the test.

• What you expect the test will do for you. Ask if that is realistic.

• Any medications you are taking.

• Whether you are pregnant or have other medical conditions.

• Your decision to accept the test.

If a test seems risky and not likely to change the recommended treatment, ask your doctor if you can avoid it. Try to agree on the best approach. **No test can be done without your permission.**

Once you agree to a test, ask what you can do to reduce the chance of errors. Ask about food, exercise, alcohol, or medications to avoid before the test. After the test, ask to review the results. Take notes for your home records. If the results are unexpected and the error rate of the test is high, consider redoing the test before basing further treatment on the results.

Shared Decisions About Medications

The first rule of medications is to know why you need each drug *before* you put it in your mouth, rub it on your skin, or whatever. The same as with medical tests, there are a few things you always need to know about medications.

Learn the basics.

• What is the name of the drug and why do I need it?

• How long does it take to work?

• How long will I need to take it?

• Are there non-drug alternatives?

Consider the risks and benefits.

• How much will this drug help?

• Are there side effects or other risks?

• Could this drug react with other drugs I am currently taking?

Ask about costs.

• How much does it cost?

• Is a generic drug available (same formula but at a lower cost)?

• Is there a similar drug that will work almost as well and be less expensive?

• Can I start with a prescription for a few days to make sure this medication agrees with me?

Medical Ping-Pong

Shared decision-making requires two-way communication, like playing a game of ping-pong.

Ping: You describe your symptoms, main concern, and hunches.

Pong: Your doctor makes a diagnosis and describes treatment options.

Ping: You tell your doctor your personal preferences or ask about other options.

Pong: Your doctor restates the options and how they relate to your preferences.

Ping: You accept one of the recommended options or learn more about what you should do.

With good two-way discussion, the chances are better that you will end up with the treatment plan that is best for you.

Let your doctor know:

- Your concerns about the drug.

- What you expect it will do.

- All other medications you are taking (including over-the-counter drugs).

- Whether or not you plan to fill the prescription and take the drug as prescribed.

Talk to your pharmacist.

Your pharmacist can be an excellent source for the most current information about over-the-counter and prescription drugs. By talking to your pharmacist about the medication recommended by your doctor, you can benefit from additional health care advice.

Shared Decisions About Surgery

Every surgery has risks. Only you can decide if the benefits are worth the risks. Are you willing to live with your problem or do you want to have the operation? The choice is yours.

Learn the basics.

- What is the name of the surgery?

- Get a description of the surgery.

- Why does my doctor think I need it?

- Is this surgery the common treatment for this problem? What are my other options?

- Are there alternative surgical approaches (such as using a laparoscope)?

Consider the risks and benefits.

- How many similar surgeries has this doctor performed?

- What is the success rate? What does success mean?

- What can go wrong? How often does this happen?

- How will I feel afterward? How long will it be until I'm fully recovered?

- How can I best prepare for the surgery and the recovery period?

- Can I avoid a general anesthetic?

Let your doctor know:

- How much the problem bothers you. Are you willing to put up with the symptoms to avoid surgery?

- Your concerns about the surgery.

- If you do not want to have the surgery at this time.

- If you want a second opinion. A second opinion is useful if you have any doubt that the proposed surgery is the best option for your problem. If you want a second opinion, ask your primary care doctor or your surgeon to recommend another specialist. Ask that your test results indicating the need for surgery be sent to the second doctor. Consider getting an opinion from a different type of doctor who treats similar problems.

Once you understand the risks and benefits of surgery, the decision is yours.

Become Skilled at Obtaining Health Care

If you have ever thought that the cost of your medical care doesn't matter because our public health care system pays the bills, please think again. We all pay for health care through our taxes to the government.

As medical costs go up, there is less money available for housing, education, wage increases, etc. These costs do affect us all.

Even though we don't pay individually for our medical care, the costs incurred from increasing demand do affect the ability of our health care system to provide the high quality of care that we are accustomed to. Wise and responsible health care consumers know about the cost of care and how to best use the system in an efficient and cost-effective way.

By each of us being a wise user, we can contribute to keeping the access to quality care for ourselves and for future generations.

Nine Ways to Safeguard Your Health and Cut Costs (but not quality)

1. Stay healthy. Healthy lifestyles and regular preventive services are the best ways to keep healthy and keep costs down. See Chapter 2. Also see Chapters 16, 17, and 18 for ideas on how to stay healthy your whole life.

2. Use self-care when you can. Every time you successfully manage a health problem at home, you reduce the cost of health care for yourself and others.

3. Get your professional care from a primary caregiver. Family physicians and other primary care providers are the best place to start for most health problems. See page 4 for more information.

4. Reduce your use of medical tests. Don't agree to expensive medical tests until you understand how they will help you. Unnecessary tests are often done because "it is standard practice." The only good reason to have a test is if the results of a test will alter your treatment and the benefits of the test outweigh the risks. No test can be done without your consent. See page 7 for more information.

5. Reduce your use of costly drugs. Ask your doctor or pharmacist about every prescribed medication. Ask what would happen if you chose not to take the medication. Don't expect to get a prescription for every illness; sometimes self-care or non-drug remedies are all you need. See page 8 for more information.

6. Use specialists only for special problems. Specialists are doctors with in-depth training and experience in a particular area of medicine. For example, a cardiologist has years of special training to deal with heart problems. A visit to a specialist usually costs the health system more than a visit to your family doctor, and the tests and treatment may be more expensive. Your family doctor can help you decide if and when you need the services of a specialist for a particular medical problem.

7. Use emergency services wisely. In life-threatening situations, modern emergency services are worth their weight in gold. However, emergency rooms cost two to three times more for common services than a doctor's office. Also, your records are not available, so emergency room doctors have no information on your medical history.

Hospital emergency rooms are set up to handle trauma and life-threatening cases. They are not set up to care for minor medical problems; and they do not work on a first-come, first-served basis. During busy times, people with minor illnesses may wait for hours.

Use good judgment in deciding to use emergency services. Whenever you feel you can apply home treatment safely and wait to see your regular doctor, do so. However, if you feel that it is an emergency situation, by all means go to the emergency department.

Prepare for the emergency room:

• Call ahead, if possible, to let them know you are coming.

• Call your doctor, if possible. He or she may meet you at the ER or call in important information.

• If there is time, take this book and your medical records with you:

  ○ Use page 1, the Healthwise Approach, to help you think through the problem and report symptoms to the doctor.

  ○ Use page 2, the Ask-the-Doctor Checklist, to organize questions for the doctor.

  ○ See pages 7 and 8 to review the medical test checklist.

  ○ Keep an updated home medical record, listing medications, past test results, and treatments, and bring it with you to the ER so the doctor can review it. Information about your allergies, medications, and conditions may be critical.

  ○ As soon as you arrive, tell the emergency room staff why you think it is an emergency.

Medical Specialists
Cardiologist: heart
Dermatologist: skin
Endocrinologist: diabetes and hormonal problems
Gastroenterologist: digestive system
Geriatrician: older adults
Gynecologist: female reproductive system
Internist: internal medicine
Neurologist: brain and nervous system
Oncologist: cancer
Ophthalmologist: eyes
Orthopedist: bones and joints
Otolaryngologist: ears, nose, and throat
Pediatrician: children
Psychiatrist: mental and emotional problems
Respirologist: lungs
Rheumatologist: arthritis and other connective tissue disorders
Urologist: urinary and male reproductive system

8. Use hospitals only when you need them. Almost half of all health care costs are for hospitalizations.

If you do need in-patient care, get in and out of the hospital as quickly as possible. This will help reduce both costs to the health care system and your risk of hospital-acquired infections.

Don't check in just for tests. Hospitalization is no longer needed for most medical tests. Ask if the tests can be done on an out-patient basis. If you agree to control your diet and activities, the doctor will usually support your request.

Try to avoid additional days in the hospital by bringing in extra help at home. Ask about home nursing services to help while you recover. With help available, many patients can shorten a hospital stay.

Hospitals are not the only choice for people with a terminal illness. Many people choose to spend their remaining time at home with people they know and love. Special arrangements for the needed care can be made through hospice care programs in most communities. Try "Hospice" in the Yellow Pages or ask your doctor.

Hospital Consumer Skills

When you need to be in the hospital, good consumer skills can help improve the quality of care you receive. However, if you are very sick, ask your spouse or a friend to help watch out for your best interests.

- Ask "why?" Don't agree to anything unless you have been given good reason. Agree only to those procedures that make sense for you.

- Provide an extra level of quality control. Check medications, tests, injections, and other treatments to

Wise Use of Ambulance Services

Call 911 or your local emergency department to dispatch an ambulance if:

Someone has symptoms of a heart attack: severe chest pain, sweating, shortness of breath. See page 91.

There is severe bleeding or blood loss. See page 216.

Someone is unconscious or is having significant difficulty breathing.

Someone is having a seizure.

You suspect a spinal or neck injury.

Do not call an ambulance if:

It is not an emergency.

Ambulance services are a precious and costly resource. If it is not an emergency, you may be preventing someone else from getting the emergency care they need to save their life.

see if they are correct. Your diligence can improve the quality of the care you receive.

- Know your rights. Remember that your care is a shared responsibility. Ask the hospital what you can expect, and be open about your health condition, such as whether you smoke, are on medications, or if you are seeing a specialist for care. The care you receive depends upon the information you provide—that's your responsibility.

- Be friendly and respectful toward the nurses and the aides. It can help make your stay in the hospital more pleasant for you and the staff.

9. Get smart about your medical needs. Learn as much as you can about your medical problem. Your research may turn up new options. See "Do Your Own Research" on page 14.

Remember—You Can...

- Ask to be spoken to in words you can understand.

- Ask for a clear and truthful explanation about what is wrong with you.

- Ask to read your medical records.

- Ask about the benefits and risks of a treatment and its alternatives.

- Ask about the cost of a test or treatment and if there is any charge to you.

- Share in all treatment decisions.

- Refuse any medical procedure.

Avoid Health Fraud and Quackery

Millions of people are taken in each year by medical fraud and worthless health products.

Bogus "cures" are advertised for many chronic problems, especially arthritis, cancer, baldness, impotence, or other conditions, targeting people who are ready to try anything. Unfortunately, those cures rarely help and often (one out of ten) can cause harmful side effects.

Be suspicious of products that:

- Advertise by testimonials.

- Claim to have a secret ingredient.

- Are not evaluated in prominent medical journals.

- Claim benefits that seem too good to be true.

- Are available only by mail.

Be suspicious of any doctor who:

- Prescribes medicines or gives injections at every visit.

- Promises a no-risk cure.

- Suggests something that seems unethical or illegal.

Trust Your Common Sense

Medicine is not as magical as we once thought. If someone takes time to explain a problem or a treatment to us, we can usually make a pretty good decision about what is best for us.

Use your common sense to become a working partner with your health care providers. The best medical tests, diagnosticians, and medical specialists are not enough. Good health care also requires your own common sense. It will help you find the care that is right for you and avoid services that you don't need.

If you trust your common sense, you are on your way to becoming a wise health care consumer.

Do Your Own Research

If you have a complicated problem, or want to know more about your options:

- Start by asking your doctor for any written information you could borrow.

- Review the introduction to the Self-Care Resources section on page 302 and the books and other publications on the pages that follow.

- Use your local library to help find additional information on your health problem.

- Call your hospital's medical library and ask if the librarian could help you look up answers to your questions.

- If your health plan or community health department has a health information resource line, call and ask if they can help.

- If you find something interesting, make a copy for your doctor and discuss it at your next visit.

Notes

Notes

*If I'd known I was going to live this long, I'd have
taken better care of myself.*
Eubie Blake

Chapter 2

Prevention and Early Detection

Prevention works! You and your family can save a lot of pain, worry, and money by avoiding health problems in the first place. If you can't prevent a problem altogether, the next best thing is to discover it early, when it is easy to treat. This chapter helps you do both.

Ten Ways to Stay Healthy

1. Immunize. Immunizations are the best bargain in health care. When you immunise, you prevent illness for your family and help prevent epidemics in your community. See page 18.

2. Keep moving. Any way you define it, fitness is essential to good health. Even moderate exercise makes a huge difference both in how you feel and what illnesses you get. For a three-part fitness plan, see page 241.

3. Eat right. Eating a well-balanced, low-fat diet of wholesome foods will keep you energetic and free of many illnesses. See Chapter 17. Consider breast-feeding your baby to help keep him or her in the best health. See page 150.

4. Control stress. Even with a hectic and hurried lifestyle, you can prevent stress from undermining your health. See page 248 for relaxation skills.

5. Be smoke-free. Smokers who quit gain tremendous health benefits. So do people who avoid second-hand smoke. See page 105.

6. Avoid drugs and excess alcohol. When you say "no" to drugs and limit what you drink, you prevent accidents and illnesses and avoid a lot of problems for yourself and your family. For more on drug and alcohol problems, see page 271.

7. Put safety first. Safety at home, at work, and at play, safe driving, firearm safety, and safe sex will all help keep you healthy.

8. Pursue healthy pleasures. Enjoy social activities with friends and family, take naps, relax during meals, play with kids, care for a pet—they all can add to your health. See Resource 122 on page 309.

9. Think well of yourself. A good self-image is the foundation of good health. For more on self-esteem and wellness, see page 283.

10. Promote peace. Peace on earth begins at home. Seek nonviolent ways of resolving conflicts at home, at school, at work, and in your community. See page 283.

Immunizations

Immunizations work by helping your immune system recognize and quickly attack diseases before they can cause problems. Some immunizations are given in a single shot while others require several shots over a period of time.

Childhood immunizations protect against pertussis (whooping cough), diphtheria, tetanus, polio, measles, mumps, rubella, and *haemophilus influenzae* type b. Booster shots for diphtheria and tetanus are needed every 10 years to maintain lifelong protection.

If your children are immunized, these serious illnesses will not be a problem. There is no need to delay immunizations because of colds or other minor illnesses.

> Contact your local health unit or public health office for a current provincial immunization schedule.

Be sure to keep good records. Children often need to show immunization records at school entry.

Diphtheria, Pertussis, and Tetanus (DPT)

Infectious diseases like diphtheria and pertussis were major killers before the DPT vaccine was developed. With proper immunization, these diseases are rare. The DPT vaccine also protects against tetanus ("lockjaw"), a bacterial infection that can result when a wound is contaminated. The bacteria enter the body through cuts and thrive only in the absence of oxygen. So, the deeper and narrower the wound, the greater the possibility of tetanus.

Childhood immunizations for these diseases are given together with a series of shots starting at age two months.

The first booster for diphtheria and tetanus is given between ages 14 and 16. After that, get a Td (tetanus and diphtheria) booster every 10 years.

Keeping up to date with Td boosters is important because tetanus can be fatal. If it has been at least five years since your last shot, and you have a wound (especially a puncture wound) that is very dirty or that you suspect may be contaminated, get a Td booster.

Polio

Polio is a viral illness that leads to loss of mobility or paralysis. It is rare today because of the polio vaccine. The first vaccine is given at age two months, and the series of immunizations gives lifelong immunity.

Nonimmunised adults need immunization only if they have a high risk of polio exposure, for example with foreign travel.

Measles, Mumps, and Rubella (MMR)

MMR is an immunization for measles, mumps, and rubella (German measles) (see page 165). Two shots are now recommended (check with your local health unit or public health office for recommended ages for receiving MMR). If both doses are given, no further MMR immunization is needed.

If you don't have records showing that you received two doses of MMR vaccine, and you did not have these illnesses as a child, discuss your need for immunization with your health care provider. Adults born after 1956 who have not been immunized or not had the illnesses will need one shot.

Hepatitis B Virus (HBV)

The hepatitis B virus causes serious and sometimes fatal liver disease. Vaccination against HBV prevents infection and its complications. See page 199.

It is recommended that all children age 10 to 13 be vaccinated against HBV. Check with your local health unit or public health department for the recommended age for receiving HBV. Three shots provide long-term immunity. Immunization is also recommended for:

- People in high-risk groups.

- Health care workers exposed to blood and body fluids.

- People planning extended travel to China, Southeast Asia, and other areas where HBV infection rates are high.

Haemophilus influenzae Type b (Hib)

Haemophilus influenzae type b disease is different than the flu. It is a serious bacterial illness that causes meningitis and may lead to brain damage and death. Most serious Hib disease affects children between six months and one year of age. Check with your local health unit or public health office for the recommended age for Hib immunizations. Children over five and adults need immunizations only if they have sickle cell anemia or spleen problems.

Immunizations After Age 65

Annual influenza vaccinations are recommended for everyone age 65 and older. The vaccines are most effective when given in the autumn.

A one-time pneumococcal vaccine is recommended for those 65 and older. This is especially important if you have a chronic respiratory disease such as emphysema or chronic bronchitis.

Reactions to Childhood Immunizations

Temporary, mild reactions to immunizations are common. Babies may develop a fever after the vaccinations, or may have some soreness, redness, or swelling where the shot was given. A mild rash or fever may develop 10 to 14 days after the MMR vaccine is given. The rash will go away without treatment. The hepatitis B vaccine may cause nausea, mild fever, or rash.

- Acetaminophen, given at the time of the shot and 4 and 8 hours after immunizations, may soothe the discomfort and relieve fever. Also see page 161.

- Keep written notes on any reactions you observe.

- Tell your health care provider if you think the reactions are excessive.

Younger people with chronic diseases, especially respiratory illnesses, should also consider receiving annual flu shots and the pneumococcal vaccine.

Other Immunizations

If you are in close contact with people who have an infectious disease or you are planning travel to areas where illnesses such as malaria, typhoid, and yellow fever are common, talk with your health unit or public health office to ask if other immunizations are needed.

Tuberculin Test

A tuberculin test is a skin test for tuberculosis (see page 107), not an immunization. A positive result does not necessarily mean that you have tuberculosis, but it does mean the bacteria have probably entered your body. Whether you should be tested depends on the prevalence of tuberculosis in your area and your risk of exposure. Once you have had a positive skin test, the test should not be repeated. Subsequent tests will always be positive and may cause more severe reactions.

Screening and Early Detection

Another way to protect your health is to detect illness early, when it may be easier to treat. You can do this in two ways: by participating in preventive health care and by becoming a good observer of your body and your health.

Be Wise, Immunize

1. Immunizations are effective. They do prevent disease.

2. Immunizations cost very little—much less than treating the illnesses they prevent.

3. The risks are low. Reactions are usually mild and short-lasting.

4. Immunizations reduce the risk of epidemics.

Preventive Health Care

Many doctors used to recommend a complete physical every year. The Canadian Task Force on Periodic Health Examinations now recommends that your doctor provide specific medical exams based on your age, gender, and risk factors. These periodic exams are more effective than annual physical exams in detecting treatable illness. Some of these periodic exams include:

- Blood pressure checks. See page 24 about measuring blood pressure.

- Cholesterol testing. See pages 257 to 259 about cholesterol and cholesterol testing.

- Vision. See Chapter 7 about eye problems.

- Hearing. See Chapter 7 about ear problems.

- Dental checkup. See pages 235 to 240 about dental problems.

- Pap test. See page 172 abut pelvic exams and Pap tests.

- Breast exam. See pages 168 to 170 about breast exams and mammograms.

- Prostate-specific antigen (PSA) testing. See pages 192 to 194 about prostate problems.

Although national guidelines for periodic tests and exams are provided by the Canadian Task Force on Periodic Health Examinations, application of these guidelines may vary from province to province. While this book provides general information and recommendations for exams and tests, you may wish to consult your health care provider about what periodic exams are best for you and when it is recommended to have them.

Periodic self-exams are also an important part of staying healthy. See the breast self-exam on page 168 and the testicular self-exam on page 188. If you have high blood pressure, see page 26.

Other Recommended Tests and Exams

Infants

Well-baby visits are recommended at two weeks and at 2, 4, 6, 9, 12, 15, 18, and 24 months of age. Your doctor may recommend a different schedule. Babies at high risk for hearing problems may be tested during this time.

Children Age 2 to 5

Discuss the frequency of visits with your health professional. A vision test is recommended at age three to four. Some childhood immunizations are also given at this age. See page 18.

Regular blood pressure checks are recommended after age three and may be done during visits for other reasons.

Children Age 6 to 18

Discuss the frequency of visits with your health professional. A tetanus booster is recommended between ages 14 and 16. Blood pressure checks can be done during any visit.

Pap tests are recommended before age 18 if a female is sexually active. See page 172.

Pregnant Women

Discuss the frequency of visits and testing with your doctor. During the first prenatal visit, blood tests, urinalysis, blood pressure, and screening for hepatitis B are recommended. Additional tests are needed during the pregnancy.

Vital Signs

With a few tools and an eye for observation, you can help detect and monitor health problems in your family. Everyone needs to know how to take a temperature and count pulse and respiration rates. It is also good to learn how to take your own blood pressure. You may even want to learn to do simple ear exams. The tools you need are inexpensive and usually come with instructions.

Temperature

A normal temperature ranges from 36.5° to 37.5°C (97.6° to 99.6°F) and for most people is 37°C (98.6°F). Temperature varies with time of day and other factors, so don't worry about minor changes.

Whenever a person feels hot or cold to your touch, it is a good idea to take and record his temperature. If you have to call your doctor during an illness, knowing the exact temperature will be very helpful.

Centigrade-Fahrenheit Conversion Chart		
°C		°F
36.9	=	98.5
37.2	=	99.0
37.5	=	99.5
37.8	=	100.0
38.1	=	100.5
38.3	=	101.0
38.6	=	101.5
38.9	=	102.0
39.2	=	102.5
39.4	=	103.0
39.7	=	103.5

There are three recommended ways to take a temperature:

• Orally (in the mouth)

• Axillary (under the armpit)

• Using an electronic oral or ear thermometer or temperature strip

Unless otherwise specified, **all temperatures in this book are oral Centigrade (Celsius) readings, with Fahrenheit in parentheses.** If you take an axillary temperature, adjust it accordingly.

Thermometer reads 38.3°C

Oral temperatures are recommended for adults and children age six years and older.

- Clean the thermometer with soapy water or rubbing alcohol.

- Hold it firmly at the end opposite the bulb and shake the mercury down to 35°C (95°F) or lower.

- Do not drink hot or cold liquids beforehand.

- Place the bulb under the tongue and close the lips around it. Do not bite it. Breathe through the nose and do not talk.

- Wait three to five minutes.

Axillary temperatures are less accurate and about 1° lower than oral. They are safer for small children who will not hold still while you use an oral thermometer.

- Use an oral thermometer. Shake it down to below 35°C (95°F).

- Place the thermometer in the armpit and have the child cross her arm across the chest and hold her opposite upper arm.

- Wait five minutes.

How to Read a Thermometer

- Roll the thermometer until you can see the thin ribbon of mercury. Note that the thermometer is marked from 35° to 42°C (92° to 108°F).

- Each large mark indicates one degree of temperature. Each small mark indicates 0.1°C (0.2°F).

Electronic thermometers are convenient and easy to use. They are quite accurate, but some are expensive. Temperature strips should only be used to measure axillary (armpit) temperature. They are inaccurate when used on the forehead.

Taking a pulse

Taking a Pulse

The pulse is the rate at which your heart is beating. As the heart forces blood through your body, you can feel a throbbing in the arteries wherever they come close to the skin surface. The pulse can be taken at the wrist, neck, or upper arm.

Certain illnesses can cause the pulse to increase, so it is helpful to know what your resting pulse rate is when you are well. The pulse rate rises about 10 beats per minute for every degree of fever.

Normal Resting Pulse		Normal Resting Respiration	
Infant - 1 year	100 - 160 beats/minute	Infant - 1 year	40 - 60 breaths/minute
1 - 6 years	65 - 140 beats/minute	1 - 6 years	18 - 26 breaths/minute
7 - 10 years	60 -110 beats/minute	7 - adult	12 - 24 breaths/minute
11 - adult	50 - 100 beats/minute		

- Count the pulse after the person has been sitting or resting quietly for 5 to 10 minutes.

- Place two fingers gently against the wrist as shown (don't use your thumb).

- If it is hard to feel the pulse in the wrist, locate the carotid artery in the neck, just to either side of the windpipe. Press gently.

- Count the beats for 30 seconds, then double the result for beats per minute.

Counting Respiration Rates

Your respiration rate is how many breaths you take in a minute. It increases with fever and some illnesses. The best time to count respiration is when a person is resting, perhaps after taking the pulse while your fingers are still on their wrist. The person's breathing is likely to change if they know you are counting it.

- Count the number of times the chest rises for one full minute.

- Notice whether there is any sucking in beneath the ribs or any apparent wheezing or difficulty breathing.

Measuring Blood Pressure

Blood pressure is the force of the blood pulsing against the walls of your arteries. The pressure when the heart beats is called the systolic pressure (the first number in blood pressure readings). The pressure between beats, when the heart is at rest, is called the diastolic pressure. A blood pressure reading below 140/90 is considered normal for an adult over 18. See page 26 for information about high blood pressure.

Blood pressure cuff

Most people with good hearing can learn to measure blood pressure using a stethoscope and a blood pressure cuff (sphygmomanometer). Electronic blood pressure cuffs are also available, which do not require a stethoscope or good hearing.

- Ask your pharmacist to recommend a blood pressure kit and show you how to use it.

- Regular in-home blood pressure monitoring is recommended for anyone who has heart disease or high blood pressure.

Fever

A fever is an abnormally high body temperature. It is a symptom, not a disease. A fever is one way your body fights illness. A temperature up to 38.9°C (102°F) is generally not harmful, though it may be uncomfortable. Most healthy adults can tolerate a fever as high as 39° to 40°C (103° to 104°F) for short periods of time without problems.

For specific fever guidelines for children under age four, see page 161.

Home Treatment

- Drink more liquids, especially water.

- Take and record the temperature every two hours and whenever symptoms change.

- For fevers that cause discomfort, sponge with lukewarm water and take acetaminophen, aspirin, or ibuprofen to lower fever. Do *not* give aspirin to children or teens under age 20.

- Watch for signs of dehydration. See page 33.

- See Chapter 6 for more home treatment of colds and flu.

When to Call a Health Professional

- Fever over 40°C (104°F) does not go down after two hours of home treatment.

- Persistent fever. Many viral illnesses, especially the flu, cause fevers of 38°C (102°F) or higher for short periods of time (up to 12 to 24 hours). Call a doctor if the fever stays:

  ○ 38.9°C (102°F) or higher for two full days

  ○ 38.3°C (101°F) or higher for three full days

  ○ 37.8°C (100°F) or higher for four full days

- Fever over 39°C (103°F) with dry skin, even under the armpits (possible heat stroke, see page 223).

- If fever occurs with other signs of a bacterial infection. See page 88.

- If fever occurs with the following symptoms:

  ○ Very stiff neck and headache. See "Encephalitis and Meningitis" on page 96.

  ○ Shortness of breath and cough. See Bronchitis on page 89 and Pneumonia on page 98.

° Pain over eyes or cheekbone. See Sinusitis on page 99.

° Painful or burning urination. See Urinary Tract Infections on page 181.

° Abdominal pain, nausea, and vomiting. See Stomach Flu and Food Poisoning on page 41, or Appendicitis on page 31.

• If fever is associated with disturbing or unexplained symptoms.

High Blood Pressure

High blood pressure (hypertension) occurs when the pressure of your blood against the artery walls is higher than normal. For more information about blood pressure, see page 24.

Doctors rate blood pressure for adults over 18 in the following categories:

• Normal: below 130/85

• High-normal: 130–139/85–89

• High: over 140/90

High blood pressure usually has no symptoms. However, it increases your risk of stroke, heart attack, and kidney disease. Risks of these diseases are lowest for people whose blood pressure is below 120/80.

Risk factors for high blood pressure include:

• Overweight

• Family history of high blood pressure

• African-American origin

• Inactive lifestyle

• Excess alcohol intake

• Excess sodium (salt) intake

• Use of certain medications, including birth control pills, weight loss pills, steroids, and anti-inflammatories

In some cases, high blood pressure can be prevented. Many people with high blood pressure can control it by changing their lifestyle and may not require medication.

Taking the following steps is especially important if you are in one of the high-risk groups listed above.

Prevention

• Lose weight if you are overweight. This is especially important if you tend to gain weight around the waist rather than in the hips and thighs. A weight loss of only 10 pounds can lower blood pressure.

• Limit your alcohol intake to two drinks or less per day. Too much alcohol increases blood pressure. Drinking less alcohol may also help you lose weight.

• Exercise regularly. Thirty to 45 minutes of brisk walking three to five times a week will help lower your blood pressure (and will also help you lose weight).

• Reduce your salt intake. See page 262.

• Make sure you get enough potassium, calcium, and magnesium in your diet. Potassium-rich foods include orange juice and potatoes. Magnesium-rich foods include leafy green vegetables and whole grains. See page 261 for calcium-rich foods.

• Reduce the saturated fat in your diet. Saturated fat is found in animal products (milk, cheese, and meat). Limiting these foods will help you lose weight and also lower your risk of heart disease. See page 256.

• Stop smoking. Smoking increases your risk of heart disease and stroke. See page 105 for tips on quitting.

Home Treatment

• Follow the prevention tips above even more closely if you have high blood pressure.

• Take any prescribed blood pressure medications exactly as directed.

When to Call a Health Professional

• If you have had two or more consistent blood pressure readings of 140 or higher systolic or 90 or higher diastolic. Call if either one or both numbers are high.

• To learn how to take your blood pressure at home. See page 24.

A great step towards independence
is a good-humored stomach.
Seneca

Chapter 3

Abdominal Problems

Abdominal problems can be hard to pin down. Stomach cramps due to gas pain, which is not often serious, can be much more painful than the early stages of appendicitis, a much more serious problem. Fortunately, most abdominal problems are minor and require only home treatment.

When you have stomach pain, note the location and severity of the pain, and any other symptoms, such as fever. Review page 30 and note your observations to help you or your doctor figure out the cause.

Remember that abdominal pain is difficult even for a doctor to evaluate. In addition to the information in the When to Call a Health Professional sections of this chapter, call your doctor whenever stomach pain:

• Is severe or persistent.

• Increases over several hours.

• Localizes to one area of the abdomen (e.g., upper right, lower left). See page 31.

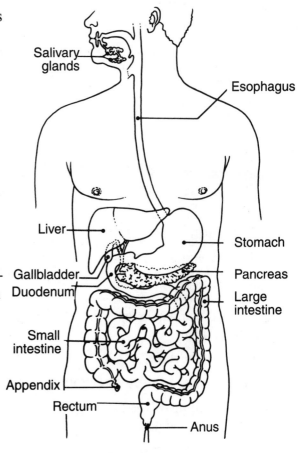

Salivary glands
Esophagus
Liver
Stomach
Gallbladder
Pancreas
Duodenum
Large intestine
Small intestine
Appendix
Rectum
Anus

Digestive tract

Abdominal Problems

Symptoms	Possible Causes
Nausea or vomiting	See Nausea and Vomiting, p. 40; watch for Dehydration, p. 33. Medication reaction. Call your doctor or pharmacist. See Antibiotics, p. 297.
Bowel Movements	
Frequent, watery stools	See Diarrhea, p. 35; Stomach Flu and Food Poisoning, p. 41. Watch for Dehydration, p. 33. See Antibiotics, p. 297.
Stools are dry and difficult to pass	See Constipation, p. 32.
Bloody or black, tarry stools	See Ulcers, p. 43.
Pain during bowel movements; bright red blood on surface of stool or on toilet paper	See Hemorrhoids, p. 37.
Abdominal Pain	
Pain and tenderness in the lower right abdomen with nausea, vomiting, and fever	See Appendicitis, p. 31; Urinary Tract Infections, p. 181.
Bloating with diarrhea, constipation, or both	See Irritable Bowel Syndrome, p. 39.
Burning or discomfort just below the breastbone	See Heartburn, p. 36; Ulcers, p. 43; Chest Pain, p. 91.
Pain in lower abdomen and lower back just before menstrual period	See Menstrual Cramps, p. 179.
Urination	
Pain or burning on urination	See Urinary Tract Infections, p. 181; Prostate Problems, p. 191; Sexually Transmitted Diseases, p. 198.
Difficulty urinating or weak urine stream (men)	See Prostate Problems, p. 191.
Blood in the urine	See p. 182.
Abdominal Lumps or Swelling	
Painless lump or swelling in groin that comes and goes	See Hernia, p. 190.
Blow to the stomach; very rigid or distended abdomen	See Blunt Abdominal Wounds, p. 210. Watch for Shock, p. 231.

Appendicitis

The appendix is a small sac extending from the large intestine. It is normally self-cleaning and does not cause problems. However, if its opening becomes blocked (usually by bowel material), bacteria can build up and the appendix may become inflamed and infected. This condition is known as appendicitis.

Appendicitis is most common in young people age 10 to 30, although it does occur in younger children and older adults. It is rare before age two. Since small children often cannot describe pain well, their cases may become quite serious before they are diagnosed.

Once appendicitis begins, it usually worsens until the appendix ruptures, which spreads the infection to the other abdominal organs.

However, the appendix rarely ruptures within the first 24 hours. Observing the symptoms for 8 to 12 hours is usually safe and is often necessary to confirm the diagnosis. In most cases, appendicitis requires surgery.

Symptoms of appendicitis may include:

- Pain that begins around the navel or upper stomach and moves (localizes) to the lower right abdomen over the course of 2 to 12 hours.

- Nausea, vomiting, loss of appetite, and constipation. Diarrhea is sometimes present, but usually indicates the pain is due to some other cause.

- Low-grade fever (37.8° to 38.3°C or 100° to 101°F).

Home Treatment

- Check the vital signs. See page 22.

- Keep a careful record of the following symptoms:

  ○ Abdominal pain and tenderness

  ○ Nausea, vomiting, constipation, or diarrhea

  ○ Fever

- Keep the patient quiet and in a comfortable position.

- Try to identify or rule out other causes of abdominal pain, such as stomach flu (see page 41) or overeating.

Abdomen

- Do not give laxatives. They can stimulate the intestine and cause the appendix to rupture sooner.

- Do not give strong pain medication. The location and severity of pain are diagnostic clues and strong pain relievers may mask them.

- Do not apply heat to the abdomen.

When to Call a Health Professional

- If you suspect appendicitis. Review your observations of the symptoms with your doctor.

- If there is severe, increasing, and continuous pain in the lower right abdomen for more than four hours.

- If any stomach pain localizes to a specific point in the abdomen.

Constipation

Constipation occurs when bowel movements are difficult to pass. Some people are overly concerned with frequency because they have been taught that a healthy person has a bowel movement every day. This is a misconception. Most people pass stools anywhere from three times a day to three times a week. If your stools are soft and pass easily, you are not constipated.

Constipation may be accompanied by cramping and pain in the rectum from the strain of trying to pass hard, dry stools. There may be some bloating and nausea. There may also be small amounts of bright red blood on the stool caused by slight tearing as the stool is pushed through the anus. This should stop when the constipation is controlled.

Rarely, a stool may become lodged in the rectum (impacted). If this happens, mucus and fluid may leak out around the stool, or there may be leaking of stool (fecal incontinence).

Lack of fibre and inadequate water in the diet are common causes of constipation. Other causes include travel, lack of exercise, delaying bowel movements, medications, pain due to hemorrhoids, and laxative overuse. Irritable bowel syndrome (see page 39) may also cause constipation.

Stress related to toilet training may contribute to constipation in young children. Children who ignore the urge to pass stools because they are involved in play or other activities may become constipated. Children and adults may get constipated because they are reluctant to use toilets away from home.

Prevention

- Eat plenty of high-fibre foods such as fruits, vegetables, and whole grains. Other ways to add fibre include (also see page 255):

  ○ A bowl of bran cereal with 10 grams of bran per serving.

  ○ 30 ml (2 tablespoons) of bran added to cereal or soup.

  ○ 30 ml (2 tablespoons) of psyllium (found in Metamucil and other bulk-forming agents) mixed in water. Start with one tablespoon or less, taken two to three times daily. Increase the amount slowly, and decrease if you develop bloating.

- Avoid foods that are high in fat and sugar.

- Drink 1½ to 2 litres (quarts) of water and other fluids every day. (However, some people find milk constipating.)

- Exercise more. A walking program would be a good start. See page 241.

- Go when you feel the urge. Your bowels send signals when a stool needs to pass. If you ignore the signal, the urge will go away and the stool will eventually become dry and difficult to pass.

Home Treatment

- Set aside relaxed times for having bowel movements. Urges usually occur sometime after meals. Establishing a daily routine, after breakfast, for example, may help.

- Drink two to four extra glasses of water per day, especially in the morning.

- Add fruits, vegetables, and high-fibre foods, such as bran cereal, beans, or prunes, to your diet.

- If necessary, use a stool softener or very mild laxative, such as milk of magnesia. Ask your pharmacist about a product to use. Do not use mineral oil or any other laxative for more than two weeks without consulting your doctor. See page 295.

For babies and children up to age two:

- Make sure you are adding the correct amount of water to the baby's formula.

- Give one to two ounces of water before feeding.

- After age six months, give 2.5 to 60 ml (½ to 2 ounces) of prune juice (increase amount slowly over time). At age nine months, add 25 to 45 ml (1½ to 3 tablespoons) of strained prunes per day.

When to Call a Health Professional

- If acute constipation persists after following the above treatment for one week for adults or three days for infants.

- If bleeding is heavy (more than a few bright red streaks), if the blood is dark red or brown, or if blood is mixed in the stool.

- If bleeding persists longer than two to three days after constipation has improved, or if bleeding occurs more than once.

- If sharp or severe pain occurs in the abdomen.

- If constipation and major changes in bowel movement patterns persist longer than two weeks without clear reason.

- If you experience fecal incontinence.

- If you are unable to have bowel movements without using laxatives.

Dehydration

Dehydration occurs when your body loses too much water. When you stop drinking water or lose large amounts of fluids through diarrhea, vomiting, or sweating, the body cells reabsorb fluid from the blood and other body tissues. When too much water is lost, the blood vessels may collapse. Without medical attention, death may result.

Dehydration is very dangerous for infants, small children, and older adults. Watch closely for its early signs anytime there is an illness that causes high fever, vomiting, or diarrhea. The early symptoms are:

- Dry mouth and sticky saliva
- Reduced urine output with dark yellow urine

Prevention

- Prompt home treatment for illnesses that cause diarrhea, vomiting, or fever will help prevent dehydration.

  ○ Diarrhea, page 35

  ○ Vomiting, page 40

  ○ Diarrhea and vomiting in children, page 159

  ○ Fever, page 25

  ○ Fever in children, page 161

- To prevent dehydration during hot weather and exercise, drink about 2 litres (8 to 10 glasses) of fluids (water and/or rehydration drinks) each day. Drink extra water before exercise and every half hour during activity.

Home Treatment

Treatment of mild dehydration involves stopping the fluid loss and gradually replacing lost fluids.

- To stop vomiting or diarrhea, stop all solid food for several hours or until you are feeling better. Take frequent, small sips of water or a rehydration drink.

Rehydration Drinks

When you have diarrhea or are vomiting, your body can lose large amounts of water and essential minerals called electrolytes. If you are unable to eat for a few days, you are also losing nutrients. This happens faster and is more serious in infants, young children, and older adults.

A rehydration drink (Pedialyte, Gastrolyte) replaces fluids and electrolytes in amounts that are best used by your body. Sports drinks (Gatorade, PowerAde, All Sport) and other sugared drinks will replace fluid, but most contain too much sugar (which can make the diarrhea worse) and not enough of the other essential ingredients. Plain water won't provide any necessary nutrients or electrolytes.

Rehydration drinks won't make the diarrhea or vomiting go away faster, but they will prevent serious dehydration from developing.

You can make an inexpensive home-made rehydration drink. However, *do not* give this homemade drink to children under age 12.

Measure all ingredients precisely. Small variations can make the drink less effective or even harmful.

- 1 litre (quart) water
- 2.5 ml (½ teaspoon) baking soda
- 2.5 ml (½ teaspoon) table salt
- 45 to 60 ml (3 to 4 tablespoons) sugar
- If available, add 1.25 ml (¼ teaspoon) salt substitute ("Lite Salt")

• When the vomiting or diarrhea is controlled, take water or diluted broth or sports drinks a sip at a time until the stomach can handle larger amounts.

• If vomiting or diarrhea lasts longer than 24 hours, sip a rehydration drink to restore lost electrolytes. See page 36 for a drink you can make at home. Do not give the homemade drink to children under 12.

• Watch for signs of more severe dehydration (see below).

For infants and children under four:

• Give small sips of a rehydration drink (Pedialyte, Gastrolyte) if vomiting or diarrhea has lasted longer than two to four hours. See page 159 for home treatment of vomiting or diarrhea in children.

When to Call a Health Professional

• If someone cannot hold down even small sips of liquid after 12 hours of no food or drink.

• If the following signs of severe dehydration develop:

  ◦ Sunken eyes

  ◦ Sunken soft spot on an infant's head

  ◦ Little or no urine for eight hours

  ◦ Skin that is doughy or doesn't bounce back when pinched

  ◦ Low blood pressure and rapid heart rate

  ◦ Lethargy

• If vomiting lasts longer than 24 hours in an adult.

• If severe diarrhea (large loose stools every one to two hours) lasts longer than two days in an adult.

Diarrhea

Diarrhea is an increase in the frequency of bowel movements and the discharge of watery, loose stools. The person with diarrhea may also have abdominal cramps and nausea.

Diarrhea occurs when the intestines push stools through before the water in them can be reabsorbed by the body. It is your body's way of quickly clearing out any viruses or bacteria.

Most diarrhea is caused by viral stomach flu (gastroenteritis). Some medications, especially antibiotics, may also cause diarrhea. For some people, emotional stress, anxiety, or food intolerance may bring on the condition. Irritable bowel syndrome (see page 39) may also cause diarrhea.

Drinking untreated water that contains the *giardia lamblia* parasite can also cause diarrhea that develops one to four weeks later.

Since most cases of diarrhea are viral, they will clear up in a few days with good home treatment.

Home Treatment

For home treatment for diarrhea in **infants and children under age four**, see page 159.

- Put your stomach at rest. Stop all solid food for several hours or until you are feeling better. Take frequent, small sips of water or a rehydration drink.

- Since diarrhea may sometimes speed recovery of the underlying problem, avoid antidiarrheal drugs for the first six hours. After that, use them only if there are no other signs of illness, such as fever, and if cramping or discomfort continues. See antidiarrheal preparations on page 292.

- Begin eating mild foods, such as broth, tea, and dry toast the next day or sooner, depending on how you feel. Avoid spicy foods, carbonated beverages, alcohol, and caffeine until 48 hours after all symptoms have disappeared. Milk products may need to be temporarily stopped.

- Take care to avoid dehydration. See page 33.

When to Call a Health Professional

- If the stools are black or bloody. However, Pepto-Bismol or other medications containing bismuth can cause stools to look black.

- If abdominal pain or severe discomfort accompanies diarrhea and is not relieved by passing stools or gas.

- If diarrhea is accompanied by fever of 38.5°C (101°F) or higher, chills, vomiting, or fainting.

- If signs of severe dehydration appear. See page 35.

- If severe diarrhea (large loose stools every one to two hours) lasts longer than two days in an adult.

- If mild diarrhea continues for one to two weeks without obvious cause.

- If diarrhea occurs after drinking untreated water.

Heartburn

Heartburn (indigestion) is caused by stomach acids backing up into the lower esophagus, the tube that leads from the mouth to the stomach. The medical term for heartburn is gastro-esophageal reflux disease (GERD). The acids produce a burning sensation and discomfort between the ribs just below the breastbone. Another symptom is sour or bitter fluid backing up into the throat or mouth. Heartburn can occur after overeating and as a side effect of many medications. Consult your physician or pharmacist.

Don't be concerned if you experience heartburn now and then; nearly everyone does (25 percent of pregnant women have it every day). However, months of heartburn can injure the esophageal lining.

Most cases of heartburn can be prevented by following the home treatment tips below.

Home Treatment

• Eat smaller meals, and avoid late-night snacks.

• Avoid foods that bring on heartburn. Alcohol, caffeine, chocolate, orange and tomato juices, peppermint- and spearmint-flavored foods, fatty or fried foods, and carbonated drinks may make heartburn worse.

• Avoid alcohol, which irritates your stomach and esophagus and may make your symptoms worse.

• Stop smoking. This is especially important because smoking promotes heartburn. Quitting will often relieve heartburn completely.

• If you are overweight, lose weight, even a few pounds. Being overweight can worsen heartburn.

• Avoid tight-fitting clothes, such as tight belts and waistbands.

• Raise the head of your bed six inches by placing a foam wedge or thick telephone books under the mattress or legs of the bed frame.

• Don't lie down too soon after eating. Try to stay upright for at least two to three hours after each meal. Avoid large meals and snacks before bedtime.

• Try acetaminophen rather than aspirin, ibuprofen, naproxen, or other anti-inflammatory drugs, which can upset the stomach.

• Take an over-the-counter product for heartburn. Antacids, such as Maalox, Mylanta, TUMS, and Gelusil, neutralize stomach acid. Acid controllers, such as Pepcid AC, reduce the production of stomach acid. Ask your pharmacist for advice in choosing one of these medications, and follow the package instructions and your doctor's advice for their use.

When to Call a Health Professional

• If pain occurs with shortness of breath or other symptoms that suggest heart problems. See Chest Pain on page 91.

• If stools are deep red, black, or tarry. If there are small amounts of bright red blood on stool or toilet paper, see Hemorrhoids, below.

• If you suspect that a prescribed medication is causing heartburn. Antihistamines, birth control pills, some sleeping pills, and anti-inflammatory drugs including aspirin, ibuprofen, and naproxen can sometimes cause heartburn.

• If you have difficulty swallowing, especially bread and meat.

• If heartburn persists for one to two weeks despite home treatment. Call sooner if symptoms are severe or are not relieved at all by antacids or acid controllers. See Ulcers on page 43.

Hemorrhoids

Hemorrhoids and piles are two terms used to describe inflammation and swelling in the veins around the anus. Hemorrhoids may develop either inside or outside the anus. Straining to pass hard, compacted stools sometimes causes these veins to become enlarged and inflamed.

The symptoms of hemorrhoids are tenderness or pain and sometimes bleeding. There may be a small lump at the opening to the anus. Hemorrhoids generally last several days and often recur.

Anal itching is usually caused by other conditions. Skin may become irritated by any fecal seepage that comes with diarrhea or by irritating foods in the diet, such as spicy food or coffee. If the anus is not kept clean, itching may result. However, trying to keep the area too clean by rubbing with dry toilet paper or using excess soap will injure the skin. It is important to be gentle with the skin in the anal area.

Prevention

- Keep your stools soft. Include plenty of water, fresh fruits and vegetables, and whole grains in your diet. Add up to two tablespoons of bran or Metamucil (psyllium) to your diet each day. Also see Constipation on page 32.

- Try not to strain during bowel movements. Take your time and never hold your breath.

Home Treatment

- Keep the anal area clean, but even more importantly, be gentle. Warm baths are soothing and cleansing, especially after a bowel movement. Sitz baths (hot baths with just enough water to cover the anal area) are helpful for hemorrhoids but may worsen anal itching. Try premoistened tissues (baby wipes) instead of toilet paper.

- Apply zinc oxide (paste or powder) or petroleum jelly to the painful area after drying. This protects against further irritation and eases the passage of stools.

- Wear cotton underwear and loose clothing.

- Relieve itching by using cold compresses on the anus for 10 minutes four times a day.

- Ease itching and irritation with zinc oxide, petroleum jelly, hydrocortisone (0.5%), or an over-the-counter medicated cream or suppository (Anusol, Tucks, Preparation H, etc.). Avoid products with a local anesthetic, which can cause an allergic reaction. These products will have the suffix "-caine" in the name or ingredients. Consult your pharmacist for the product that is best for you.

When to Call a Health Professional

- If bleeding is heavy (more than a few bright red streaks), if the blood is dark red or brown, or if blood is mixed in the stool.

- If any bleeding continues for longer than one week or occurs more than once despite home treatment.

- If a lump on the anus is increasing in size or becoming more painful.

- If pain is severe or lasts longer than one week.

- If bleeding occurs for no apparent reason, and is not associated with straining to pass stools.

Irritable Bowel Syndrome

Irritable bowel syndrome (IBS) is one of the most common disorders of the digestive tract. Symptoms of IBS often increase with stress or after eating, and include:

- Abdominal bloating, pain, and gas

- Mucus in the stool

- Feeling that a bowel movement hasn't been completed

- Irregular bowel habits, with constipation, diarrhea, or both

IBS is a functional bowel disorder, which means that function of the digestive tract is impaired. There are no physical signs of this disorder and no tests that diagnose it.

IBS can persist for many years. An episode may be milder or more severe than the one before it, but the disorder itself does not worsen over time. It does not lead to more serious diseases such as cancer.

Prevention

There is no way to prevent IBS. However, because symptoms often worsen or improve due to diet, stress, medications, exercise, or for unknown reasons, identifying those things that trigger your symptoms may help you avoid or minimize attacks.

Home Treatment

If constipation is the main symptom:

- Try an over-the-counter fibre supplement or bulk-forming agent that contains psyllium or methylcellulose. Examples include Metamucil, Exlax, and Citrucel.

- Add fibre-rich foods to your diet slowly so they do not worsen gas or cramps. See page 255.

- Use laxatives (e.g., Feen-A-Mint, Correctol) only on a doctor's recommendation.

If diarrhea is the main symptom:

- Avoid foods that make diarrhea worse. Try eliminating one at a time, then add it back gradually. If a food doesn't seem to be related to symptoms, there is no need to avoid it. Many people find the following foods or drinks worsen their symptoms:

  ○ Alcohol, caffeine, nicotine

  ○ Beans, broccoli, apples

  ○ Spicy foods

  ○ Foods high in acid, such as citrus fruit

  ○ Fatty foods, including bacon, sausage, butter, oils, and anything deep-fried

- Avoid dairy products that contain lactose (milk sugar) if they seem to worsen symptoms. However, get enough calcium in your diet from other sources. Yogurt may be a good choice, because some of the lactose has already been digested by the yogurt cultures.

- Avoid sorbitol, an artificial sweetener found in some sugarless candies and gum and in some medications.

- Add more starchy food (bread, rice, potatoes, pasta) to your diet.

- If diarrhea persists, an over-the-counter medication such as loperamide (Imodium) may help. Check with your doctor if you are using it twice a month or more.

To reduce stress:

- Keep a record of the life events that occur with your symptoms. This may help you see any connection between your symptoms and stressful occasions.

- Get regular, vigorous exercise such as swimming, jogging, or brisk walking to help reduce tension.

- See page 247 for more tips on managing stress. Also see Resource 114 on page 308.

When to Call a Health Professional

Call your doctor for an urgent care appointment:

- If you have continuous moderate to severe pain localized to any part of the abdomen accompanied by a fever of 38.1°C (100.5°F) or higher not due to any other reason (such as stomach flu) and chills or yellowing of the eyes and skin (jaundice).

- If pain is so severe that treatment is needed, or if symptoms gradually or suddenly become worse.

- If there is blood in the stool that is not obviously related to hemorrhoids that have been diagnosed by a doctor.

- If you have been diagnosed with IBS and your symptoms change significantly from their usual pattern.

If none of these more serious symptoms are present, try to rule out other causes of stomach problems (e.g., eating a new food, nervousness, stomach flu). Try home treatment for a week. If there is no improvement, or if your symptoms worsen, call for an appointment.

Nausea and Vomiting

Nausea is a very unpleasant feeling in the pit of the stomach. Someone who is nauseated may feel weak and sweaty and produce lots of saliva. Intense nausea often leads to vomiting, which forces stomach contents up the esophagus and out the mouth. Home treatment will help ease the discomfort. Nausea and vomiting may be caused by:

- Viral stomach flu or food poisoning (see page 41)

- Stress or nervousness

- Medications (especially antibiotics, anti-inflammatories, and narcotic pain medications)

- Pregnancy (see page 174)

- Diabetes

- Migraine (see page 124)

- Head injury (see page 221)

Nausea and vomiting can also be signs of other serious illnesses.

For home treatment for vomiting in children under age four, see page 159.

Home Treatment

- If vomiting is severe and persistent, stop all solid food for several hours or until you are feeling better. Take frequent small sips of water or a rehydration drink (see page 34).

- Drink only clear noncarbonated liquids such as water, weak tea, diluted juice, or broth for the next 12 to 24 hours. Start with a few sips at a time and increase gradually.

- If vomiting lasts longer than 24 hours, sip a rehydration drink to restore lost fluids and nutrients. See page 34.

- Rest in bed until you are feeling better.

- Watch for and treat early signs of dehydration (see page 34). Infants, children, and older adults can quickly become dehydrated from vomiting.

- When you are feeling better, begin eating clear soups, mild foods, and liquids until all symptoms are gone for 12 to 48 hours, depending on how you feel. Jell-O, dry toast, crackers, and cooked cereal are good choices.

When to Call a Health Professional

- If vomiting is severe or violent (shoots out in large quantities).

- If there is blood in the vomit. It may look like red or black coffee grounds.

- If vomiting occurs with fever and increasing pain in the lower right abdomen. See Appendicitis on page 31.

- If pain localizes to one area of the abdomen rather than generalized cramping.

- If vomiting occurs with severe headache, sleepiness, lethargy, or stiff neck.

- If vomiting lasts longer than 24 hours in an adult.

- If signs of severe dehydration develop. See page 34.

- If nausea and vomiting persist longer than two hours after a head injury, or if violent vomiting lasts longer than 15 minutes. Limited nausea or vomiting at first is usually not serious. See Head Injuries on page 221.

- If you suspect that medication is causing the problem. Antibiotics and anti-inflammatory medications (aspirin, ibuprofen, naproxen, etc.) may cause nausea or vomiting. Learn which of your medications can cause these symptoms.

Stomach Flu and Food Poisoning

Stomach flu and food poisoning are different ailments with different causes. However, many people confuse the two because the symptoms are so similar. Most people who get food poisoning attribute their symptoms of nausea, vomiting, diarrhea, and stomach pain to a sudden case of stomach flu, and vice versa. The disagreeable symptoms discourage you from eating until the problem clears up.

Stomach flu is usually caused by a viral infection in the digestive system, hence the medical name, viral gastroenteritis. To prevent stomach flu, you must avoid contact with the virus, which is not always easy to do.

Food poisoning is caused by bacteria that grow in food that is not handled or stored properly. Bacteria can grow rapidly when certain foods, especially meats, shellfish, dairy products, and sauces, are not handled properly during preparation or are kept at temperatures between 4° and 60°C (40° and 140°F). The bacteria produce a poison (toxin) that causes an acute inflammation of the intestines.

Suspect food poisoning when symptoms are shared by others who ate the same food, or after eating unrefrigerated foods. Symptoms of food poisoning may not begin for 6 to 48 hours after eating. Nausea, vomiting, and diarrhea may last from 12 to 48 hours for common food poisoning. Please notify your local health unit or public health office if you suspect food poisoning.

Botulism is a rare but often fatal type of food poisoning. It is generally caused by improper home canning methods for low-acid foods like beans and corn. Bacteria that survive the canning process may grow and produce toxin in the jar. Symptoms include blurred or double vision, muscle weakness, and headache.

Prevention

To prevent food poisoning:

- Follow the 2-hour rule. Don't eat meats, dressing, salads, or other foods that have been kept for more than two hours between 4° and 60°C (40° and 140°F).

- Be especially careful with large cooked meats like your holiday turkey, which require a long time to cool. Thick parts of the meat may stay over 4°C (40°F) long enough to allow bacteria to grow.

- Use a thermometer to check your refrigerator. It should be between 0° and 4°C (32° and 40°F).

- Defrost meats in the refrigerator or by microwaving, not on the kitchen counter.

- Wash your hands, cutting boards, and counter tops frequently. After handling raw meats, especially chicken, wash your hands and utensils before preparing other foods.

- Reheat meats to over 60°C (140°F) for 10 minutes to destroy any bacteria. Even then, the toxin may not be destroyed.

- Cook hamburger well done. Cook chicken until the juices run clear.

- Cover meats and poultry during microwave cooking to heat the surface of the meat.

- Do not eat raw eggs or sauces made with raw eggs.

- Keep party foods on ice.

- When you eat out, avoid rare and uncooked meats. Eat salad bar and deli items before they get warm.

- Discard any cans or jars with bulging lids or leaks.

- Follow home canning and freezing instructions carefully. Contact your local health unit/public health office for further advice.

Home Treatment

- Viral stomach flu will usually go away within 24 to 48 hours. Good home care can speed recovery. For adults and children age four and older, see Nausea and Vomiting on page 40 and Diarrhea on page 35. For children younger than four years, see page 159.

- Watch for and treat early signs of dehydration (see page 34). Infants, children, and older adults can quickly become dehydrated from diarrhea and vomiting.

- If you suspect food poisoning, check with others who may have eaten the same food. If possible, save a sample of the food for analysis in case symptoms do not improve.

When to Call a Health Professional

- If vomiting lasts longer than one day in an adult.

- If severe diarrhea (large loose stools every one to two hours) lasts longer than two days in an adult.

- If signs of severe dehydration develop. See page 35.

- If you suspect food poisoning from a canned food, or have symptoms of botulism (blurred or double vision, difficulty swallowing or breathing). If you still have it, take a food sample with you for testing.

Ulcers

An ulcer (peptic ulcer) is a sore or crater in the lining of the gastrointestinal tract. Ulcers may develop in the stomach (gastric ulcers) or in the upper part of the small intestine (duodenal ulcers). Ulcers develop when something damages the protective lining and allows stomach acid to eat away at it. Factors that increase the risk of ulcers include:

- Regular use of aspirin, ibuprofen, and other non-steroidal anti-inflammatory drugs (NSAIDs), such as indomethacin, naproxen, clinoril, etc.

- Smoking

- Infection with bacteria called *Helicobacter pylori*

Symptoms of an ulcer may include a burning or sharp pain in the abdomen between the navel and the end of the breastbone. The pain often occurs between meals and may wake you during the night. The pain can usually be relieved by eating something or taking an antacid. Ulcers may also cause heartburn, nausea or vomiting, and a bloated or full feeling during or after meals.

Ulcers can cause bleeding in the stomach, which may produce black or tarry bowel movements. Without treatment, ulcers may occasionally cause obstruction or break through (perforate) the stomach wall. Bleeding and perforation are serious situations that require immediate treatment.

Home Treatment

- Avoid foods, especially alcohol, caffeine, and spicy foods, that seem to bring on symptoms. It isn't necessary to eliminate any particular food from your diet if it doesn't cause you problems. Avoid frequent servings of milk products.

- Try eating smaller, more frequent meals. If it doesn't help, return to a regular diet.

- Stop smoking. People who smoke are twice as likely to develop ulcers as nonsmokers. Smoking also slows healing of ulcers.

- Do not take aspirin, ibuprofen, naproxen, or other anti-inflammatory drugs. Try acetaminophen instead.

- Antacids are usually needed to neutralize stomach acid and allow the ulcer to heal. Talk with your doctor about the best dose. You may need frequent large doses. Nonabsorbable antacids like Maalox, Mylanta, and Gelusil are often best. If you are on a low-salt diet, talk with your doctor or pharmacist before choosing an antacid. Some antacids have a high sodium content.

- Too much stress may slow ulcer healing. Practise the relaxation techniques on page 248.

When to Call a Health Professional

- If pain occurs with shortness of breath or other symptoms that suggest heart problems. See Chest Pain on page 91.

- If pain localizes to one area of the abdomen.

- If increasing pain in the lower right abdomen occurs with vomiting and fever.

- If stools are deep red, black, or tarry, which usually means there is blood in the stool. Ulcers are one of many possible causes of this condition, which needs to be evaluated.

- If you have an ulcer and develop sudden, severe abdominal pain that is not relieved by your usual home treatment.

- If you suspect an ulcer, and your symptoms have not improved after two weeks of home treatment. Your doctor can evaluate your symptoms and prescribe a treatment plan that may include antacids or other medications.

- To discuss your use of prescription anti-inflammatory drugs.

Urinary Incontinence

If you suffer from loss of bladder control (urinary incontinence), you are not alone. Many people are coping with this problem.

Many cases of incontinence can be controlled, if not cured outright. Temporary incontinence can be caused by water pills (diuretics) and many other common medications. Constipation, urinary infections, stones in the urinary tract, or extended bed rest are other causes. If the underlying problem is corrected, the incontinence can be cured.

There are three types of bladder control problems:

Stress incontinence occurs when small amounts of urine leak out during exercise or when you cough, laugh, or sneeze. This is common in women, and men may experience it after prostate surgery. This type of incontinence is often helped by Kegel exercises (page 46).

Urge incontinence happens when the need to urinate comes on so quickly there is not enough time to get to the toilet. **Overflow incontinence** occurs when the bladder cannot empty itself completely.

Home Treatment

- Don't let incontinence embarrass you. Take charge and work with your doctor to treat any underlying conditions that may be causing the problem.

- Don't let incontinence keep you from doing the things you like to do. Absorbent pads or briefs, such as Attends and Depend, are available in pharmacies and supermarkets.

- Avoid coffee and other drinks that contain caffeine, which overstimulates the bladder. Do not cut down on overall fluids; you need about two quarts a day to keep the rest of your body healthy.

- Practise "double-voiding." Empty your bladder as much as possible, relax for a minute, and then try to empty it again.

- Urinate on a schedule, perhaps every three to four hours during the day, whether the urge is there or not. This may help you to restore control.

- Keep skin in the genital area dry to prevent rashes. Vaseline or Desitin ointment will help.

- Pay special attention to any medications you are taking, including over-the-counter drugs, since some affect bladder control.

- Incontinence is sometimes caused by a urinary tract infection. If you feel pain or burning when you urinate, see page 181.

When to Call a Health Professional

- If you experience more than one episode of urinary incontinence, even in small amounts.

- If you feel that you cannot completely empty your bladder.

Kegel Exercises

Kegel exercises can help cure or improve stress incontinence by strengthening the muscles that control the flow of urine.

- Locate the muscles by repeatedly stopping your urine in mid-stream and starting again. The muscles that you feel squeezing around your urethra and anus are the ones to focus on.

- Practise squeezing these muscles while you are not urinating. If your stomach or buttocks move, you are not using the right muscles.

- Hold the squeeze for three seconds, then relax for three seconds.

- Repeat the exercise 10 to 15 times per session. Do at least three Kegel exercise sessions per day.

Kegel exercises are simple and effective and can be done anywhere and anytime. No one will know you are doing them except you.

Stand up straight!
Mom

Chapter 4

Back and Neck Pain

Although back and neck pain are usually preventable, most of us will suffer from one or both at some time in our lives. Fortunately, 9 out of 10 acute back injuries will heal on their own within 8 to 12 weeks.

By following the prevention and home treatment guidelines in this chapter, you can recover from most back and neck pain and prevent it from recurring.

Quick Reference Guide:

- First aid for back pain, page 48.

- Back pain due to arthritis, page 63.

- Neck pain, page 57.

Back Pain

Your back includes the bones of the spine (vertebrae that support body weight), their joints (facets that guide the direction of the movement of the spine), the discs that separate the vertebrae and absorb shock as you move, and the muscles and ligaments that hold it all together. One or more of these structures can be injured.

- You can strain or sprain the ligaments or muscles from a sudden or improper movement, or by overuse.

- You can damage your discs the same way so that they tear or stretch. If the tear is large enough, it may press against a nerve. The nerve may also become irritated due to swelling or inflammation of the other parts of the back.

Any of these injuries can result in two or three days of acute pain and swelling in the injured tissue, followed by slow healing and a gradual reduction in pain. The pain may be felt in the low back, in the buttock, or down the leg (sometimes called sciatica). The goals of self-care are to relieve pain, promote healing, and avoid reinjury.

First Aid for Back Pain

When you first feel a catch or strain in your back, try these steps to avoid or reduce expected pain. These are the most important home treatments for the first few days of back pain. Also see Home Treatment on page 55.

First Aid #1: Ice
As soon as possible, apply ice or a cold pack to your injured back (10 to 15 minutes every hour). Cold limits swelling, reduces pain, and speeds healing.

Ice

First Aid #2: Relax
Lie flat on your stomach with your arms beside your body and your head to one side. If this causes more pain, try to find the most comfortable position. Relax for one to two minutes.

Relax

First Aid #3: Pelvic tilts
This exercise gently moves the spine and stretches the lower back.

- Lie on your back with knees bent and feet flat on the floor.

- Slowly tighten your stomach muscles and press your lower back against the floor. Hold for 10 seconds (do not hold your breath). Slowly relax.

Pelvic tilt

First Aid #4: Walk
Take a short walk (three to five minutes) on a level surface (no inclines) every three hours. Walk only distances you can manage without pain, especially leg pain.

Walk

In addition to the injuries discussed above, back pain can also be caused by conditions that affect the bones and joints of the spine. Arthritis pain may be a steady ache, unlike the sharp, acute pain of strains, sprains, or disc injuries. If you think your back pain may be caused by arthritis, combine the self-care guidelines for back pain with those for arthritis on page 64. Osteoporosis weakens the bones of the spine, which can cause bone degeneration, and lead to varying degrees of pain. See page 71.

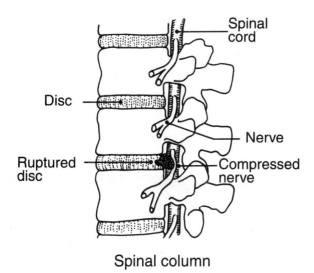

Spinal column

Prevention

The frequency of back pain has increased dramatically in all developed countries. The more time we spend sitting at desks, in cars, or in front of the TV, the more we must do to prevent back pain. Good posture and body mechanics will reduce the stress on your back. Exercise (stretching, strengthening, and aerobic exercise)

Sciatica

Sciatica is an irritation of the sciatic nerve, which runs from the lower back down through the buttocks and to the feet. It can result when an injured disc presses against the nerve. Its main symptom is radiating pain, numbness, or weakness that can be worse in the leg than in the back. In addition to the Home Treatment for back pain on page 55, the following may help:

- Avoid sitting if possible, unless it is more comfortable than standing.

- Alternate lying down with short walks. Increase the distance as you are able to tolerate without pain.

- An ice or cold pack will probably do the most good placed in the middle of your lower back. See page 77.

---

will help maintain your flexibility, strengthen the muscles that support your spine, and maintain your overall fitness. Maintaining an ideal body weight also reduces the load on your lower back.

Back Posture

Improper posture puts too much stress on your back and can lead to discomfort and damage. The key to good back posture is to keep the right amount of curve in your lower back. Too much curve ("swayback") or too little curve ("flat back") can result in problems. The right amount of curve is called the "neutral position."

Standing and Walking

When you stand and walk with good posture, your ear, shoulder, hip, and ankle should be in a line. Do not lock your knees. Keep your lower back in the neutral position.

Sitting

When you sit, keep your shoulders back and down, chin back, abdomen in, and your lower back supported in the neutral position. Slouching can stress the ligaments and muscles in your lower back.

- Avoid sitting in one position for more than one hour at a time. Get up or change positions often.

- If you must sit a lot, the exercises on page 53 are particularly important.

- If your chair doesn't give enough support, use a small pillow or rolled towel to support your lower back.

- See the illustration of proper sitting posture on page 58.

- To rise from a chair, keep your back in the neutral position and scoot forward to the edge of the chair. Use your leg muscles to stand up without leaning forward at the waist.

- For driving, pull your seat forward so that the pedals and steering wheel are within comfortable reach. Your forearms should be parallel to the floor. Stop often to stretch and walk around.

Sleeping

A firm bed is better than a soft mattress or waterbed. Sleep so that your back is in the neutral position.

- If you sleep on your back, you may want to use a towel roll to support your lower back or a pillow under your knees.

- If you sleep on your side, try placing a pillow between your knees.

- Sleeping on your stomach is fine if it doesn't increase your back or neck pain.

- To rise from bed, lie on your side, bend both knees, and drop your feet over the side of the bed as you push with both arms to sit up. Scoot to the edge of the bed and position your feet under your buttocks. Stand up, keeping your back in the neutral position.

Sleeping positions

Body Mechanics

Good body mechanics means practicing good posture during daily activities. Use good body mechanics all the time, not just when you have back pain.

- Keep your back in the neutral position.

- When you must stay in one position for long periods, take regular breaks to stretch and restore the neutral position of your back.

- When standing for long periods, stand with one foot on a small stool.

Lifting

- Keep your upper back straight and your lower back in the neutral position. Do not bend forward from the waist to lift.

- Bend your knees and let your arms and legs do the work. Tighten your buttocks and abdomen to further support your back.

- Keep the load as close to your body as possible, even if it is light.

- While holding a heavy object, turn your feet, not your back. Do not turn or twist your body.

- Never lift a heavy object above shoulder level.

- Get close to objects you need to reach. Use a stool or ladder for items that are above your head, and place it close to what you are doing.

- Use a hand truck or ask someone to help with heavy or awkward objects.

Exercises to Prevent Back Pain

Both the exercises in this chapter and general aerobic exercise (such as walking, swimming, cycling) are important to prevent back injury and pain. They will also speed your recovery from injuries and decrease chronic pain.

Do not do these exercises if you have just injured your back. Instead, see First Aid for Back Pain on page 50.

- You do not need to do every exercise. Do the ones that help you the most.

- If any exercise causes increasing or continuing back pain, stop the exercise and try something else. Stop any exercise that causes the pain to radiate away from your spine into your buttocks or legs, either during or after the exercise.

- Start with five repetitions three to four times a day, and gradually increase to 10 repetitions. Do all exercises slowly.

Proper lifting posture

Stretching and strengthening exercises help keep your back healthy.

Flexion exercises stretch the lower back muscles and strengthen the stomach muscles.

Extension exercises strengthen your lower back muscles and stretch the stomach muscles and ligaments.

Flexion Exercises

1. Curl-ups

Curl-ups strengthen your abdominal muscles, which work with your back muscles to support your spine.

• Lie on your back with knees bent (60° angle) and feet flat on the floor, arms crossed on your chest. Do not hook your feet under anything.

• Slowly curl your head and shoulders up until your shoulder blades barely rise from the floor. Keep your lower back pressed to the floor. To avoid neck problems, remember to lift your shoulders and do not force your head up or forward. Hold for 5 to 10 seconds (do not hold your breath), then curl down very slowly.

2. Knee-to-Chest

The knee-to-chest exercise stretches the low back and hamstring muscles and relieves pressure on the bone facets where the vertebrae come together.

• Lie on your back with knees bent and feet close to your buttocks.

• Bring one knee to your chest at a time, keeping the other foot flat on the floor (or the other leg straight, whichever feels better on your lower back). Keep your lower back pressed to the floor. Hold for 5 to 10 seconds.

• Relax and lower knee to starting position.

2. Knee-to-chest

1. Curl-ups

3. Press-ups

4. Shoulder lifts

5. Backward bend

Extension Exercises

3. Press-ups

Begin and end every set of exercises with a few press-ups.

- Lie face down with arms bent, hands at shoulders with palms flat on floor.

- Lift yourself up on your elbows, keeping lower half of body relaxed. If it's comfortable, press your chest forward.

- Keep hips pressed to the floor. Feel the stretch in your lower back.

- Lower upper body to the floor. Repeat slowly 3 to 10 times.

4. Shoulder Lifts

Shoulder lifts will strengthen the back muscles that support the spine.

- Lie face down with your arms beside your body.

- Lift your head and shoulders straight up from the floor as high as you can without pain. Keep your torso and hips pressed to the floor.

5. Backward Bend

Practise the backward bend at least once a day and whenever you work in a bent-forward position.

- Stand upright with your feet slightly apart. Back up to a counter top for greater support and stability.

- Place your hands in the small of your back and gently bend backward. Keep your knees straight (not locked) and bend only at the waist. See illustration. Hold the backward stretch for one to two seconds.

Additional Strengthening and Stretching Exercises

6. Prone Buttocks Squeeze

This exercise strengthens the buttocks muscles, which support the back and help you lift with your legs.

- Lie flat on your stomach with your arms at your sides.

- Slowly tighten your buttocks muscles and hold for 5 to 10 seconds (do not hold your breath). Relax slowly.

- You may need to place a small pillow under your stomach for comfort.

7. Pelvic Tilts

See illustration on page 48.

8. Hamstring Stretch

This exercises stretches the muscles in the back of your thigh, which allow you to bend your legs while keeping your back in the neutral position.

- Lie on your back in a doorway with one leg through the doorway on the floor. Put the leg you want to stretch straight up with the heel resting on the wall next to the doorway.

- Keep the leg straight and slowly move your heel up the wall until you feel a gentle pull in the back of your thigh. Do not overstretch.

- Relax in this position for 30 seconds, then bend the knee to relieve the stretch. Repeat with the other leg.

9. Hip Flexor Stretch

This exercise stretches the muscles in the front of your hip, to avoid "sway-back" caused by tight hip muscles.

- Kneel on one knee with your other leg bent and foot in front of you. Keep your back in the neutral position.

- Slowly shift your weight onto your front foot, keeping your back in the neutral position. Hold for 10 seconds. You should feel a stretch in the groin of the leg you are kneeling on. Repeat with the other leg.

8. Hamstring stretch

9. Hip flexor stretch

Exercises to Avoid

Many common exercises actually increase the risk of low back pain. Avoid the following:

- Straight leg sit-ups

- Bent leg sit-ups during acute back pain (may be safe if back is kept in neutral position)

- Leg lifts (lifting both legs while lying on your back)

- Lifting heavy weights above the waist (military press, biceps curls while standing)

- Any stretching done while sitting with the legs in a V

- Toe touches while standing

Home Treatment

Immediately after an injury and for the next few days, the most important home treatment includes:

- Get in a comfortable position and apply cold to the injured area. See the icing guidelines on page 48. Apply cold packs or ice for 15 to 20 minutes three to four times a day or up to once an hour for at least the first three days. Cold decreases inflammation, swelling, and pain.

- Sit or lie in positions that are most comfortable and reduce your pain, especially any leg pain.

- Do not sit up in bed, and avoid soft couches and twisted positions. Avoid positions that worsen your symptoms, such as sitting for long periods of time. Follow the posture and body mechanics guidelines discussed earlier.

- Do the first aid exercises on page 48 three to four times a day.

- Bed rest can help relieve back pain but may not speed healing. Stick with what makes you feel better. Unless you have severe leg pain, one to three days of rest should relieve pain. More than three days is not recommended and could actually delay healing. Try one of the following positions (see illustrations on page 50):

  ○ Lie on your back with your knees bent and supported by large pillows, or lie on the floor with your legs on the seat of a sofa or chair.

  ○ Lie on your side with your knees and hips bent and a pillow between your legs.

  ○ If it doesn't increase your pain, lie on your stomach.

- Take aspirin or ibuprofen regularly as directed (pages 295 and 296). Call your doctor if you've been told to avoid anti-inflammatory medications. Acetaminophen may also be used. Take these medications sensibly. Masking the pain completely might allow movement that could lead to reinjury.

- As soon as you can, take short walks (three to five minutes every three hours) on level surfaces (no inclines) to keep your muscles strong. Only walk distances that you can manage without pain, especially leg pain.

- Relax your muscles. See page 248 for progressive muscle relaxation.

After two to three days of home treatment:

- Continue daily walks (increase to 5 to 10 minutes three to four times a day) and the exercises above.

- Try swimming, which is good for your back. It may be painful immediately after a back injury, but lap swimming or kicking with swim fins is often helpful to prevent back pain from recurring.

- When your pain has improved, begin easy exercises that do not increase your pain. One or two of the exercises in the Prevention section (pages 49 to 55) may be helpful. Start with five repetitions twice a day and increase to 10 repetitions as you are able.

- See Resources 28 to 30 on page 304.

When to Call a Health Professional

- If you have loss of bowel or bladder control. Although constipation and frequent or urgent urination are common in people with low back pain, any new problems with bowel or bladder control should be discussed with your doctor.

- If you have new numbness in the genital or rectal area.

- If you have leg weakness that is not solely due to pain. Many people with low back pain say their legs feel weak. However, significant leg weakness should be evaluated, especially if you are unable to bend your foot upward, get up out of a chair, or climb stairs.

- If someone falls from more than three metres height.

- If you have new or increased back pain with unexplained fever, painful urination, or other signs of urinary tract infection. See page 181.

- If you have a dramatic increase in your chronic back pain, especially if it is unrelated to a new or changed physical activity.

- If you have a history of cancer or HIV infection and develop a new or increased back pain.

- If you have new back pain that does not improve after one week of home treatment, contact your doctor for advice.

- If you develop a new, severe pain in your lower back that does not increase with movement and is not related to stress or muscle tension.

- If chronic back pain does not improve after two weeks of home treatment.

Medical Doctors

In addition to diagnosing the cause of back pain and evaluating back injuries, a medical doctor may also:

- Help you develop an individualized exercise and home care plan or modified work plan if needed.

- Prescribe muscle relaxants, anti-inflammatory drugs, and pain relievers. Note: If you do get a strong painkiller or muscle relaxer, avoid postures and activities that could reinjure your back.

- Suggest physical therapy.

- Recommend back surgery.

Physical Therapists

After the initial first-aid actions, a physical therapist with training in orthopedic treatment can help you:

• Identify specific muscle or disc problems.

• Provide other therapies, such as ultrasound or manual therapy, if you aren't improving.

• Help you improve your posture and customize an exercise program for recovery and long-term protection.

Other Professionals

Chiropractors, acupuncturists, massage therapists, and others may also provide short-term relief. If there is no great improvement in six visits, see your doctor.

Back Surgery

Doctors recommend back surgery much less often now than in the past. Rest, posture changes, and exercise can relieve 90 percent of back problems, even disc problems.

Surgery is often appropriate for certain conditions that do not improve with the usual treatment. If you do plan to have surgery, the posture and body mechanics guidelines and exercises in this chapter are still important. A strong, flexible back is important to a quick recovery after surgery.

Neck Pain

Neck pain and stiffness are usually caused by strain or spasm of the neck muscles or inflammation of the neck joints. It may occasionally be due to arthritis or damage to the discs between the neck (cervical) vertebrae. Neck movement may be limited, usually more to one side than the other. Neck problems often cause headaches or pain in the shoulder, upper back, or down the arm.

Neck pain and headaches are sometimes related to tension in the trapezius muscles, which run from the back of the head across the back of the shoulder. When you have neck pain, these muscles may also feel tight and painful.

Neck muscle strain may be due to:

• Forward head posture

• Sleeping on a pillow that's too high, too flat, or doesn't support your head

• Sleeping on your stomach or with the neck twisted or bent

• Extended periods of the "thinker's pose" (resting your forehead on your upright fist or arm)

• Watching TV or reading lying down with the neck in an awkward position

• Stress

• A workstation that puts the neck in an awkward position

• Other pressures on the neck muscles

• Injury that causes sudden movement of the head and neck (whiplash) or a direct blow to the neck

• Strenuous activity with the upper body and arms

Meningitis is a serious illness that causes a severe stiff neck with headache and fever. If these three symptoms occur together, see a doctor promptly.

Prevention

Good posture, body mechanics, and exercise are important to preventing neck pain. Most neck pain that isn't due to arthritis or an injury is completely avoidable.

If pain is worse at the **end of the day**, evaluate your posture and body mechanics during the day.

• Sit straight in your chair with your low back supported. Avoid sitting for long periods without getting up or changing positions. Take mini-breaks several times each hour to stretch your neck muscles.

• If you work at a computer, adjust the monitor so that the top of the screen is at eye level. Use a document holder that puts the copy at the same level as the screen.

• If you use the telephone a lot, consider a headset or speaker phone.

• Adjust your car seat to a more upright position that supports your head and lower back.

If neck stiffness is worse **in the morning**, check your sleeping posture (and your activities the day before).

• Improve your sleeping support. A hard mattress or special neck support pillow may solve the problem (try before buying). Or, you can fold a towel lengthwise into a four-inch wide pad, wrap it around your neck, and pin it for good support.

• Avoid pillows that force your head forward when you are sleeping on your back.

• When sleeping on your side, make sure your nose is in line with the centre of your body.

• If stress is a factor, practise the progressive muscle relaxation exercises on page 248.

• Strengthen and protect your neck by doing neck exercises once a day. See page 60.

Proper sitting posture

Home Treatment

Much of the home treatment for back pain is also helpful for neck pain, including the guidelines on posture, body mechanics, and ice. Also see page 55.

- Place a cold pack over painful muscles for 10 to 15 minutes at a time, as often as once an hour. It will help decrease any pain, muscle spasm, or swelling. If the problem is near the shoulder or upper back, it will usually help more to ice the back of the neck.

- Keep your head and neck in the neutral position over your body. Avoid slouching or forward head posture.

- Use aspirin, ibuprofen, or acetaminophen to help relieve pain.

- Walking is also helpful in relieving and preventing neck pain. The gentle swinging motion of your arms often relieves pain. Start with short walks of 5 to 10 minutes, three to four times a day.

- If neck pain occurs with headache, see Tension Headaches on page 125.

- Once the pain subsides, do the prevention exercises on page 60. Start with five repetitions twice a day. Gradually increase to 10 repetitions. Stop doing any exercise that causes pain.

- See Resource 95 on page 307.

When to Call a Health Professional

- Call your doctor *immediately* if a stiff neck occurs together with headache and fever. Also see "Encephalitis and Meningitis" on page 96.

- If the pain extends or shoots down one arm, or you have numbness or tingling in your hands.

- If you develop new weakness in the arms or legs.

- If a blow or injury to the neck (whiplash) has caused new pain.

- If you are unable to manage the pain with home treatment.

- If the pain has lasted two weeks or longer without improvement despite home treatment.

- If someone falls from more than three metres height.

Neck Exercises

You do not need to do every exercise. Stick with the ones that help you the most. Stop any exercise that increases pain. Start with five repetitions twice a day. Do each exercise slowly.

1. Dorsal glide: Sit or stand tall, looking straight ahead (a "palace guard" posture). Slowly tuck your chin as you glide your head backwards over your body. Hold for a count of five, then relax. Repeat 6 to 10 times. This stretches the back of the neck. If you feel pain, do not glide so far back. Some people find this exercise easier while lying on their back with ice on the neck.

2. Chest and shoulder stretch: Sit or stand tall and glide your head backward as in exercise 1. Raise both arms so that your hands are next to your ears. As you exhale, lower your elbows down and back. Feel your shoulder blades slide down and together. Hold for a few seconds. Relax and repeat.

3. Shoulder lifts: Lie face down with your arms beside your body. Lift your head and shoulders straight up from the floor as high as you can without pain. Keep your torso and hips pressed to the floor. Repeat 6 to 10 times.

4. Hands on head: Move your head backward, forward, and side to side against gentle pressure from your hands, holding each position for several seconds. Repeat 6 to 10 times.

Dorsal glide

Chest and shoulder stretch

Shoulder lifts

*I don't deserve this award, but then I have arthritis
and I don't deserve that either.*
Jack Benny

Chapter 5

Bone, Muscle, and Joint Problems

Our aches and pains remind us that life isn't always easy. But pain can be managed. This chapter covers pain from arthritis to ankle sprains. The focus is less on reducing pain and more on limiting its impact on our quality of life. As with most chapters in this book, we hope you rarely have to refer to these pages. But when you do, we hope these guidelines will make your life more comfortable.

Arthritis

Arthritis refers to a variety of joint problems that cause pain, swelling, and stiffness. Simply put, arthritis means inflammation of a joint. Arthritis can occur at any age, but it affects older people the most.

There are over 100 different types of arthritis, each with its own specific symptoms. Little is known about what causes most types. Some seem to run in families; others seem to be related to imbalances in body chemistry or immune system problems.

The chart on page 62 describes the three most common kinds of arthritis. Osteoarthritis is the most common type and can usually be successfully managed at home. Rheumatoid arthritis and gout will improve with a combination of self-care and professional care.

Prevention

It may not be possible to prevent arthritis, but you can prevent a lot of pain by being kind to your joints. This is especially important if you already have arthritis.

- Modify activities that cause repeated jarring, such as high-impact aerobic activities, to low-impact activities if they cause pain.

- Control your weight.

- Exercise regularly.

While repeated jarring activities can increase joint pain, regular exercise can relieve or prevent it. Exercise is needed to nourish the joint cartilage and remove waste products. It also strengthens the muscles around the joint. Strong muscles support the joint and reduce injuries caused by fatigue. Stretching maintains your range of pain-free motion.

Home Treatment

- A warm shower or bath may help relieve morning stiffness. Try to avoid sitting still after a warm shower or bath.

- If the joint is not swollen, apply moist heat for 20 to 30 minutes two to three times a day. Do not apply heat to a swollen, inflamed joint.

- Put each of your joints gently through its full range of motion one to two times each day.

- Rest sore joints. Avoid activities that put weight or strain on the joint for a few days. Take short rest breaks from your regular activities throughout the day.

Common Types of Arthritis

Type	Cause	Symptoms	Comments
Osteoarthritis	Breakdown of joint cartilage	Pain, stiffness, and swelling; common in fingers, hips, and knees.	Most common type in women and men between the ages of 45 and 90.
Rheumatoid Arthritis	Inflammation of the membrane lining the joint (synovium)	Pain, stiffness, swelling in multiple joints; joints may be "hot" and red; common in hands, wrists, and feet.	Occurs most often around age 30 to 40; more common in women.
Gout	Build-up of uric acid crystals in the joint fluid	Sudden onset of burning pain, stiffness, and swelling; common in big toe, ankle, knee, wrist, elbow.	Most common in men over 40; may be aggravated by alcohol and organ meats.

- Apply cold packs to inflamed, swollen joints for 10 to 15 minutes, once an hour. Cold will help relieve pain and reduce inflammation (although it may be uncomfortable for the first few minutes).

- Regular exercise is important to help maintain strength and flexibility in the muscles and joints. Strengthening exercises prevent the muscle decline that leads to loss of function. Try low-impact activities, such as swimming, water aerobics, biking, or walking.

- Acetaminophen can provide safe pain relief for osteoarthritis. Aspirin or ibuprofen also help ease pain, but can cause stomach upset. Do not use anti-inflammatory medications (aspirin, ibuprofen, etc.) together. See page 295 for the symptoms of aspirin overdose.

- Enroll in an arthritis self-management program. Participants usually have less pain and fewer limitations on their activities. See Resource 24 on page 304.

When to Call a Health Professional

- If you have fever or skin rash along with severe joint pain.

- If the joint is so painful that you cannot use it.

- If there is sudden, unexplained swelling, redness, or pain in any joint.

- If there is severe pain and swelling in multiple joints.

- If you experience sudden back pain that occurs with numbness in the legs or loss of bowel or bladder control.

- If joint pain continues for over six weeks and home treatment is not helping.

- If you experience side effects of large doses of aspirin or other arthritis medication (stomach pain, nausea, persistent heartburn, or dark tarry stools). Do not exceed recommended doses of over-the-counter medications without your doctor's advice.

Bunions and Hammertoes

A **bunion** is a swelling of the joint at the base of the big toe. The big toe may bend toward and overlap the other toes. A **hammertoe** is a toe that bends up permanently at the middle joint. Both conditions are usually irritated by wearing shoes that are too short or narrow. These problems sometimes run in families.

Prevention

- Wear shoes with no heel (or a low heel) and a roomy toe box. Tennis or basketball court shoes are often best. Make sure that your shoes fit properly. Tight or high-heeled shoes increase the risk of bunions and hammertoes and irritate them if they are already present.

Home Treatment

Once you have a bunion or hammer-toe, there is usually no way to completely get rid of it. Home treatment will help keep it from getting worse.

• Wear low-heeled, roomy shoes that have good arch supports.

• Cushion the bunion or hammertoe with moleskin or donut-shaped pads to prevent rubbing and irritation.

• Cut out the area over the bunion or hammertoe from an old pair of shoes to wear around the house, or wear comfortable sandals that don't press on the area.

• Try aspirin, ibuprofen, or acetaminophen to relieve pain. Ice or cold packs may also help.

When to Call a Health Professional

• If severe pain in the big toe came on suddenly, and you have not been diagnosed with gout.

• If severe pain interferes with walking or daily activities.

• If the big toe begins to overlap the second toe.

• If you have diabetes, poor circulation, or peripheral vascular disease. Irritated skin over a bunion or hammer toe can easily become infected in people with these conditions.

• If pain does not respond to home treatment in two to three weeks.

Hammertoe

Bunion

Bursitis and Tendinitis

A bursa is a small sac of fluid that helps the muscles slide easily over other muscles or bones. Injury or overuse of a joint or tendon may result in pain, redness, heat, and inflammation of the bursa, a condition known as bursitis. Bursitis often develops quickly, over just a few days, often after a specific injury or excessive use (overuse).

Tendons are tough, rope-like fibres that connect muscles to bones. Injury or overuse may cause pain, tenderness, and inflammation in the tendons or the tissues surrounding them, a condition known as tendinitis. Both bursitis and tendinitis can also be related to job, sports, or household activities that require repeated twisting or rapid joint movements.

Bursitis and tendinitis can occur at several different places in the body, and can occur together in one place. The same home treatment is good for both problems.

Prevention

Regular warm-ups and stretching may help prevent bursitis or tendinitis. Warm up well before exercising, gradually increase the intensity of the activity, and stretch afterwards. See page 66 for additional joint-specific prevention tips.

Home Treatment

Bursitis or tendinitis will usually go away or at least subside in a few days or weeks if you avoid the activity that caused it.

The most common mistake in recovery is thinking that the problem is gone when the pain is gone. Chances are, bursitis or tendinitis will recur if you do not take steps to strengthen and stretch the muscles around the joint, and change the way you do some activities.

- Rest the inflamed area. Change the way you do the activity that causes pain so that you can do it without pain. See page 66 for joint-specific guidelines. To maintain fitness, substitute activities that don't stress the inflamed area.

**Bone, Muscle, and
Joint Problems**

In many cases, you can determine the cause of bone, muscle, or joint problems by thinking back to how the pain started.

Traumatic injuries (turning an ankle or twisting a knee) usually cause **Strains, Sprains, or Fractures**. See page 74.

A single episode of overuse or repeated heavy use of a joint can cause **Bursitis or Tendinitis**. See page 64.

Joint pain that comes on gradually and seems unrelated to any specific injury may be due to **Arthritis** (see page 61) or poor posture (see page 49).

- As soon as you notice pain, apply ice or cold packs for 10-minute periods, once an hour or as often as you can for 72 hours. Continue applying ice (15 to 20 minutes, three times a day) as long as it relieves pain. See page 77. Although heating pads or hot baths may feel good, ice or cold packs will relieve inflammation and speed healing.

- Aspirin, ibuprofen, or naproxen may help ease pain and inflammation, but don't use medication to relieve pain while you continue overusing a joint. See page 296 for dosage.

- Gently move the joint through as full a range of motion as you can without pain several times a day to prevent stiffness. As the pain subsides, continue stretching and add exercises to strengthen the affected muscles.

- Warm up before and stretch after the activity. Apply ice to the injured area after exercise to prevent pain and swelling.

- Gradually resume the activity at a lower intensity. Increase slowly and only if pain does not recur.

In addition to the general prevention and home treatment information for bursitis and tendinitis above, the following tips will be useful if you have a specific joint problem.

Wrist pain may be due to one of the following common types of tendinitis. Though this is not the same as carpal tunnel syndrome, the same home care may help. See page 68.

Elbow pain is often due to one of the following common types of tendinitis in the forearm muscle tendons. **Tennis elbow** causes pain on the *outside* of the elbow where the muscles that bend the wrist back are attached. **Golfer's elbow** causes pain on the *inside* of the elbow where the muscles that bend the wrist down are attached.

- Strengthen the wrist, arm, shoulder, and back muscles to help protect the elbow.

- A brace or elbow sleeve may help relieve pain.

- Use tools with larger handles.

- Use a two-handed tennis backhand and a midsize, more flexible racquet.

- Avoid hitting divots in golf.

- Avoid side-arm pitching and throwing curve balls.

- Support a sore elbow with a sling for one to two days. To prevent stiffness, do not use a sling for more than two days and do range-of-motion exercises daily.

Shoulder pain that occurs on the outside of the upper arm is often due to tendinitis or bursitis in the shoulder joint. Pain on the top of the shoulder closer to the neck is often due to tension in the trapezius muscles, which extend from the back of the head down to the tip of the shoulders. See Neck Pain on page 57.

- Use proper throwing techniques for baseball and football.

- Use a different swim stroke: breast stroke or sidestroke instead of the crawl or butterfly.

- To prevent stiffness, do not rest a sore shoulder with a sling for more than two days. Keep the elbow at your side, not in front of your body. Do range-of-motion exercises 10 times daily.

Hip pain: Tendinitis or bursitis in the hip can cause pain at the side of the hip when rising from a chair and taking the first few steps, while climbing stairs, or while driving. If pain is severe, sleeping on your side may also be painful. Pain in the front of the hip may also be due to arthritis. See page 61.

- Wear well-cushioned shoes and avoid high heels.

- Walk up and down stairs one at a time, leading with your strong leg, until the pain is gone.

- Avoid activities that force one side of the pelvis higher than the other, such as running in only one direction on a track or working sideways on a slope. Keep the pelvis level.

- Sleep on your uninjured side with a pillow between your knees, or on your back with pillows beneath your knees.

- See the hip stretches on pages 54 and 244. Stretch after activity, when your muscles are warm.

Knee pain may be caused by bursitis or tendinitis. See Knee Problems on page 69.

Heel or foot pain may be due to plantar fasciitis or to Achilles tendinitis. See page 72. Pain in the front of the lower leg may be due to shinsplints. See page 70.

When to Call a Health Professional

- If there is fever, rapid swelling, redness, or an inability to use a joint.

- If severe pain continues when the joint is at rest and you have applied ice.

- If the problem is severe and you can think of no injury or activity that might have caused it.

- If the pain persists for two weeks or longer despite home treatment. Your doctor or physical therapist can help you develop a specific exercise and home treatment plan.

Carpal Tunnel Syndrome

The carpal tunnel is a narrow passageway of bone and ligament in your wrist. The median nerve, which controls sensation in your fingers and some muscles in the hand, passes through this tunnel along with some of the finger tendons. Repeated motion or use of the hand or wrist may cause the tendons to become inflamed and press the nerve against the bone. This is known as carpal tunnel syndrome (CTS).

Pressure on the nerve causes the following symptoms of CTS:

- Numbness or tingling in one or both hands except for the little finger.

- Wrist pain that may also affect your fingers and radiate up your arm. The pain is often greater at night and early in the morning.

Carpal tunnel syndrome can be caused by anything that causes pressure on the nerve, such as obesity, swelling due to repetitive use of the hand and wrist, a cyst on the tendon, rheumatoid arthritis, or other conditions. Pregnancy, diabetes, an underactive thyroid, and taking birth control pills also may increase the risk of CTS.

Prevention

- Take frequent breaks (five minutes each hour) from repetitive hand motions. Stretch your fingers and thumb and change your grip often.

- Avoid repetitive hand motions with a bent wrist. Keep your wrist straight for the following activities:

  ○ Writing, typing, drawing, knitting, crocheting, needlepoint

  ○ Driving

  ○ Using power tools, pliers, or scissors

  ○ Playing piano or other musical instruments

- Learn to type with a soft touch.

- Maintain good posture. Avoid rounding your shoulders or slouching. See page 58.

Home Treatment

- Don't ignore wrist pain. If possible, stop the activity that triggered the problem. If the symptoms decrease, resume the activity gradually with a greater effort to keep your wrist straight.

- If you cannot stop the activity, try to change the way you do it so that your wrist is not stressed. Alternate tasks so that you don't spend more than one to two hours doing an activity involving your hands.

- Gently warm up your hands before starting work. Do some wrist circles and stretch your fingers and wrists. Repeat every hour.

- Use a wrist rest pad with your computer keyboard to help maintain the straight alignment of your wrist, but don't lean on it continuously.

- Use aspirin, ibuprofen, or acetaminophen to relieve pain.

- Apply ice or a cold pack to the palm side of the wrist. See "Ice and Cold Packs" on page 77.

- A wrist splint that keeps your wrist straight or slightly extended (bent backward no more than 15 degrees) may help relieve pain. Try to combine a splint with a real effort to change the activities that cause you pain. Wear the splint at night and when doing heavy lifting. You can buy a splint at a pharmacy or hospital supply store.

- When the pain is gone, begin arm and upper body strengthening exercises so you can maintain good posture and a straight wrist without the splint.

- Some people find that 50 mg of vitamin B_6 (pyridoxine) taken twice a day helps relieve wrist pain. (Talk with your doctor before taking B_6.) The scientific proof of this is not clear, but it may help.

- Reducing the salt in your diet (see page 262) may help reduce water retention and relieve swelling in the wrist.

- Avoid sleeping on your hands.

When to Call a Health Professional

A health professional can confirm the diagnosis, properly fit you with a splint or, in severe cases, recommend a surgical solution. Call a health professional:

- If the pain or numbness is severe and is not relieved by rest, changing positions, ice, or a normal dose of aspirin, ibuprofen, or acetaminophen.

- If your hand grip becomes weak.

- If minor symptoms do not improve after one month of prevention and home treatment.

- If any numbness remains after one month of home treatment. Long-term numbness can lead to *permanent* loss of some hand function.

Knee Problems

The knee is a vulnerable joint. It is basically just two long leg bones held together with ligaments and muscles. Problems develop when we put too much stress on the joint. The three most common knee problems are:

- Strained or sprained ligaments and muscles caused by a blow to the knee, forcing it in a direction that it does not normally bend. See Strains, Sprains, and Fractures on page 74.

- Kneecap pain, also known as patellofemoral pain. This problem causes pain around or behind the kneecap when running downhill, going up or down stairs, or after sitting for long periods of time.

- Patellar tendinitis, also known as jumper's knee, is an inflammation of the tendon that attaches the kneecap (patella) to the shinbone (tibia). It is common among basketball and volleyball players.

Prevention

- The best way to prevent knee problems is to strengthen and stretch the leg muscles, especially the front and back of the thigh (quadriceps and hamstring). See page 244.

- Avoid deep knee bends.

- Avoid running downhill unless you are fully conditioned.

- Avoid wearing shoes with cleats in contact sports.

- Wear shoes with good arch supports. Replace running shoes every 300 to 500 miles.

- Avoid high-heeled shoes.

- Also see Bursitis and Tendinitis on page 64.

Home Treatment

- Apply ice to your knee. See "Ice and Cold Packs" on page 77.

- Reduce by at least half the activities that cause pain.

- A brace or elastic or neoprene sleeve or a band with a hole for the kneecap that holds the kneecap in place may help ease pain during activity. You can buy one at a pharmacy or sporting goods store.

- Stretch the front and back of your thigh (quadriceps and hamstring) muscles after exercise, when they are warm. See pages 54 and 244.

- Also see Sprains on page 74 and Bursitis and Tendinitis on page 64.

- If knee pain is not related to exercise or due to a recent or past injury, see Arthritis on page 61.

When to Call a Health Professional

- If the knee wobbles from side to side or "gives out."

- If you felt or heard a "pop" during a knee injury which was followed by immediate swelling.

- If you are unable to straighten the knee, or if the joint "locks."

- If knee is red, hot, swollen, and painful to touch.

- If pain is severe or does not improve substantially within two to five days.

Muscle Cramps and Leg Pain

Leg and muscle cramps ("charley horse" or "stitch") are common. They often occur during exercise, especially during hot weather, or at night. Dehydration or low levels of potassium in the body and using a muscle that is not stretched well may cause cramps.

Pain in the front of the lower leg may be due to shinsplints, especially if you have recently increased your exercise.

Arthritis can also cause leg pain (see page 61). Leg pain that runs from the buttocks down the back of the leg and into the foot may be due to sciatica. See page 49.

Phlebitis, an inflammation of a vein, also causes leg pain, usually in the calf of one leg. This condition can be serious if blood clots formed in the vein break loose and lodge in the lungs. It is most common after surgery or prolonged bed rest. Hardening of the arteries (atherosclerosis) in the leg can also cause pain that is worse during activity and is relieved by rest.

Prevention

- Warm up well and stretch before any activity. Stretch after exercise to keep hot muscles from shortening and cramping.

- Drink extra water before and during exercise, especially during hot or humid weather.

- Include plenty of potassium in your diet. Bananas, orange juice, and potatoes are good sources.

- To avoid stomach cramps ("stitches") during exercise, do side stretches before exercising and learn to breathe with your lower lungs. See page 248.

- If cramps wake you at night, take a warm bath and do some stretching exercises before going to bed. Keep your legs warm while sleeping.

Growing Pains

Children age 6 to 12 often develop harmless "growing pains" in their legs at night. The cause is unknown. A heating pad, acetaminophen, or gentle massage of the legs may help.

Home Treatment

If there is pain, swelling, or heaviness in the calf of one leg only, or other symptoms that cause you to suspect phlebitis (see When to Call a Health Professional below), call your doctor before attempting home treatment.

• Follow the prevention guidelines.

• Gently stretch the cramping muscle. Rub or massage the cramp.

• To stretch the calf, straighten your leg, grab your foot, and pull it toward you.

• Drink some extra water. Cramps are often related to dehydration.

• The best treatment for shinsplints is ice, aspirin, ibuprofen, or acetaminophen, and a week or two of rest followed by a gradual return to exercise.

When to Call a Health Professional

• If you have the following symptoms:

  ◦ Pain deep in the leg or calf

  ◦ Heat, redness, or pain along the course of a leg vein

  ◦ Swelling of one leg

  ◦ Leg is white or blue and cold

  ◦ Shortness of breath or chest pain

• If leg cramps worsen or persist in spite of the prevention and home treatment.

• If cramps or leg pain occur repeatedly during even mild exercise, such as walking, even if relieved by rest.

Osteoporosis

Osteoporosis or "brittle bones" is a condition that affects 25 percent of women over age 60. It is much less common and not as severe in men. It is more common after menopause, when estrogen levels decline. Osteoporosis is caused by loss of bone mass and strength. Bones weakened by osteoporosis are easily broken. Risk factors for osteoporosis include thin body frame, Asian or Caucasian race, family history, inactivity, and eating disorders. Women who smoke, drink, or regularly miss periods are also at greater risk. Hyperthyroidism may also cause osteoporosis.

Osteoporosis is a silent disease; there may be no symptoms until a bone breaks and the condition is recognized after X-rays. The first sign may be hip or low back pain, or painful swelling of a wrist after a fall.

Prevention

Start to build sturdy bones in childhood. Peak bone mass is reached during your twenties and thirties. These steps can help you build and keep strong bones throughout your life.

• Get regular weight-bearing exercise, such as walking. Exercise helps keep bones strong. See Chapter 16.

• Get plenty of calcium in your diet. The average North American diet contains about 500 mg per day, but the 1996 Canadian Consensus

Guidelines recommends a prevention dose of calcium at 1,000 mg to 1,500 mg per day along with vitamin D 400 to 800 units/day. Pregnant women and breast-feeding mothers should get about 1,200 mg per day. After menopause, 1,000 to 1,500 mg are recommended. The best source of calcium is low-fat dairy products. Milk, cheese, and yogurt are the richest sources of calcium. Vitamin D, which helps us use calcium, is added to milk. See page 261.

- If you are unable to get all the calcium you need from your diet, take two to three calcium carbonate tablets (TUMS) each day with meals or with milk. TUMS have 200 mg of calcium per tablet. Don't take more than four to six tablets per day, and drink lots of water, because they can cause constipation.

- Don't smoke, and drink alcohol only in moderation (one drink per day), if at all.

When to Call a Health Professional

- If you are at risk of osteoporosis and are nearing menopause, talk with your doctor about estrogen or hormone replacement therapy. It is the most effective way to prevent osteoporosis. See page 177.

- If a fall causes hip pain or if you are unable to get up after a fall.

- If you have sudden, unexplained back pain that does not improve after two to three days of home treatment.

Plantar Fasciitis

Plantar fasciitis is a condition that occurs when the thick, fibrous tissue that covers the bottom of your foot (plantar fascia) becomes inflamed and painful. Athletes (especially runners), middle-aged people, and those who are overweight tend to develop plantar fasciitis. Repetitive exercises such as running and jumping sports can lead to heel pain and plantar fasciitis.

An excessive inward rolling of the foot during walking or running (called pronation) can also cause heel pain and plantar fasciitis. Pronation can be due to poor arch support, worn-out shoes, tight calf muscles, or by running downhill or on uneven surfaces.

Achilles tendinitis can cause pain in the back of the heel.

A **heel spur** is a calcium buildup that may occur where the plantar fascia attaches to the heel. It does not change the treatment of plantar fasciitis.

Prevention

- Stretch your Achilles tendon and calf muscles several times a day (see page 244). Stretching is important for both athletes and nonathletes.

- Maintain a reasonable weight for your height.

- Wear shoes with well-cushioned soles and good arch supports. Replace athletic shoes every few months because padding wears out.

- Establish good exercise habits. Increase mileage slowly, limit your running and training on hilly terrain, and run on softer surfaces (grass or dirt) rather than concrete. Cross-train by alternating running with different sports.

Home Treatment

Treat heel pain when it first appears to keep plantar fasciitis or other problems from becoming chronic.

- Reduce all weight-bearing activities to a pain-free level.

- Apply ice to your heel. See "Ice and Cold Packs" on page 77.

- You may wish to try an over-the-counter arch support.

- Do not go barefoot until the pain is completely gone. Wear shoes or arch-supporting sandals during all weight-bearing activities, even going to the bathroom during the night.

- Take aspirin, ibuprofen, or naproxen to relieve pain.

- Stretch the calf muscles. See page 244.

- For achilles tendinitis, try putting heel lifts or heel cups in both shoes. Use them only until the pain is gone (continue other self-care).

- Avoid "running through the pain." Reduce your activity to a level that does not cause pain. Try low-impact activities such as cycling or swimming to speed healing.

- Do not return to high-impact activity until you have been pain-free for one week. When you do return, start slowly and ice your heel afterward. If the pain recurs, start home treatment again.

When to Call a Health Professional

- If heel pain occurs with fever, redness or heat in your heel, or if there is numbness or tingling in your heel.

- If pain continues when you are not standing or bearing any weight on your heel.

- If heel pain persists for one to two weeks despite home treatment.

Sports Injuries

Injuries are common among physically active people. Most sports injuries are due to either traumatic injury or overuse and can be avoided by proper conditioning, training, and equipment.

Traumatic injuries:

Strains, Sprains, and Fractures, page 74.

Stress fractures, page 75.

Overuse injuries:

Bursitis and Tendinitis, page 64.

Tennis or golfer's elbow, page 66.

Patellar tendinitis, page 69.

Achilles tendinitis, and plantar fasciitis, page 72.

Prevention

- Warm up before exercise. Cold, stiff muscles and ligaments are more susceptible to injury. Cool down and stretch after activities. See page 243.

- Increase the intensity and duration of activities and exercise gradually. As your fitness level improves, you will be able to do increasingly strenuous exercise without injury.

- Use proper sports techniques and equipment. For example, wear supportive, well-cushioned shoes for running, aerobics, and walking; use a two-handed tennis backhand stroke; wear protective pads for rollerskating. Make sure that your bicycle's seat and handlebars are adjusted properly for your body.

- Alternate hard workouts with easier ones to let your body rest. For example, if you run, alternate long or hard runs with shorter or easier ones. If you lift weights, don't work the same muscles two days in a row.

- Cross-train (do several activities regularly) to rest your muscles. Alternate days of walking with biking, running, or swimming.

- Don't ignore aches and pains. A few days of reduced activity or rest, ice, and other home treatment when you feel the first twinge of pain may help you avoid more serious problems.

Home Treatment

The biggest home treatment challenge for most sports injuries is to get enough rest to allow healing without losing overall conditioning. This approach is called relative rest.

- Keep the rest of your body fit by cross-training with activities that don't stress the injured area: swimming or biking for sore ankles or feet; walking or biking for sore shoulders or elbows. Don't hurry the return to the activity that caused the injury. Cross-training can maintain your level of fitness.

- Resume your regular activity gradually. Start with a slow, easy pace and increase only if you have no pain.

- Break your sport down into components. If you can throw a ball a short distance without pain, try increasing the distance. If you can walk comfortably, try jogging. If you can jog without pain, try running.

- Also see Bursitis and Tendinitis on page 64.

- See below for tips on deciding whether a bone is broken.

Strains, Sprains, and Fractures

A **strain** is an injury caused by overstretching a muscle.

A **sprain** is an injury to the muscle and the ligaments, tendons, or soft tissues around a joint.

A **fracture** is a broken bone.

All three injuries cause pain and swelling. Unless a broken bone is obvious, it may be difficult to tell if an injury is a strain, sprain, or fracture. Injuries often involve all three. Rapid swelling often indicates a more serious injury.

Most minor strains and sprains can be treated at home, but severe sprains and fractures need professional care. Apply home treatment while you wait to see your doctor.

You may have a severe sprain or broken bone if:

• The injured area is visibly swollen.

• The injured area is twisted or bent out of shape or a bone is poking through the skin.

• The injured area is black and blue.

• The pain from the injury prevents normal use of the limb, such as walking.

Splinting

Splinting immobilizes a suspected fracture to prevent further injury. There are two ways to immobilize a fracture: tie the injured limb to a stiff object, or fasten it to some other part of the body. Do not tie too tight.

For the first method, tie rolled-up newspapers or magazines, a stick, a cane, or anything that is stiff to the injured limb with a rope, a belt, or anything else that will work.

Position the splint so the injured limb cannot bend. A general rule is to splint from a joint above the fracture to a joint below it. For example, splint a broken forearm from above the elbow to below the wrist.

For the second method, tape a broken toe to the next toe or immobilize an arm by tying it across the victim's chest.

A **stress fracture** is a weak spot or small crack in a bone caused by repeated overuse. Stress fractures in the small bones of the foot are common during intensive training for basketball, running, and other sports. The main symptom is persistent foot pain and tenderness that increases during use. There may be no visible swelling.

Prevention

• Make sure you can always see where you are walking. Don't climb stairs with both hands full.

• Don't carry objects that are too heavy.

• Use a stepstool. Do not stand on chairs or other objects.

• See prevention tips for Sports Injuries on page 74.

Home Treatment

Generally speaking, if the injury is to a muscle, ligament, tendon, or bone, the basic treatment is the same. It is a two-part process: **RICE** (rest, ice, compression, elevation) to treat the acute pain or injury; and **MSA** (movement, strength, alternate activity) to help the injury heal completely and to prevent further problems.

Begin the RICE process immediately for most injuries. If you suspect a fracture, splint the affected limb to prevent further injury (at left).

If the sprain is to a finger or part of the hand, remove all rings immediately. See page 76.

Removing a Ring

If you did not remove a ring before a sprained finger started to swell, try the following method to remove it:

• Stick the end of a slick piece of string, such as dental floss, under the ring toward the hand.

• Starting at the knuckle side of the ring, wrap the string snugly around the finger toward the end of the finger, wrapping beyond the knuckle. Each wrap should be right next to the one before.

• Grasp the end of the string that is stretched under the ring and start unwrapping it. Push the ring along ahead of the unwrapped string as you unwrap it until the ring passes the knuckle.

Start wrapping here

Removing a ring

R. Rest. Do not put weight on the injured joint for at least 24 to 48 hours.

• Use crutches to support a badly sprained knee or ankle.

• Support a sprained wrist, elbow, or shoulder with a sling, which helps the injury heal faster.

• Rest a sprained finger or toe by taping it to a healthy one.

Injured muscle, ligament, or tendon tissue needs time and rest to heal. Stress fractures need rest for two to four months.

I. Ice. Cold will reduce pain and swelling and promote healing. Heat feels nice, but it does more harm than good until all of the swelling is gone.

• Apply ice or cold packs immediately to prevent or minimize swelling. For difficult-to-reach injuries, a cold pack works best. See "Ice and Cold Packs" on page 77.

C. Compression. Wrap the injury with an elastic (Ace) bandage or compression sleeve to immobilize and compress the sprain. Don't wrap it too tightly, which can cause more swelling. Loosen the bandage if it gets too tight. A tightly wrapped sprain may fool you into thinking you can keep using the joint. With or without a wrap, the joint needs total rest for one to two days.

Ice and Cold Packs

Ice can relieve pain, swelling, and inflammation from injuries and other conditions such as arthritis. Apply ice consistently and thoroughly as long as you have symptoms. Use either a commercial cold pack or one of the following:

• Ice towel: Wet a towel with cold water and squeeze it until it is just damp. Fold the towel, place it in a plastic bag, and freeze it for 15 minutes. Remove the towel from the bag and place it on the affected area.

• Ice pack: Put about a pound of ice in a plastic bag. Add water to barely cover the ice. Squeeze the air out of the bag and seal it. Wrap the bag in a wet towel and apply to the affected area.

• Homemade cold pack: See instructions on page 287.

Ice the area at least three times a day. For the first 72 hours, ice for 10 minutes once an hour. After that, a good pattern is to ice for 15 to 20 minutes three times a day: In the morning, in the late afternoon after work or school, and about one-half hour before bedtime. Also ice after any prolonged activity or vigorous exercise.

Always keep a damp cloth between your skin and the cold pack, and press firmly against all the curves of the affected area. Do not apply ice for longer than 15 to 20 minutes at a time, and do not fall asleep with the ice on your skin.

E. Elevation. Elevate the injured area on pillows while you apply ice and anytime you are sitting or lying down. Try to keep the injury at or above the level of your heart to help minimize swelling.

• Aspirin, ibuprofen, or naproxen may help ease inflammation and pain. Do not use drugs to mask the pain while you continue to use the injured joint. Do not give aspirin to children or teens under age 20. Review guidelines on pages 295 and 296.

• The use of heat (hot water bottle, warm towel, heating pad) after 48 hours of cold treatments is controversial. Some experts think it will increase swelling; others think it may speed healing. If you use heat, do not apply anything that is uncomfortably warm.

Begin the **MSA** process as soon as the initial pain and swelling have subsided. This may be in two days or up to a week or longer, depending on the location and severity of the injury. Resume sports and activities slowly. Any increased pain may be a sign you need to rest a while longer.

M. Movement. Resume a full range of motion as soon as possible after an injury. After one to two days of rest, begin moving the joint. If an activity causes pain, stop it and give the joint more rest. Gentle stretching will prevent scar tissue (formed as the injury heals) from limiting movement later.

S. Strength. Once the swelling is gone and range of motion is restored, begin gradual efforts to strengthen the injured area.

A. Alternate activities. After the first few days, but while the injury is still healing, phase in regular exercise using activities or sports that do not place a strain on the injured part. See page 74.

When to Call a Health Professional

• Call for immediate care if a bone is poking through the skin, or if a limb below the injury is white, cold, or numb.

• If you suspect a severe sprain or fracture (see page 74), call for an urgent-care or same-day appointment. After you have splinted the injury and applied ice, a short delay in receiving professional care will not affect the outcome.

• If a sprained joint is very unstable, won't support your weight, or wobbles from side to side.

• If you cannot bear weight on a sprained ankle after 24 hours, or if it hurts to bear weight after three days.

• If pain is still severe after two days of home treatment.

• If a sprain does not improve after four days of home treatment.

Weakness and Fatigue

Weakness is a lack of physical strength causing inability or difficulty in moving arms, legs, or other muscles.

Fatigue is feeling tired or exhausted, or a lack of energy.

Unexplained muscle weakness is usually more serious than fatigue. It may be due to metabolic problems such as diabetes (see page 266), thyroid problems, kidney problems, or stroke. Call your doctor immediately.

Fatigue, on the other hand, can usually be treated with self-care. Most fatigue is caused by lack of exercise, stress or overwork, poor sleep, depression, worry, or boredom. Colds and flu may sometimes cause fatigue and weakness, but the symptoms disappear as the illness runs its course.

Prevention

• Regular exercise is your best defense against fatigue. If you feel too tired to exercise vigorously, try a short walk.

• Eat a well-balanced diet. See Chapter 17.

• Make sure you are getting enough sleep. See page 280.

• Deal with feelings of depression. See page 276.

Home Treatment

- Follow the prevention guidelines above and be patient. It may take a while to feel energetic again.

- Listen to your body. Alternate rest with exercise.

- Limit drugs that might contribute to fatigue. Tranquilizers and cold and allergy medications are particularly suspect.

- Reduce your use of caffeine, nicotine, and alcohol.

- Cut back on watching television. Spend that time with friends, new activities, or travel to break the fatigue cycle.

When to Call a Health Professional

- If you have unexplained muscle weakness in one area of your body.

- If severe fatigue causes you to limit your usual activities for longer than two weeks despite home treatment.

- If you experience sudden, unplanned weight loss.

- If you do not feel more energetic after six weeks of home treatment.

Chronic Fatigue Syndrome

Chronic fatigue syndrome (CFS) is a flu-like illness that causes severe fatigue lasting longer than six months. Other symptoms include mild fever, sore throat, painful lymph glands, muscle weakness and pain, headaches, and sleep problems.

CFS is difficult to diagnose. There is no definitive lab test. Many other illnesses, such as depression, thyroid disorders, or mononucleosis, cause similar symptoms. A CFS diagnosis is made only after fatigue and other symptoms continue for at least six months and other possible causes have been ruled out.

The fatigue and other symptoms usually develop quickly in a previously healthy person. Treatment is focused on adequate rest, balanced diet, and mild exercise. No medications are known to cure CFS. Treatment of the individual symptoms can be effective. For treatment of depression, which develops in about half of CFS patients, see page 276.

Call your doctor if unexplained fatigue is severe, persistent, and interferes with your activities for more than two weeks despite home treatment.

Life is made up of sobs, sniffles, and smiles,
with sniffles predominating.
O. Henry

Chapter 6

Chest and Respiratory Problems

Chest and respiratory problems can be as simple as a minor cold or as life-threatening as a heart attack. For most respiratory problems, including allergies, colds, sore throats, sinusitis, and tonsillitis, this chapter will help you decide what to do at home and when to call your doctor.

Start this chapter with a look at the chart on the next page. From asthma to pneumonia and from heart attack to heartburn, the chart will lead you to the information you need the most. If you don't find what you are looking for, please check the index.

Allergies

Allergies come in many forms. Hay fever is the most common allergy. Symptoms include itchy, watery eyes, sneezing, runny, stuffy, or itchy nose, temporary loss of smell, headache,

and fatigue. Dark circles under the eyes ("allergic shiners") or postnasal drip may also accompany hay fever. A child with allergies may snore, wake with a sore throat, breathe through the mouth, and frequently rub her nose. Allergy symptoms are often like cold symptoms, but usually last longer.

The most common causes of allergies are particles in the air, such as pollen, house dust mites, mold or mildew, and animal dander. Allergies seem to run in families. Parents with hay fever often have children with allergies. Hay fever usually develops in the early teens, but can occur at any age.

You can often discover the cause of an allergy by noting when symptoms occur. Symptoms that occur at the same time each year (especially during spring, early summer, or early fall) are often due to grass, weed, or tree pollen. Allergies that persist all year long may be due to dust mites in

Chest, Respiratory, Nose, and Throat Problems

Chest and Respiratory Symptoms	Possible Causes
Wheezing or difficulty breathing	See Allergies, p. 81; Asthma, p. 85; Bronchitis, p. 89; Pneumonia, p. 98.
Rapid, shallow, labored breathing	See Pneumonia, p. 98.
Chest-wall pain with cough, fever, and yellow-green or rusty sputum	See Bronchitis, p. 89; Pneumonia, p. 98.
Burning, pain, or discomfort behind the breastbone	See Heartburn, p. 36; Chest Pain, p. 91.
Chest pain with sweating or rapid pulse	Possible heart attack. Call for help. See CPR, p. 204.
Coughing	See Coughs, p. 94.

Nose and Throat Symptoms	Possible Causes
Stuffy or runny nose with watery eyes, sneezing	See Allergies, p. 81; Colds, p. 92.
Cold symptoms with fever, headache, body aches, fatigue	See Influenza, p. 96.
Thick green, yellow, or grey nasal discharge with fever and facial pain	See Sinusitis, p. 99.
Foul odour from nose; swollen, inflamed nasal tissue	See Objects in the Nose, p. 227; Sinusitis, p. 99.
Pale, bluish nasal tissue	See Allergies, p. 81.
Sore throat	See Sore Throat, p. 101; Tonsillitis, p. 103.
Sore throat with white spots on tonsils, swollen glands, fever of 101° or higher	See Strep Throat, p. 101.
Swollen tonsils, sore throat, fever	See Tonsillitis, p. 103.
Swollen lymph nodes in the neck	See Swollen Glands, p. 102; Tonsillitis, p. 103.
Hoarseness, loss of voice	See Laryngitis, p. 97.

household dust, mold spores, or animal dander. Animal allergy is often easy to detect; symptoms clear up when you stay away from the animal.

Life-Threatening Allergic Reactions

A few people have severe allergies to insect stings or certain foods or drugs, especially penicillin. For these people, the allergic reaction is sudden and severe, and may cause difficulty breathing and a drop in blood pressure (anaphylactic shock).

An anaphylactic reaction is a medical emergency and prompt care is needed. If you have had a severe allergic reaction, doctors suggest that you carry an epinephrine syringe (EpiPen, Ana-Kit) designed to self-administer a shot that will decrease the severity of the reaction. If you have had an allergic reaction to a drug, wear a medical identification bracelet that will tell health professionals about your allergy if you cannot.

It is critical that parents of children with such conditions notify the school and ensure that the school staff are educated about the particular allergic reaction and how to give the EpiPen or Ana-Kit.

Prevention

• There is no practical prevention for hay fever. Avoiding the substance that causes allergy attacks will help. See page 265 for more information on food allergies.

• If you or your spouse have a history of allergies, consider breast-feeding your infants. There is some evidence that feeding only breast milk during the first six months of life may reduce a child's risk of developing food allergies.

Home Treatment

If you can discover the source of your allergies, avoiding that substance is the best treatment. Keep a record of your symptoms and the plants, animals, foods, or chemicals that seem to trigger them.

If your symptoms are seasonal and seem to be related to pollen:

• Keep your house and car windows closed. Keep bedroom windows closed at night.

• Limit the time you spend outside when pollen counts are high. Dogs and other pets may bring large amounts of pollen into your house.

If your symptoms are year-round and seem to be related to dust:

• Keep the bedroom as dust-free as possible, since most of your time is spent there.

• Avoid carpeting, upholstered furniture, and heavy draperies that collect dust. Vacuuming doesn't pick up dust mites.

• Cover your mattress and box spring with dust-proof cases and wipe them clean weekly. Avoid wool or down blankets and feather pillows. Wash all bedding weekly in hot water.

• Consider using an air conditioner or air purifier with a special HEPA filter. Rent one before buying to see if it helps.

If your symptoms are year-round and worse during damp weather, they may be related to mold or mildew:

• Keep the house well-ventilated and dry. Keep the humidity below 50 percent. Use a dehumidifier during humid weather.

• Use an air conditioner, which removes mold spores from the air. Change or clean heating and cooling system filters regularly.

• Clean bathroom and kitchen surfaces often with bleach to reduce mold growth.

If you are allergic to a pet:

• Keep the animal outside, or at least out of the bedroom.

• If your symptoms are severe, the best solution may be to get rid of the pet.

General information on avoiding irritants:

• Avoid yardwork (raking, mowing), which stirs up both pollen and mold. If you must do it, wear a mask and take a non-sedating antihistamine beforehand.

• Avoid smoking and inhaling other people's smoke.

• Eliminate aerosol sprays, perfumes, room deodourizers, cleaning products, and other substances that may add to the problem.

• Antihistamines and decongestants may relieve some allergy symptoms. Use caution when taking these drugs. See pages 293 and 294.

What About Immunotherapy?

Immunotherapy involves a series of shots given to desensitize your body to an allergen. It requires regular treatments lasting up to three to four years. Because of the time and expense involved, you need a realistic idea of the benefits before agreeing to the treatment.

Immunotherapy is effective only if the specific allergen has been identified by sensitivity testing. It is 98 percent effective for allergies to bee stings and other insect venoms. For most people, it is effective against grass, tree, and weed pollens, as well as house dust, the house dust mite, and dog and cat dander.

The following factors make it more likely that immunotherapy will be worthwhile for you:

1. Your symptoms have bothered you a lot for at least two years.

2. You have tried home treatment without success.

3. You have tried both prescription and nonprescription medications without relief.

4. Immunotherapy is effective for the allergens identified by your skin tests.

• For more information on allergies, contact your local health unit/public health office, provincial Lung Association, or Allergy/Asthma Association.

When to Call a Health Professional

• Go to the Emergency Room *immediately* if signs of a severe allergic reaction develop, especially soon after taking a drug, eating a certain food, or being stung by an insect:

  ◦ Wheezing or difficulty breathing

  ◦ Swelling around the lips, tongue, or face, or significant swelling around the site of the insect sting (e.g., entire arm or leg is swollen)

  ◦ Skin rash, itching, feeling of warmth, or hives

• If symptoms worsen over time, and your home treatment doesn't help. Your doctor can recommend stronger medication or desensitizing shots. Allergy shots may help reduce sensitivity to some allergens. See page 84.

Asthma

Asthma is the Greek word for panting. A person having an asthma attack is literally panting for breath. Asthma is a condition that causes inflammation and obstruction of the airways. The muscles surrounding the air tubes (bronchial tubes) of the lungs go into spasm, the mucous lining swells, and secretions build up, making breathing quite difficult.

Asthma usually occurs in attacks or episodes. During an attack, the person may make a wheezing or whistling sound while breathing, cough a great deal, or spit up mucus. A chronic dry cough may be the only symptom.

Many things can trigger asthma, including allergens, such as dust, pollen, mold, and animal dander. In general, infections are the most common triggers of asthma. Other triggers include exercise; cigarette or wood smoke; changes in weather; colds or the flu; chemical vapors from household or workplace products; analgesics (especially aspirin), anti-inflammatories, and some medications; food preservatives and dyes; and emotional stress.

Asthma usually develops in childhood but may also begin later in life. The first episode often follows a cold or the flu. It is more common in children who are exposed to cigarette smoke in the home. Many children outgrow asthma as they get older but will still be at risk for it in adulthood.

Most children and adults can control their asthma by avoiding triggers that cause attacks and using medications to manage symptoms. Severe attacks can usually be treated with inhaled or injected medications. Asthma attacks are rarely fatal if they are treated *promptly*.

Prevention

Discover and avoid the things that cause your asthma attacks:

• Review the home treatment for allergies on page 83.

• Avoid smoke of all kinds. Stop smoking and avoid secondhand smoke. Eat, work, travel, and relax in smoke-free areas. Stay away from wood-burning stoves.

• Avoid air pollution. Stay indoors when the air pollution is high.

- Avoid strong odors, fumes, and perfume.

- Avoid breathing cold air. In cold weather, breathe through your nose and cover your nose and mouth with a scarf or cold weather mask (available at most drug stores).

- Avoid indoor pets with fur or feathers. Outdoor pets or pets such as fish or turtles may cause less trouble.

- Reduce your risk of colds and flu by washing your hands often and getting a flu shot each year.

Build up the strength of your lungs and airways:

- Get regular exercise. Swimming or water aerobics may be good choices because the moist air is less likely to trigger an attack. If vigorous exercise triggers asthma attacks, talk with your doctor. Adjusting your medication and your exercise routine may help.

- Practise roll-breathing as described on page 248.

Home Treatment

- Learn to use a peakflow metre to monitor your ability to exhale. Used regularly, this device measures your progress as you improve your ability to breathe. It also helps you tell when an attack may be coming on so you can take appropriate steps. Peakflow metres can be purchased at a community pharmacy or through a hospital respiratory department.

How to Use an Inhaler and Spacer

1. Shake the inhaler well for five seconds. Remove the protective cap and insert the mouthpiece of the inhaler into one end of the spacer. Hold the inhaler with your index finger on top and your thumb supporting the bottom.

2. Breathe out as much as possible to empty the lungs. Tilt your head back, place the mouthpiece of the spacer tube in your mouth, and close your lips around it.

3. Press down on the top of the inhaler to release a puff of medication. Breathe in slowly and deeply, filling your lungs with as much air as possible. If you hear a musical sound, you are inhaling too fast. Hold your breath for at least 10 seconds, then breathe out.

4. With your lips still closed around the mouthpiece, take two or three more deep breaths, holding each one for 10 seconds. For maximum effectiveness, wait a minute or two before taking the next puff.

5. Wash the inhaler mouthpiece, spacer, and protective caps weekly with mild soapy water and allow to air dry.

- If you have significant asthma, ask your doctor for a written care plan to guide you in adding medication as needed.

- If your child has an asthma attack, remain calm. Give the recommended medication and help the child relax. Make sure your child and his teachers or child care providers know what to do in case of an attack.

- Learn to use a metred-dose inhaler. Inhalers help get the right amount of medication to the airways. However, it takes some skill to use the inhaler correctly. A device called a spacer is now recommended for use with an inhaler (see page 86). Ask your health care professional to watch you use your inhaler and spacer to make sure you are doing it right.

- Ask your health professional about anti-inflammatory inhalers.

- People with asthma usually do better in warm, moist air than in cold, dry air. If you're feeling "tight," stand or sit in a warm shower for 5 to 10 minutes.

- Increase your fluid intake to help thin bronchial mucus.

- Aspirin and ibuprofen can cause severe reactions in some people with asthma. Use them with caution and discuss them with your doctor. If you find that these medications bother you, avoid using them.

- Do not use over-the-counter cold and cough medicines unless your doctor tells you to do so.

- Practise the relaxation exercises on pages 248 to 250.

- Follow the prevention tips above.

- Work in partnership with your doctor to maximize your control over your asthma.

- To get more information on managing asthma, contact your local health unit or public health office, provincial Lung Association, or Allergy/Asthma Association.

When to Call a Health Professional

- If acute asthma symptoms have occurred for the first time.

- If asthma symptoms fail to respond to your usual treatment, or if the attack is severe (peak flow is less than 50 percent of best).

- If sputum becomes discolored, particularly green, yellow, or bloody. This may be a sign of a bacterial infection (see page 88).

- If a person with asthma or other family members have not been educated about treatment, or if the medication required is not available.

- To learn exactly what to do when an attack begins. With proper training, medication, and confidence, you can often handle acute episodes without professional help.

- If you begin to use your asthma medication more often than usual, which may be a sign that your asthma is getting worse.

- To discuss allergy shots, which are sometimes helpful in preventing asthma attacks. See page 84.

- To get a referral to a support group. Talking with others who have asthma can give you information and confidence in dealing with prevention and treatment.

Bacterial Infections

Respiratory infections caused by bacteria are often hard to distinguish from those caused by viruses. In particular, a bad case of the flu (see page 96) may be hard to distinguish from a bacterial infection. Bacteria will sometimes attack the weakened system of a person with a cold or the flu. (Bacterial infections sometimes follow viral infections.)

The most common bacterial infections are ear infections and strep throat. Bronchitis, sinusitis, and pneumonia may also be caused by bacteria.

Symptoms of a bacterial infection may include:

- Fever of 40°C (104°F) or higher that does not reduce with two hours of home treatment.

- Fever over 38.3°C (101°F) with shaking chills and productive cough.

- Persistent fever. Many viral illnesses, especially the flu, cause fevers of 38.9°C (102°F) or higher for short periods of time (up to 12 to 24 hours). Call a doctor if the fever stays high:
  - 38.9°C (102°F) or higher for two full days
  - 38.3°C (101°F) or higher for three full days
  - 37.8°C (100°F) or higher for four full days

- Labored, shallow, rapid breathing with shortness of breath.

Bacterial or Viral?

Bacterial Infections

- May follow a viral infection that does not improve.

- Usually localized at a single point in the body: sinuses, ear, lungs.

- Typical bacterial infections: strep throat, ear infection.

- Antibiotics *may* help.

Viral Infections

- Usually involve different parts of the body: sore throat, runny nose, headaches, muscle aches. In the abdominal area, viruses cause nausea and/or diarrhea.

- Typical viral infections: cold, flu, stomach flu.

- Antibiotics *do not* help.

- Sputum (mucus coughed up from lungs) is yellow, green, rust-colored, or bloody, and other symptoms (fever, productive cough, severe fatigue) are worsening. Sputum that is coughed up from the lungs is more significant than mucus that has drained down the back of the throat (postnasal drip).

- Nasal discharge changes from clear to colored (yellow or green) after five to seven days of a cold, and other symptoms (such as sinus pain or fever) are worsening. If nasal discharge is colored from the start of a cold, call if it lasts longer than 7 to 10 days.

- Cough that lingers more than 7 to 10 days *after* other symptoms have cleared, especially if it is productive (bringing up sputum). A dry, hacking cough may last several weeks after a viral illness such as a cold.

- Ear pain that lasts more than 24 hours, or severe ear pain that lasts longer than one hour. If the pain is severe at night, call the next morning even if the pain has stopped. See page 114.

- Localized sinus pain persists despite two to four days of home treatment, especially if nasal discharge is colored rather than clear. See page 101.

- Sore throat lasts longer than two to three days despite home treatment, and does not "act" like a cold. See page 101.

Antibiotics are effective against bacterial infections only after they have developed, so most doctors will not prescribe them until a bacterial infection is confirmed. However, antibiotics are sometimes used to prevent recurrent sinus and ear infections. They cannot prevent complications of a viral infection. For important information about antibiotics, see page 297.

When to Call a Health Professional

Call if symptoms of a bacterial infection develop or if cough lasts more than one week. Bacterial infections need to be diagnosed and treated by a doctor.

Bronchitis

Bronchitis is an inflammation and irritation of the bronchial tubes in the lungs. It is caused most often by viruses or bacteria, but may also be caused by cigarette smoke or air pollution. It often occurs after a cold or an upper respiratory infection that does not heal completely.

The inflamed bronchial tubes secrete a sticky mucus (called sputum), which is difficult for the hairs (cilia) on the bronchi to clear out of the lungs. The productive cough that comes with bronchitis is the body's attempt to get rid of the mucus. Other symptoms include discomfort or tightness in the chest, fatigue, low fever, sore throat, runny nose, and sometimes wheezing. Severe cases may lead to pneumonia.

Bronchitis can become chronic, especially among people who smoke or who work in polluted air. Seventy-five percent of people with chronic bronchitis have a history of heavy smoking.

Chronic bronchitis may occur with emphysema or chronic asthma. Any combination of these conditions is known as chronic obstructive pulmonary disease (COPD).

Prevention

- Give proper home care to minor respiratory problems such as colds and flu. See pages 92 and 96.

- Stop smoking. People who smoke and those who live with them have more frequent bouts of bronchitis.

- Avoid polluted air.

Home Treatment

Self-care for bronchitis focuses on getting rid of the mucus in your lungs. Here is what you can do at home to speed healing.

- Increase your fluid intake to as much as 8 to 12 glasses per day (until you are urinating more than usual). Liquids help thin the mucus in the lungs so your cough can clear it out.

- Stop smoking and avoid others' smoke. Smoke irritates the lungs and slows healing.

- Breathe moist air from a humidifier, hot shower, or a sink filled with hot water. The heat and moisture will liquefy mucus and help the cough bring it up.

- Get some extra rest. Let your energy go to healing.

- Have someone massage your chest and back muscles. The massage increases blood flow to the chest and helps you relax.

- Take aspirin, ibuprofen, or acetaminophen to relieve fever and body aches. Do not give aspirin to children and teens younger than 20.

- If a dry, unproductive cough keeps you awake, take a cough syrup containing dextromethorphan. Avoid products containing more than one active ingredient. See page 294.

When to Call a Health Professional

If the following signs of a bacterial infection develop:

- Fever of 38°C (104°F) or higher that does not reduce with two hours of home treatment.

- Fever over 38.3°C (101°F) with shaking chills and productive cough.

- Persistent fever. Many viral illnesses, especially the flu, cause fevers of 38.9°C (102°F) or higher for short periods of time (up to 12 to 24 hours). Call a doctor if the fever stays high:
  - 38.9°C (102°F) or higher for two full days
  - 38.3°C (101°F) or higher for three full days
  - 37.8°C (100°F) or higher for four full days

- Labored, shallow, rapid breathing with shortness of breath.

- Sputum (mucus coughed up from lungs) is yellow, green, rust-colored, or bloody, and other symptoms (fever, productive cough, severe fatigue) are worsening. Sputum that is coughed up from the lungs is more significant than mucus that has drained down the back of the throat (postnasal drip).

- Cough that lingers more than 7 to 10 days.

- If the sick person is an infant, an older adult, or is chronically ill, especially with lung problems.

Chest Pain

CALL 911 OR OTHER EMERGENCY SERVICES IMMEDIATELY if chest pain is crushing or squeezing, increases in intensity, or occurs with any of the symptoms of a heart attack:

• **Sweating**

• **Shortness of breath**

• **Pain radiating to the arm, neck, or jaw**

• **Nausea or vomiting**

• **Dizziness**

• **Rapid and/or irregular pulse**

Chest pain is a key warning sign of a heart attack, but it may also be caused by other problems.

Pain that increases when you press on the site is probably chest wall pain, which may be caused by strained muscles or ligaments in the chest wall. A shooting pain that lasts a few seconds, or a quick pain at the end of a deep breath, is usually not a cause for concern. Hyperventilation (see page 224) can also cause chest pain.

Chest pain can be associated with other disorders. With pleurisy or pneumonia (see page 100), the pain will get worse with a deep breath or cough; heart pain will not. An ulcer (see page 43) can cause chest pain that is worse on an empty stomach. Gallbladder pain may worsen after a meal or in the middle of the night. Heartburn or indigestion can also cause chest pain. See page 36.

Angina is pain, pressure, heaviness, or numbness behind the breastbone or across the chest. It is caused by poor circulation to the heart muscle due to artherosclerosis (hardening of the arteries) in the arteries that supply blood to the heart. It is a symptom of coronary artery disease. The symptoms of angina may radiate to the neck, jaws, shoulders, arms, or wrists. It may be brought on by stress or exertion and is relieved by rest and use of prescribed medication.

A **heart attack** (myocardial infarction) is caused by blocked blood flow to the heart muscle. The pain of a heart attack is similar to that of angina. Both heart attack and angina pain usually last longer than five minutes and occur with other symptoms such as sweating, nausea, or shortness of breath. However, unlike angina, the pain of a heart attack is usually not relieved by rest.

Lifestyle factors that may increase your risk of a heart attack include:

• Smoking

• High blood pressure

• High cholesterol

• Inactive lifestyle

• High stress levels

Home Treatment

For chest wall pain caused by strained muscles or ligaments:

• Use pain relievers such as aspirin, ibuprofen, or acetaminophen.

• Ben-Gay or Vicks VapoRub A-535 may soothe sore muscles.

• Avoid the activity that strains the chest area.

When to Call a Health Professional

CALL 911 OR EMERGENCY SERVICES IMMEDIATELY if symptoms of a heart attack are present (see page 91). See CPR on page 204.

- If your chest pain has been diagnosed by a doctor and he has prescribed a home treatment plan, follow it. Call 911 or emergency services if the pain worsens or you develop any of the heart attack symptoms on page 91.

- If you suspect angina and your symptoms have not been diagnosed, call your doctor immediately.

- If symptoms of angina do not respond to your prescribed treatment, or if the pattern of your angina changes.

If minor chest pain occurs *without* the symptoms of a heart attack, call a health professional:

- If the person has a history of heart disease or blood clots in the lungs.

- If chest pain is constant, nagging, and not relieved by rest.

- If chest pain occurs with symptoms of pneumonia. See page 98.

- If any chest pain lasts 48 hours without improvement.

Colds

The common cold is caused by any one of 200 viruses. The symptoms of a cold are a runny nose, red eyes, sneezing, sore throat, dry cough, headache, and general body aches. There is a gradual one- or two-day onset. As a cold progresses, the nasal mucus may thicken. This is the stage just before a cold dries up. A cold usually lasts about one or two weeks.

Colds occur throughout the year, but are most common in late winter and early spring. The average child has six colds a year; adults have fewer.

Using a mouthwash will not prevent a cold and antibiotics will not cure one. There is no cure for the common cold. If you catch one, treat the symptoms.

Sometimes a cold will lead to a bacterial infection (see page 88) such as bronchitis or pneumonia. Good home treatment of colds can help prevent complications.

If someone seems to have a cold all the time, or if cold symptoms last two weeks or more, suspect allergies (see page 81) or sinusitis (see page 99).

Prevention

- Eat well and get plenty of sleep and exercise to keep up your resistance.

- Wash your hands often, particularly when you are around people who have colds.

- Keep your hands away from your nose, eyes, and mouth.

- Stop smoking.

- Consider breast-feeding your baby. Breast-fed babies seem to have fewer, milder colds.

Home Treatment

. Home treatment for a cold will help relieve symptoms and prevent complications.

- Get extra rest after work or school. Slow down just a little from your usual routine. It isn't necessary to stay home in bed, but take care not to expose others.

- Drink plenty of liquids. Hot water, herbal tea, or chicken soup will help relieve congestion.

- Take aspirin, ibuprofen, or acetaminophen to relieve aches. Do not give aspirin to children and teens under age 20.

- Humidify the bedroom and take hot showers to relieve nasal stuffiness.

- Watch the back of your throat for postnasal drip. If streaks of mucus appear, gargle to prevent a sore throat.

- Use disposable tissues, not handkerchiefs, to reduce spreading the virus to others.

- If your nose is red and raw from rubbing with tissues, put a bit of petroleum jelly on the sore area.

- Avoid cold remedies that combine drugs to treat many different symptoms, such as decongestants, antihistamines, and pain relievers. Treat each symptom separately. Take a decongestant for stuffiness, a cough medicine for a cough. See Home Treatment for coughs on page 94.

- Avoid antihistamines. They are not an effective treatment for colds.

- Use nasal decongestant sprays for only three days or less. Continued use may lead to a "rebound" effect, when the mucous membranes swell up more than before using the spray. See page 293 for nose drops you can make at home.

When to Call a Health Professional

If the following signs of a bacterial infection develop:

- Fever of 38°C (104°F) or higher that does not reduce with two hours of home treatment.

- Fever over 38.3°C (101°F) with shaking chills and productive cough.

- Persistent fever. Many viral illnesses, especially the flu, cause fevers of 38.9°C (102°F) or higher for short periods of time (up to 12 to 24 hours). Call a doctor if the fever stays high:
  ○ 38.9°C (102°F) or higher for two full days
  ○ 38.3°C (101°F) or higher for three full days
  ○ 37.8°C (100°F) or higher for four full days

- Labored, shallow, rapid breathing with shortness of breath.

- Sputum (mucus coughed up from lungs) is yellow, green, rust-colored, or bloody, and other symptoms (fever, productive cough, severe fatigue) are worsening. Sputum that is coughed up from the lungs is more significant than mucus that has drained down the back of the throat (postnasal drip).

- If facial pain, fever, and other signs of sinusitis develop. See page 99.

- Nasal discharge changes from clear to colored (yellow or green) after five to seven days of a cold, and other symptoms (such as sinus pain or fever) are worsening. If nasal discharge is colored from the start of a cold, call if it lasts longer than 7 to 10 days.

- Cough that lingers more than 7 to 10 days.

Coughs

Coughing is the body's way of removing foreign material or mucus from the lungs. Coughs have distinctive traits you can learn to recognize.

Productive coughs produce phlegm or mucus (sputum) that comes up from the lungs. This kind of cough generally should not be suppressed; it is needed to clear mucus from the lungs.

Nonproductive coughs are dry coughs that do not produce sputum. A dry, hacking cough may develop toward the end of a cold or after exposure to an irritant, such as dust or smoke. Dry coughs that follow viral illnesses may last up to several weeks and often get worse at night.

A chronic dry cough may be a sign of mild asthma. See page 85. Some medications can cause chronic cough.

Prevention

- Don't smoke. A dry, hacking "smoker's cough" means your lungs are constantly irritated.

- Increase fluid intake to as much as 2 litres (8 to 10 glasses) of water every day. You are drinking enough if you are urinating more often than usual.

Home Treatment

- Drink lots of water. Water helps loosen phlegm and soothe an irritated throat. Dry, hacking coughs respond to honey in hot water, tea, or lemon juice. (Do not give honey to children under one year of age.)

- Cough drops can soothe irritated throats, but most have no effect on the cough-producing mechanism. Expensive medicine-flavored cough drops are not any better than inexpensive candy-flavored ones or hard candy.

- Elevate your head with extra pillows at night to ease a dry cough.

- Use an over-the-counter cough suppressant containing dextromethorphan to help quiet a dry, hacking cough so you can sleep. If you have a productive cough, don't suppress it so much that you are no longer bringing up mucus. See Cough Preparations on page 293.

- For coughs caused by inhaled irritants (smoke, dust, or other pollutants), avoid exposure or wear a face mask.

When to Call a Health Professional

If the following signs of a bacterial infection develop:

- Fever of 40°C (104°F) or higher that does not reduce with two hours of home treatment.

- Fever over 38.3°C (101°F) with shaking chills and productive cough.

- Persistent fever. Many viral illnesses, especially the flu, cause fevers of 38.9°C (102°F) or higher for short periods of time (up to 12 to 24 hours). Call a doctor if the fever stays high:
  - 38.9°C (102°F) or higher for two full days
  - 38.3°C (101°F) or higher for three full days
  - 37.8°C (100°F) or higher for four full days

- Labored, shallow, rapid breathing with shortness of breath.

- Sputum (mucus coughed up from lungs) is yellow, green, rust-colored, or bloody, and other symptoms (fever, productive cough, fatigue) are worsening. Sputum that is coughed up from the lungs is more significant than mucus that has drained down the back of the throat (postnasal drip).

- Cough that lingers more than 7 to 10 days. A dry, hacking cough may last several weeks after a viral illness such as a cold.

- If any cough lasts more than four weeks.

Description and Treatment of Coughs

Type of Cough	Possible Causes
Loud cough like a seal's bark	See Croup, p. 157.
Dry cough in the morning that gets better as day goes on	Dry air; cigarette smoking. Increase fluids. Humidify the bedroom. Stop smoking. See Coughs, p. 94.
Hacking, dry, nonproductive cough; may be worse at night	Common for several weeks following a viral illness. May be due to postnasal drip, smoking, or mild asthma. Increase fluids. Try a decongestant. Stop smoking. See Coughs, p. 94; Asthma, p. 85.
Productive cough following a cold or flu	See Bronchitis, p. 89; Pneumonia, p. 98; Sinusitis, p. 99.
Dry, sudden-onset cough after a choking episode, most often in an infant or toddler	Foreign object in the throat. See Choking, p. 214.

Influenza (Flu)

Influenza, or flu, is a viral illness that commonly occurs in the winter and affects many people at once (epidemic). (The name "influenza" comes from the Italian word for "influence.")

Influenza has symptoms similar to a cold, but they are usually more severe and come on quite suddenly.

The flu is commonly thought of as a respiratory illness, but the whole body can be affected. Symptoms include fever (38.3° to 40°C or 101° to 104°F), chills, muscle aches, headache, pain in the muscles around the eyes, fatigue and weakness, sneezing, and runny nose. Symptoms may last five to seven days. Most other viruses, such as colds, have milder symptoms that don't last as long.

Although a person with the flu feels very sick, it seldom leads to more serious complications. The illness is usually dangerous only for infants, older adults, and people with chronic diseases.

Prevention

- Get a flu shot each autumn if you are over 65, if you have a chronic illness, such as asthma, heart disease, or diabetes, or if you are a health care worker who might expose high-risk people to the flu if you catch it. The flu shot is available from most health units/public health offices or family physicians.

- Keep up your resistance to infection with a good diet, plenty of rest, and regular exercise.

- Avoid exposure to the virus. Wash your hands often and keep your hands away from your nose, eyes, and mouth.

Home Treatment

- Get plenty of rest.

- Drink extra fluids, at least one glass of water or juice every waking hour.

Encephalitis and Meningitis

Encephalitis is an inflammation of the brain that may occur following a viral infection, such as chicken pox, flu, measles, mumps, or cold sores (herpes simplex).

Meningitis is a viral or bacterial illness that causes inflammation around the tissues surrounding the brain and spinal cord. It may follow an infection, such as an ear or sinus infection, or a viral illness.

Encephalitis and meningitis are serious illnesses with similar symptoms. Call a health professional *immediately* if the following symptoms develop, especially following a viral illness or a mosquito bite:

- Severe headache with stiff neck, fever, nausea, and vomiting

- Drowsiness, lethargy, confusion, or delirium

- Bulging soft spot on an infant's head (when the baby is not crying)

• Take acetaminophen, aspirin, or ibuprofen to relieve fever, headache, and muscle aches. (Do not give aspirin to children and teens under age 20.)

When to Call a Health Professional

It is common for adults with influenza to have high fevers (up to 39.4°C or 103°F) for three to four days. When trying to decide if you need to see a doctor, consider the likelihood that you have the flu versus a possible bacterial infection. If it is the flu season, and many people in your community have similar symptoms, it is likely that you have the flu. However, if you have any concerns, or any of the following signs of a bacterial infection, contact your doctor.

• Fever of 40°C (104°F) or higher that does not reduce with two hours of home treatment.

• Fever over 38.3°C (101°F) with shaking chills and productive cough.

• Persistent fever. Flu may cause fevers 38.9°C (102°F) or higher for three to four days. However, unless you are sure you have flu, it may be wise to call your doctor if a fever stays high:
  ○ 38.9°C (102°F) or higher for two full days
  ○ 38.3°C (101°F) or higher for three full days
  ○ 37.8°C (100°F) or higher for four full days

• Labored, shallow, rapid breathing with shortness of breath.

• Sputum (mucus coughed up from lungs) is yellow, green, rust-colored, or bloody, and other symptoms (fever, productive cough, severe fatigue) are worsening. Sputum that is coughed up from the lungs is more significant than mucus that has drained down the back of the throat (postnasal drip).

• Cough that lingers more than 7 to 10 days.

• If facial pain, fever, and other signs of sinusitis develop. See page 99.

• If the person seems to get better, then gets worse again.

• If flu-like symptoms or a red rash occur four days to three weeks after being bitten by a tick. See page 145.

Laryngitis

Laryngitis is an infection or irritation of the voice box (larynx). The most common cause is a viral infection or a cold. It can also be caused by allergy, excessive talking, singing, or yelling, cigarette smoke, or reflux of acid from the stomach into the throat. Heavy drinking or smoking can lead to chronic laryngitis.

Symptoms include hoarseness or loss of voice, the urge to clear your throat, fever, tiredness, pain in the throat, and coughing.

Prevention

• To prevent hoarseness, stop shouting as soon as you feel minor pain. Give your vocal cords a rest.

Home Treatment

- Laryngitis will usually heal in 5 to 10 days. Medication does little to speed recovery.

- If hoarseness is caused by a cold, treat the cold (see page 92). Hoarseness may last up to a week after a cold.

- Rest your voice by not shouting and by talking as little as possible. Do not whisper, and avoid clearing your throat.

- Stop smoking and avoid other people's smoke.

- Humidify the air with a humidifier, or take a hot shower.

- Drink lots of liquids.

- To soothe the throat, gargle with warm salt water (5 ml in a half-litre of water) or drink honey in hot water, lemon juice, or weak tea.

- If you suspect stomach acid problems may be contributing to your laryngitis, refer to the remedies for heartburn on page 36.

When to Call a Health Professional

- If signs of a bacterial infection develop. See page 88.

- If hoarseness persists for three to four weeks.

Pneumonia

Pneumonia is an infection or inflammation of the smallest air passages in the lungs (alveoli). These passages fill up with pus or mucus, preventing oxygen from reaching the blood. It can be caused by a variety of bacteria or viruses.

Pneumonia may follow or accompany a cold, flu, or bronchitis. Someone who has bacterial pneumonia is usually very sick, and symptoms may include:

- Fever (over 38.3°C or 101°F) and shaking chills

- Productive cough with yellow, green, rust-colored, or bloody sputum (mucus coughed up from lungs)

- Pain in the chest wall, especially when coughing or taking a deep breath

- Labored, shallow, or rapid breathing

- Fatigue that is worse than you would expect from a cold

- Sweating and flushed appearance

- Loss of appetite or upset stomach

Prevention

- Keep up your resistance to infection with a good diet, plenty of rest, and regular exercise.

- Take care of minor illnesses. Don't try to "tough them out." See home treatment for colds on page 93 and flu on page 96.

- Avoid smoke and other irritants.

- If you are over age 65, or if you have chronic lung disease (asthma, emphysema), get a pneumococcal vaccination. See page 20.

Home Treatment

Call a health professional if you suspect pneumonia. If pneumonia is diagnosed, follow the home treatment below.

- Increase your fluid intake to 8 to 12 glasses of water a day (until you are urinating more than usual). Extra fluids help thin the mucus.

- Get lots of rest. Don't try to rush recovery.

- Take the entire course of all prescribed medications.

- Stop smoking.

When to Call a Health Professional

- If you suspect pneumonia.

- If there is rapid or labored breathing during any respiratory illness.

Sinusitis

Sinusitis is an inflammation or infection of the sinuses. The sinuses are cavities, or hollow spaces, in the head that are lined with mucous membranes. The sinuses usually drain easily unless there is an inflammation or infection. Sinusitis may follow a cold and is often associated with hay fever, asthma, or any air pollution that causes inflammation. It can occur in infants and children but is more common in adults.

The key symptom of sinusitis in adults is pain in the cheekbones and upper teeth, in the forehead over the eyebrows, or around and behind the eye. In children, a chronic stuffy nose is a common symptom. There may also be headache, fever (if the sinuses are infected), mucus running down the back of the throat (postnasal drip), and sore throat or cough. Sinus headaches may occur on rising and get worse in the afternoon or when bending over.

If there is a bacterial infection, antibiotics may be needed.

Sinus cavities

Prevention

- Treat colds promptly. Blow your nose gently. Do not close one nostril when blowing your nose.

- Drink plenty of extra fluids when you have a cold, to help keep mucus thin and draining.

- Stop smoking. Smokers are more prone to sinusitis.

Home Treatment

Some nasal stuffiness and facial pressure are common with a cold. Home treatment will often get your sinuses draining normally again.

- Drink extra fluids to keep mucus thin. Drink a glass of water or juice every waking hour.

- Breathe moist air from a humidifier, hot shower, or sink filled with hot water.

- Increase home humidity, especially in the bedrooms.

- Take an oral decongestant or use a decongestant nasal spray (see page 293). Do not use a nasal spray for more than three days. Avoid products containing antihistamines.

- Take aspirin, acetaminophen, or ibuprofen for headache.

- Check the back of your throat for postnasal drip. If streaks of mucus appear, gargle with warm water to prevent a sore throat.

- Elevate your head at night.

- Salt water (saline) irrigation helps wash mucus and bacteria out of the nasal passages. Use an over-the-counter saline nasal spray or a homemade solution (see page 293):
  - Use a bulb syringe and gently squirt the solution into the nose, or snuff the solution from the palm of your hand one nostril at a time.
  - Blow the nose gently afterward. Repeat two to four times a day.

When to Call a Health Professional

- If cold symptoms last longer than 10 to 14 days or worsen over time.

- If there is a severe headache, different from a "normal" headache, that is not relieved by acetaminophen, aspirin, or ibuprofen.

- If there is increased facial swelling or blurring or changes in vision.

- If nasal discharge changes from clear to colored (yellow or green) after five to seven days of a cold, and other symptoms (such as sinus pain or fever) are worsening. If nasal discharge is colored from the start of a cold, call if it lasts longer than 7 to 10 days.

- If facial pain, especially in one sinus area or along the ridge between the nose and lower eyelid, persists after two to four days of home treatment. If you also have a fever and coloured nasal discharge, call in one to two days.

- If sinusitis symptoms persist after you have taken a full course of antibiotics.

Sore Throat and Strep Throat

Most sore throats are caused by viruses and sometimes accompany a cold. A mild sore throat is often due to low humidity, smoking, air pollution, or perhaps yelling. People who have allergies or stuffy noses may breathe through their mouths while sleeping, causing a mild sore throat.

Another common cause of sore throat is stomach acid that refluxes into the throat. Although this is often associated with heartburn or an "acid" taste in the mouth, sometimes a sore throat is the only symptom.

Strep throat is a sore throat caused by streptococcal bacteria. It is more common in children ages 4 to 11, and is less common in older children and adults. Symptoms of strep throat include sore throat with two of these three:

- Fever of 38.3°C (101°F) or higher (fever may be lower in adults)

- White or yellow coating on the tonsils

- Swollen glands in the neck

In children, other symptoms may include general body aches, headache, stomachache, nausea, vomiting, runny nose, or listlessness. Strep throat is treated with antibiotics to prevent rheumatic fever. Antibiotics are effective in preventing rheumatic fever if started within nine days of the sore throat.

If a sore throat is accompanied by runny or stuffy nose and cough, it may be due to a virus, and antibiotics will not help.

Another cause of persistent sore throat is **mononucleosis** (mono or "the kissing disease"), a viral infection. It is most common in older teens and young adults. In addition to a severe sore throat and fatigue, mono symptoms often include weakness, aches, dizziness, swollen lymph nodes in the neck, and an enlarged spleen. It is diagnosed by a blood test for the Epstein-Barr virus.

Mono may last for several weeks and is usually not severe. Symptoms can recur for several months, and it is normal for the lymph nodes to remain enlarged for up to a month. There is no specific treatment except rest, plenty of fluids, and aspirin or acetaminophen for body aches.

Prevention

- Increase your fluid intake to as much as 8 to 12 glasses of water a day (until you are urinating more often than usual).

- Identify and avoid irritants that cause sore throat (smoke, fumes, yelling, etc.). Don't smoke.

- Avoid contact with people who have strep throat.

- Don't share toothbrushes, eating or drinking utensils, and avoid kissing to keep from spreading the virus or strep.

Home Treatment

Home care is usually all that is needed for viral sore throats. If you are taking antibiotics for strep throat, these tips will also help you feel better.

- Gargle with warm salt water (5 ml of salt in a half-litre of water). The salt reduces swelling and discomfort.

- If you have postnasal drip, gargle frequently to prevent more throat irritation.

- Drink more fluids to soothe a sore throat. Honey and lemon in weak tea may help.

- Stop smoking and avoid others' smoke.

- Acetaminophen will relieve pain and reduce fever. Do not give aspirin to children and teens under age 20.

- Some over-the-counter throat lozenges have a local anesthetic to deaden pain. Dyclonine hydrochloride (Sucrets Maximum Strength) and benzocaine (Chloraseptic Lozenges) are safe and effective. Regular cough drops or hard candy may also help.

- If you suspect problems with stomach acid may be contributing to your sore throat, refer to the remedies for heartburn on page 36.

When to Call a Health Professional

- If the following symptoms develop:

  ○ Excessive drooling in a small child (more than the usual amount)

  ○ Difficulty swallowing

  ○ Labored or difficult breathing

- If sore throat develops after exposure to strep throat.

- If a sore throat occurs with two of these three symptoms of strep throat:

  ○ Fever of 38.3°C (101°F) or higher (may be lower in adults)

  ○ White or yellow coating on the tonsils

  ○ Swollen glands in the neck

- If a rash occurs with sore throat. Scarlet fever is a rash that may occur when there is a strep throat infection. Like strep throat, scarlet fever is treated with antibiotics.

- If you cannot trace the cause of a sore throat to a cold, allergy, smoking, overuse of your voice, or other irritation.

- If a mild sore throat lasts longer than two weeks.

Swollen Glands

The lymph nodes are small glands in the body. The most noticeable nodes are those in the neck. The lymph nodes swell as the body fights minor infections from colds, insect bites, or small cuts. More serious infections may cause the glands to greatly enlarge and become very firm and tender.

Swelling in the glands on either side of the neck is common with a cold or sore throat. The lymph nodes in the groin may swell if there is a vaginal or other pelvic infection, or if there is a cut or sore on the leg or foot.

Lymph nodes may remain hard long after the initial infection is gone. This is especially true in children, whose glands may get smaller but remain hard and visible for several weeks.

Home Treatment

- There is no specific home treatment for swollen lymph glands. Continue treating the cold or other infection that is causing the glands to swell.

- If small hardened glands following a child's cold or minor infection are not tender, you can monitor them at home and report them at his next regular doctor visit.

Common sites of swollen lymph nodes

When to Call a Health Professional

- If the glands are large, very firm, red, and very tender.

- If swollen glands are associated with other signs of infection in a nearby cut or sore:

  - Fever of 100° or higher with no other cause

  - Swelling and tenderness

  - Discharge from the cut

  - Red streaks extending from the area

- If swollen glands continue to get bigger, or appear without apparent cause and persist two weeks or longer.

- If swollen glands appear in areas other than the ones shown.

Tonsillitis

The tonsils and adenoids are lymph tissues in the throat. They assist in the production of antibodies to fight infections. The tonsils can be seen on either side of the throat at the back of the mouth. The adenoids are higher in the throat and usually cannot be seen.

Inflammation of the tonsils (tonsillitis) or adenoids (adenoiditis) is common in children and may occur separately or together. Symptoms of tonsillitis or adenoiditis are sore throat, fever, and tiredness. It may be painful to swallow, and the tonsils are often bright red, spotted with pus, and swollen. The lymph glands in the neck may also swell. Adenoiditis can also cause headache and vomiting.

If the adenoids are chronically inflamed, the child may breathe through the mouth, snore, and have a nasal or muffled voice. Inflamed adenoids can block the eustachian tubes, contributing to ear infections. See page 114.

Tonsillitis and adenoiditis are sometimes caused by a virus. It is common to have mildly swollen and painful tonsils with a sore throat and other cold symptoms such as runny nose and cough.

A severe sore throat with very swollen tonsils, fever, and swollen glands in the neck can be due to a strep or other bacterial throat infection. See page 101 for signs of strep throat, which needs antibiotic treatment.

Surgical removal of the tonsils (tonsillectomy) or adenoids (adenoidectomy) used to be common operations for children who had frequent sore throats. Now it is thought that this lymph tissue may be helpful in fighting infection and should not be removed unless necessary. These surgeries have some risk, and should be done only for valid reasons and after discussion with your doctor. See page 105.

Home Treatment

• Home treatment is usually all that is needed for mildly swollen and painful tonsils with other cold symptoms. See page 102.

When to Call a Health Professional

• If sore throat occurs with two of these three signs, which may indicate a bacterial tonsillitis infection:

 ○ Fever of 38.3°C (101°F) or higher (may be lower in adults)

 ○ White or yellow coating on the tonsils or swollen, tender tonsils

 ○ Swollen glands in the neck

• If sore throat or tonsillitis develops after exposure to strep.

• If there are repeated bouts of tonsillitis, especially more than four or five per year.

• If a child has persistent mouth breathing, snoring, or very nasal or muffled voice.

• If you have persistent bad breath.

Adenoid
(not visible)

Posterior
pharynx

Uvula

Tonsil

Location of tonsils
and adenoids

Tonsillectomy and Adenoidectomy

It was once common to remove children's tonsils and adenoids. Today, in recognition of the risks, costs, and limited benefits, tonsillectomy and adenoidectomy are done less often, and only when the benefits greatly outweigh the risk, inconvenience, and pain.

Tonsillectomy may be recommended if at least one of the following criteria is met:

• If there have been *at least* four to six severe strep tonsillitis infections in the past year despite treatment with at least two different antibiotics.

• If the enlarged tonsils cause severe breathing difficulty or sleep disturbance.

• If there are deep pockets of infection in the tonsils that haven't responded to drug treatment.

Adenoidectomy may be recommended if at least one of the following criteria is met:

• If the enlarged adenoids are obstructing the airway, causing breathing difficulty and sleep disturbance.

• If the adenoids are believed to cause persistent ear infections despite antibiotic treatment.

If surgery is recommended without meeting one of the above criteria, a second opinion may be advisable. See page 9.

Quitting Smoking

Quitting smoking is one of the most important things you can do for your own health and the health of those around you. Smoking is a risk factor for many health problems, including heart disease, stroke, and cancer. Children who are exposed to cigarette smoke in the home have more ear infections and are more prone to other health problems. When you quit smoking, it doesn't take long for your body to start to heal and reduce your risk of health problems.

• Your risk of heart disease goes down almost immediately, and after 10 years is close to that of a non-smoker.

• Your lungs begin to heal, and after 10 to 15 years your risk of lung cancer is almost as low as that of a non-smoker.

It isn't easy to stop smoking. No single method works for everyone–some people can quit "cold turkey," others succeed by gradually cutting down over several months. No matter which method you choose, the following tips will help you get started.

Tips for Quitting

Preparation

• Decide how and when you will quit. About half of ex-smokers quit "cold turkey"; the other half cut down gradually.

The Nicotine Patch

The nicotine patch is an adhesive patch that releases nicotine into the bloodstream through the skin. Used together with a smoking cessation program, it may help some smokers gradually withdraw from nicotine addiction by supplying smaller and smaller amounts of nicotine.

First try to stop smoking without the patch. Many people succeed without it.

The patch is most useful for people who have had serious withdrawal symptoms (headaches, anxiety, depression, difficulty concentrating, insomnia) when they try to quit smoking. Generally, it is prescribed only to those who smoke more than a pack a day.

Using the patch alone is not always successful. By combining the patch with a good smoking cessation program, your chances of success can be greatly increased.

- Figure out why you smoke. Do you smoke to pep yourself up? To relax? Do you like the ritual of smoking? Does smoking help you deal with anger or negative feelings? Do you smoke out of habit, often without realizing you're doing it?

- Find a healthy alternative that accomplishes what smoking does for you. For example, if you like to have something to do with your hands, pick up something else: coins, worry beads, pen or pencil. If you like to have something in your mouth, substitute sugarless gum or minted toothpicks.

- List your reasons for quitting: for your own and your family's health, to save money, to prevent wrinkles, or whatever. Keep reminding yourself of your goal.

- Plan a healthful reward for yourself when you have stopped smoking. Take the money you save by not buying cigarettes and spend it on yourself.

- Plan things to do for when you get the urge to smoke. Urges don't last long—take a walk, brush your teeth, have a mint, or chew gum.

- Choose a reliable smoking cessation program. Good programs have at least a 20 percent success rate after one year; great programs, 50 percent. Higher numbers may be too good to be true.

- Set a quit date and stick to it. Try to choose a time that will be busy but not stressful.

- Contact your local health unit/public health office or provincial Lung Association for additional information and resources.

Action

- Know what to expect. The worst will be over in just a few days, but physical withdrawal symptoms may last one to three weeks. After that, it is all psychological. See Chapter 16 for relaxation tips.

- Remove all reminders of smoking from your surroundings. Do things that are incompatible with smoking, like bicycling or going to a movie.

- For the first few weeks, avoid situations and settings that you associate with smoking.

- Drink plenty of water to help flush the nicotine out of your system. Keep alcohol to a minimum, if any.

- Keep low-calorie snacks handy for when the urge to munch hits. Your appetite may perk up, but most people gain less than 10 pounds when they quit smoking. A healthy, low-fat diet and regular exercise will help you resist the urge to smoke and avoid unwanted pounds. The health benefits of quitting outweigh a few extra pounds.

- Get help and support. Ask an ex-smoker to help you.

- Think of yourself as an ex-smoker. Be positive.

- Be prepared for slip-ups. It often takes several tries to quit smoking permanently. If you do smoke, forgive yourself and learn from the experience. You will not fail as long as you keep trying.

- **Good luck!**

Tuberculosis

Tuberculosis (TB) is a contagious disease caused by bacteria that primarily infect the lungs. TB is spread when infected people cough or sneeze the bacteria into the air and others inhale the organisms. After infection, it can take up to two years to develop active TB, and many never do. Symptoms of active infection include a persistent cough, weight loss, fatigue, and fever.

Groups at higher risk of being infected by TB include people who are infected with the human immunodeficiency virus (HIV), IV drug users, the homeless, immigrants from countries with high rates of TB, health care workers, and older adults.

Drug treatment can cure TB but it may take up to 6 to 12 months. Many patients become discouraged and stop their treatment, increasing the risk that they will spread the infection.

To prevent TB, avoid close contact with someone who has an active infection, especially spending a long time together in a stuffy room. You cannot get TB by handling things an infected person has touched.

If you think you've had close contact with someone with active TB, contact your doctor or local health unit/public health office about a tuberculin skin test (see page 20).

Healthwise Handbook

108

You can observe a lot just by watching.
Yogi Berra (naturally)

Chapter 7

Eye and Ear Problems

From dry eyes to pinkeye and earaches to earwax, your eyes and ears can cause you trouble. With home care and patience, most of these problems will clear up. This chapter will explain what you can do at home and when to get professional help.

Conjunctivitis

Conjunctivitis, or pinkeye, is an inflammation of the delicate membrane (conjunctiva) that lines the inside of the eyelid and the surface of the eye. It can be caused by bacteria, viruses, allergies, pollution, or other irritants.

The symptoms are redness in the whites of the eyes, red and swollen eyelids, lots of tears, and a sandy feeling in the eyes. There may be a discharge that causes the eyelids to stick together during sleep and occasional sensitivity to light.

Prevention

- Wash your hands thoroughly after treating pinkeye.

- Do not share towels, handkerchiefs, or washcloths with an infected person.

- If a chemical or object gets into your eye, immediately flush it with water. See page 213 or page 227.

Home Treatment

Although most cases of conjunctivitis will clear up in five to seven days on their own, viral pinkeye can last many weeks. Conjunctivitis due to allergies or pollution will last as long as you are exposed to the irritating substance. Good home care will speed healing and bring relief.

- Apply cold or warm compresses several times a day to relieve discomfort.

Eye and Ear Problems

Eye Symptoms	Possible Causes
Red, itchy, watery eyes	See Allergies, p. 81. Think about allergy to eye care products, make-up, smoke; or contact lens irritation. Remove lenses. See p. 111.
Excessive discharge from eye; red, swollen eyelids; scratchy, sandy feeling	See Conjunctivitis, p. 109 Possible contact lens irritation, p. 111.
Pimple or swelling on eyelid	See Styes, p. 117.
Pain in the eye	See Chemical Burns to the Eye, p. 213; Migraine Headaches, p.124; Cluster Headaches, p. 125; Objects in the Eye, p. 227; consider contact lens irritation, p. 111.
Severe eye pain, blurred vision, reddened eyeball	Possible iritis. See a doctor now!
Red spot on white of eye	See Blood in the Eye, p. 112.
Blow to eye	See Bruises (black eye), p. 211.
Dry, scratchy eyes	See Dry Eyes, p. 114.

Ear Symptoms	Possible Causes
Earache and fever; pulling at ears by infants and small children, especially with inconsolable crying	See Ear Infections, p. 114.
Pain while chewing; headache	See TMJ Syndrome, p. 239.
Pain when ear is wiggled; itching or burning in ear	See Swimmer's Ear, p. 117.
Discharge from ear	See Swimmer's Ear, p. 117; eardrum rupture, p. 114.
Feeling of fullness in ear; with runny or stuffy nose, cough, fever	See Colds, p. 92; Ear Infections, p. 114.
Feeling of something in ear; as if ear is "bumping around"	See Objects in the Ear, p. 226.
Hearing loss; inattentiveness	See Earwax, p. 116; serous otitis media, p. 114.
Ringing or noise in the ears	See Tinnitus, p. 119.

- Gently wipe the edge of the eyelid with moist cotton or a clean wet washcloth to remove encrusted matter.

- Don't wear contact lenses or eye makeup until the infection is gone. Discard eye makeup after an eye infection.

- If eyedrops are prescribed, insert as follows:

  ○ Wash hands thoroughly before administering eyedrops.

  ○ For older children and adults, pull the lower lid down with two fingers to create a little pouch. Put the drops there. Close the eye for several minutes to let the drops move around.

  ○ For younger children, ask the child to lie down with eyes closed. Put a drop in the inner corner of the eye. When the child opens the eye, the drop will run in.

Inserting eyedrops

Contact Lenses

If you wear contact lenses, these tips will help you avoid problems.

- Follow the cleaning instructions for your lenses. Keep your lenses and anything that touches them (hands, storage containers, solution bottles, makeup) very clean. Wash your hands before handling your contacts.

- Use a commercial saline solution. (Generic brands are just as good as name brands.) Homemade solution is easily contaminated with bacteria.

- Insert your contacts *before* applying eye makeup. Do not apply makeup to the inner rim of the eyelid. Replace eye makeup every three to six months to reduce the risk of contamination.

- When worn for long periods of time, extended-wear lenses are more likely to cause severe eye infections. If you choose to wear them, follow the wearing and cleaning schedule your doctor recommends.

- Symptoms of a possible problem with your contacts include unusual redness, pain or burning in the eye, discharge, blurred vision, or extreme sensitivity to light. Remove your lenses and disinfect them. If symptoms persist longer than two to three hours after removing and cleaning your contacts, call your eye care professional.

- Visit your eye care professional once a year to check the condition of your lenses and the health of your eyes.

○ Be sure the dropper is clean and does not touch the eye, eyelid, or any surface. Eyedrops are washed out by normal tearing, so they will need to be replaced at least three times a day.

• Putting antibiotic ointment in the eye can be tricky, especially with children. Try to make a pouch by gently pulling down the eyelid. Apply a thin ribbon of ointment into the pouch and allow it to melt into the eye. Don't touch the eye or eyelid with the ointment tip.

• Make sure any over-the-counter medicine you use is *ophthalmic* (for eyes), not *otic* (for ears).

When to Call a Health Professional

• If there is pain in the eye (rather than irritation), blurring, or loss of vision, not cleared even momentarily with blinking.

• If the eye is painfully sensitive to light.

• If you feel there is a foreign object in the eye.

• If the eye is red and there is a thick, greenish-yellow discharge.

• If there is an abnormal difference in size of pupils.

• If the problem continues for more than three days.

Blood in the Eye

Sometimes, blood vessels in the whites of the eyes break and cause a red spot or speck. This is called a subconjunctival hemorrhage. The blood may look alarming, especially if the spot is large. It is usually not a cause for concern, and will clear up in two to three weeks.

However, if your eye is bloody and painful, if there is blood in the colored part of the eye, or if the bleeding followed a blow to the eye, call a health professional. Also call if bleeding in the eye occurs often, or occurs after you begin taking blood thinners (anticoagulants).

Dizziness

Dizziness or **lightheadedness** is usually not due to a serious problem; in fact, it is common to feel lightheaded occasionally. It is often due to a momentary drop in blood pressure and blood flow to the head that occurs when you get up too quickly from a seated or lying position. This is called orthostatic hypotension, and it is most commonly caused by medications or dehydration.

Other causes of dizziness include side effects of medications, stress, anxiety or drinking alcohol. Another less common cause is an abnormality in your heart rhythm, which usually causes recurrent spells of lightheadedness over a period of a few days.

Vertigo is a sensation that your body or the world around you is spinning. It may occur with nausea and vomiting. It may be impossible to walk when you have severe vertigo. Benign positional vertigo, the most common form, is triggered by changes in the position of the head, such as when you move your head from side to side or bend your head back to look up. Vertigo may also be caused by inflammation (called labyrinthitis) in the part of the inner ear that controls balance. Labyrinthitis is usually caused by a viral infection and sometimes occurs following a cold or the flu.

Home Treatment

Dizziness is not usually a cause for concern unless it is severe, persistent, or occurs with other symptoms.

- When you feel dizzy, sit down for a minute or two and take some deep breaths. Stand up again slowly.

Floaters and Flashes

Floaters are spots, specks, and lines that "float" across your field of vision. They are caused by stray cells or strands of tissue that float in the vitreous humor, the gel-like substance that fills the eyeball. Floaters can be annoying, but are not usually serious. However, if you see floaters or flashes of light for the first time, call your eye doctor or family doctor. If you have had floaters for some time, or if you have occasional flashes, mention it at your next routine eye exam.

- Sit up or stand up slowly to avoid the changes in blood flow to the head that can make you feel dizzy.

- Avoid head positions or changes in position that bring on vertigo. However, some experts suggest that practicing these positions may help overcome the problem.

- If you have vertigo, avoid lying flat on your back. Prop yourself up slightly to relieve the spinning sensation.

When to Call a Health Professional

- If dizziness is accompanied by headache, confusion, loss of hearing or changes in vision, weakness in the arms or legs, or numbness in any part of the body.

- If you feel like you might faint or if there is a complete loss of consciousness.

- If you have vertigo that is severe (often causing vomiting), or occurs with hearing loss or significant ear pain.

- If you suspect dizziness may be a side effect of a medication.

- If dizziness lasts more than three to five days and interferes with your daily activities.

- If you experience vertigo (sensation that the room is spinning around you) that is severe or persists for more than three days, has not been diagnosed, or is significantly different from previous episodes.

- If you have repeated spells of lightheadedness over a few days.

- If your pulse is less than 50 or more than 130 beats per minute when you are feeling lightheaded.

Dry Eyes

Eyes that don't have enough moisture in them may feel dry, hot, sandy, or gritty. Dry eyes may be due to low humidity, smoke, the natural aging process, or certain medications such as antihistamines, decongestants, and birth control pills.

Home Treatment

• Try an over-the-counter artificial tear solution, such as Isopto-Tears, Duratears, or Hypotears. These are different from drops like Visine, which reduce eye redness rather than dryness.

• Call a health professional if dry eyes are persistent and artificial tears do not help.

Eye Twitches

Eye twitches or muscle spasms around the eye are most often associated with fatigue or stress. Twitches will usually stop on their own in a short time, and they will improve with rest or reduced stress.

Call a health professional if twitches occur with redness, swelling, discharge from the eye, or fever, or if the eye twitch lasts longer than one to two weeks.

Ear Infections

A middle ear infection (otitis media) usually starts when a cold causes the eustachian tube between the ear and throat to swell and close. When the tube closes, fluid seeps into the ear and bacteria start to grow. As the body fights the infection, pressure builds up, causing pain. Antibiotic treatment stops bacterial growth, relieving pressure and pain.

Left untreated, the pressure can cause the eardrum to rupture. A single eardrum rupture (perforation) is not serious and does not cause hearing loss. Repeated ruptures may cause hearing loss.

Young children get more ear infections because they get more colds and their eustachian tubes are more easily blocked.

Symptoms of a bacterial ear infection include earache, dizziness, ringing or fullness in the ears, hearing loss, fever, headache, and runny nose. In children who can't yet talk, look for tugging on the ear as a sign of pain.

Otitis media with effusion (serous otitis) is a collection of fluid in the ear that often remains after an ear infection. There are often no symptoms, or there may be a feeling of fullness in the ear and some minor hearing loss. Effusion is not a cause for concern and may not require treatment unless it lasts longer than three months and causes significant hearing loss.

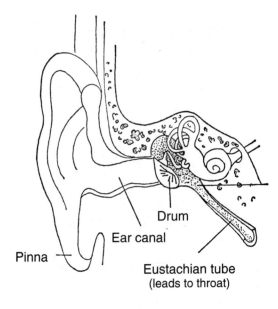

Drum

Ear canal

Pinna

Eustachian tube
(leads to throat)

Ear

Prevention

- Teach your children to blow their noses gently. This is a good idea for adults, too.

- Breast-feed your baby. Breast-fed babies have fewer ear infections.

- Feed infants in a relatively upright position to prevent milk from getting into the eustachian tubes. Do not allow infants to fall asleep with a bottle. (Nursing infants may fall asleep at the breast.)

- Avoid exposing children to cigarette smoke, which is associated with more frequent ear infections.

- Limit your child's contact with other children who have colds.

Home Treatment

- Apply heat to the ear to ease the pain. Use a warm washcloth or a heating pad set on low. Don't leave a child alone with a heating pad.

- Rest. Let your energy go to fighting the infection.

- Increase clear liquids.

- Aspirin, ibuprofen, or acetaminophen will help relieve earache. Do not give aspirin to a child or a teen under 20. See dosage on page 296.

- Oral nasal decongestants may help relieve earache pain. Avoid products that contain antihistamines.

- If dizziness occurs, see page 112.

When to Call a Health Professional

- Anytime an ear infection is suspected. If the exam confirms an infection, antibiotics may be needed.

- If a severe earache lasts longer than one hour or any earache lasts longer than 12 to 24 hours. If the pain is severe at night, call the next morning even if the pain has stopped. The infection may still be present.

- If an infant repeatedly rubs or pulls on the ear and appears to be in pain.

- If a child has an earache and fever and appears ill.

- If a headache, fever, and stiff neck are also present, which may be signs of meningitis.

- If home otoscope exam shows redness in the ear of a small child who cannot describe ear pain. See page 288.

- If you suspect an eardrum rupture. Look for a white, yellow, or bloody discharge from the ear.

- If there is no improvement after three to four days of antibiotics.

- If stuffy ears or hearing loss persist without other symptoms for more than 10 days after a cold has cleared up.

Earwax

Earwax is a protective secretion, similar to mucus or tears, that filters dust and keeps the ear clean. Normally, earwax is liquid, self-draining, and does not cause problems. Occasionally, the wax will build up, harden, and cause some hearing loss. Poking at the wax with cotton swabs, fingers, or other objects will only further compact the wax against the eardrum. Professional help is needed to remove tightly packed wax. You can handle most earwax problems by avoiding cotton swabs and following the home treatment tips below.

Children have a lot of earwax, which seems to taper off as they grow older. You should be concerned only if the earwax causes ringing or a full feeling in the ears, or some hearing loss.

Recurrent Ear Infections and Persistent Effusion

If your child has at least three ear infections in a six-month period, or has more than two infections before age six months, prophylactic antibiotics may be recommended. This is a low dose of antibiotics taken daily throughout the season when the child is prone to ear infections. It may reduce the frequency of ear infections, but may not always prevent fluid in the ear (effusion).

If infection persists after one month of continuous treatment (with at least two different antibiotics), your doctor may suggest inserting ear tubes (tympanostomy) through the eardrum to help prevent ear infections. The tubes remain in the eardrum for 6 to 12 months.

Long-term use of antibiotics may be just as effective as ear tubes in preventing infection.

In some children, effusion (fluid behind the eardrum) persists longer than three months after an ear infection. Depending on the amount of hearing loss, continued observation, antibiotics, or ear tubes may be appropriate treatment choices. If the child still has effusion and significant hearing loss after four to six months, your doctor may recommend ear tubes. Ask your doctor about the long-term risks and benefits of continued observation, antibiotic use, and ear tubes.

Home Treatment

- Warm mineral oil helps loosen wax. Wash the wax out with an ear syringe and warm mineral oil. (Cold fluid may make you dizzy.) Use very gentle force. Do not do this if there is discharge from the ear, if you suspect an ear infection or a ruptured eardrum, or if you have ear tubes.

- If the warm mineral oil does not work, use an over-the-counter wax softener, followed by gentle flushing with an ear syringe, each night for a week or two. Do not use it if you suspect infection or eardrum rupture.

When to Call a Health Professional

- If the above procedures do not work and the wax build-up is hard, dry, and compacted.

- If you suspect that earwax is causing a hearing problem.

- If the ear is sore or bleeding.

Styes

A sty is a noncontagious infection of the eyelash follicle. It looks like a small, red bump, much like a pimple, either in the eyelid or on the edge of the lid. It comes to a head and breaks open after a few days.

Styes are very common and are not a serious problem. Most will resolve with some home treatment and don't require removal.

Home Treatment

- Do not rub the eye, and do not squeeze the sty.

- Apply warm, moist compresses for 10 minutes, five to six times a day until the sty comes to a head and drains.

When to Call a Health Professional

- If the sty interferes with vision.

- If the sty gets worse despite your home treatment.

- If the redness centred on the sty spreads to involve the entire lid.

Swimmer's Ear

Swimmer's ear (otitis externa) is an infection of the outer ear canal. It often develops after water has gotten into the ear, especially after swimming. Sand or other debris that get into the ear canal may also cause swimmer's ear. Scratching the ear or injury from a cotton swab or other object may also irritate the ear canal.

Symptoms include pain, itching, and a feeling of fullness in the ear. The ear canal may be swollen. A more severe bacterial infection may cause increased pain, a discharge from the ear, and possibly some hearing loss. Unlike a middle ear infection (otitis media), swimmer's ear pain is worse when you chew and when you press on the "tag" in front of the ear or wiggle the earlobe.

Prevention

- Keep your ears dry. After swimming or showering, shake your head to remove water from the ear canal. Gently dry your ears with the corner of a tissue or towel, or use a blow-dryer on its lowest setting held several inches from the ear.

- Put a few drops of rubbing alcohol or alcohol mixed with an equal amount of white vinegar in the ear after swimming or showering. Wiggle the outside of the ear to let the liquid enter the ear canal, then tilt your head and let it drain out. You can also use over-the-counter drops (Lidosporin Otic Drops) to prevent swimmer's ear.

- Avoid cleaning the ears with cotton swabs or other objects. See page 117 for tips on removing excess earwax. Remove dirt or sand that gets into the ear while swimming by using a bulb syringe or gentle warm shower directed into the ear, then tip your head to let it drain out.

- If your ear is itchy, try over-the-counter swimmer's eardrops (see left). Use them before and after swimming or getting your ears wet.

- To insert eardrops, have the person lie down, ear facing up. Warm the drops first by rolling the container between your hands. Place drops on the wall of the ear canal in small quantities so air can escape and drops can get into the ear. Wiggling the outer ear will help.

- You may find it easier to insert eardrops in a small child by holding the child on your lap with her legs around your waist and head down on your knees.

- Apply heat to the outer ear with a warm towel or heating pad set on low to relieve discomfort. Don't leave a child alone with a heating pad. Acetaminophen or aspirin may also help. Don't give aspirin to children or to teens under age 20.

Home Treatment

- Make sure there isn't an object or insect in the ear. See Objects in the Ear on page 226.

- Gently rinse the ear using a bulb syringe and saline solution or a half-and-half solution of white vinegar and warm water.

- Avoid getting water in the ear until the irritation clears up. Cotton coated with petroleum jelly can be used as an earplug. Do not use plastic earplugs.

External canal

Eardrum

Inserting eardrops

When to Call a Health Professional

- If ear pain and itching persist or worsen despite five days of home treatment.

- If the ear canal is swollen, red, and very painful, or if there is a discharge from the ear.

- If the earache follows a cold. See page 92.

- If there is discharge from the ear following a blow or injury to that side of the head.

Tinnitus

Almost everyone has experienced an occasional ringing (or hissing, buzzing, or tinkling) in their ears. The sound usually lasts only a few minutes. If it becomes persistent, you may have tinnitus.

Tinnitus is usually caused by damage to the nerves in the inner ear from prolonged exposure to loud noise. Other, more treatable causes include excess earwax, ear infection, dental problems, and medications, especially antibiotics and large amounts of aspirin. Drinking excessive alcohol can also cause tinnitus.

Home Treatment

- Limit or avoid exposure to loud noises, such as music, power tools, gunshots, and industrial machinery.

- Cut back or eliminate caffeine, nicotine, and alcohol.

Cataracts and Glaucoma

Cataracts are cloudy areas in the lens of the eye. They may cause vision problems such as cloudy, foggy, or filmy vision; glare from lamps, sunlight, or car headlights, and double vision. They are common in older adults. Risk factors for cataracts include:

- Diabetes

- Aboriginal or African-American origin

- Use of steroids

- Smoking

- Ultraviolet light exposure (it isn't clear that protecting the eyes from sunlight reduces the risk)

Glaucoma is an eye disorder that results when there is excess pressure in the eyeball. If the pressure is not relieved, the optic nerve may be damaged, causing blindness. It has no symptoms and develops slowly over several years. Risk factors for glaucoma include:

- Family history of glaucoma

- African-American race

- Diabetes or nearsightedness

Cataracts and glaucoma are easy to detect during routine eye exams and respond well to medical treatment. Talk with your doctor about the best schedule of eye exams for you, based on your age and risk factors for these eye problems.

Call your health professional immediately if you have sudden blurry vision, loss of vision, or pain in the eye.

- Try to relax. Stress and fatigue seem to make it worse.

- Limit your use of aspirin and products containing aspirin. Many nonprescription medications contain aspirin. Check with your pharmacist if you are unsure.

When to Call a Health Professional

- If tinnitus becomes persistent and interferes with your daily activities or sleep.

- If ringing occurs with dizziness, loss of balance, vertigo, nausea, or vomiting.

- If tinnitus persistently affects only one ear.

*I'm very brave generally, only today I happen
to have a headache.*
Tweedledum in *Alice in Wonderland*

Chapter 8

Headaches

Headaches are one of the most common health complaints. Some possible causes include tension, infection, allergy, injury, hunger, changes in the flow of blood in the vessels of the head, or exposure to chemicals.

Most headaches that occur without other symptoms will respond well to self-care.

The majority of headaches—over 90 percent—are caused by tension and respond well to prevention and home care. See page 125.

An unusual headache that is very different from any you have had before, or a change in the usual pattern of your headaches is a cause for concern. See "Headache Emergencies." However, if you have had similar headaches before and your doctor has recommended a treatment plan for them, emergency care may not be needed.

Headache Emergencies

Call your doctor now if you have:

• A very sudden, "thunderclap" headache.

• A sudden, severe headache unlike any you have had before.

• Headache with stiff neck, fever, nausea, vomiting, drowsiness, confusion.

• Sudden, severe headache with stiff neck developing soon after the headache starts.

• Headache with weakness, paralysis, numbness, visual disturbances, slurred speech, confusion, or behaviour changes.

• Headaches following a recent fall or blow to the head. **See page 221 for information on head injuries.**

Possible Headache Causes

If headache occurs:	Possible causes
On awakening.	See Tension Headaches, p. 125; Allergies, p. 81; Sinusitis, p. 99. May also be due to low humidity.
In jaw muscles or in both temples.	See TMJ, p. 239; Tension Headaches, p. 125.
Each afternoon or evening; after hours of desk work; with sore neck and shoulders.	See Tension Headaches, p. 125.
On one side of the head.	See Migraine Headaches, p. 124; Cluster Headaches, p. 125.
After a blow to the head.	See Head Injuries, p. 221.
After exposure to chemicals (paint, varnish, insect spray, cigarette smoke).	Chemical headache. Get into fresh air. Drink water to flush poisons.
With fever, runny nose, or sore throat.	See Sinusitis, p. 99; Flu, p. 96; Sore Throat, p. 101.
With fever, stiff neck, nausea, and vomiting.	See Encephalitis and Meningitis, p. 96.
With runny nose, watery eyes, and sneezing.	See Allergies, p. 81.
With fever and pain in the cheek or over the eyes.	See Sinusitis, p. 99.
On mornings when you drink less caffeine than usual.	Caffeine withdrawal headache. Cut back slowly. See p. 125.
Following a stressful event.	See Tension Headaches, p. 125.
At the same time during menstrual cycle.	See Premenstrual Syndrome, p. 180.
With new medication.	Drug allergy. Contact doctor.
With severe eye pain.	Acute glaucoma. See doctor now!

Headaches in Children

Children's headaches rarely indicate a serious problem. They are more frequent in children whose parents often discuss their own headaches. Children tend to imitate their parents, so mention headaches as little as possible.

Emotional tension is the most common cause of headaches in children. A parent can often discover the cause of stress and help relieve it. Many times, just talking about a problem may help a child relax. Some children try to do too much, or are pushed to do too much at home or at school. Even fun activities can be overdone and cause fatigue and headaches. Encourage your children to talk openly about problems and stress at school.

Tension headaches (see page 125) are common in teenagers, and are generally caused by emotional stress related to school, sports, or relationships. Migraine headaches (see page 124) sometimes begin during the teen years.

Hunger can also cause headaches in children. A daily breakfast and a nutritious after-school snack may prevent them. Eyestrain may also cause headaches. Headaches are also common with viral illnesses that cause fever, such as colds and flu.

Home Treatment

• Talk to your child. Try to discover the source of the headache and deal with it. Let the child know you care.

Tension headaches are sometimes "attention" headaches. With quiet time and extra attention, most tension headaches in children can be managed without pain relievers.

• Play quietly with the child, or read stories together.

• If the headache is still present, have the child lie down in a darkened room with a cool cloth on the forehead.

• If non-drug treatments do not relieve the pain, try acetaminophen. See page 296 for the dose. Avoid creating the pattern of using a pill for every pain. Do not give aspirin to children.

When to Call a Health Professional

• If a headache is severe and is not relieved by relaxation or acetaminophen.

• If a severe headache occurs with signs of encephalitis or meningitis (see page 96), especially following a viral illness.

• If a child's headaches occur two to three times a week or more, or if you are using pain relievers to control a child's headaches more than once a week.

• If you cannot discover a reasonable cause. A child may share problems with someone other than a parent.

• If headaches awaken the child at night or are worse early in the morning.

• Also see "Headache Emergencies" on page 121.

Migraine Headaches

Migraine headaches have very specific symptoms including throbbing pain on one or both sides of the head and sensitivity to light or noise. Because migraines may also cause nausea or vomiting, they are sometimes called "sick" headaches. Migraines are also called vascular headaches, because they are believed to be caused by changes in the flow of blood in the vessels of the head.

Although a migraine headache comes on quite suddenly, it is sometimes preceded by visual disturbances, such as zig-zagged lines, called an aura. Dizziness and numbness on one side of the body may also precede a migraine. The headaches last from a few hours to a few days, and recur from several times a week to once every few years.

Migraines are more common in women. The headaches may begin during childhood, but most begin during the teens and early twenties.

Prevention

Keep a diary of your headache symptoms. See "Tracking Your Headaches" on page 126. Once you know what events, foods, medications, or activities bring on a headache, you may be able to prevent or limit their recurrence.

Some women find that their headaches improve if they stop taking birth control pills. Experiment with a nonhormonal form of birth control. See page 197.

Home Treatment

- At the first sign of a migraine, lie down in a darkened room with a cool cloth on your forehead. Relax your entire body, starting with the forehead and eyes and working down to the toes (see page 248). Sleeping often relieves migraines.

- Many people find aspirin, acetaminophen, or ibuprofen helps relieve a migraine.

- If a doctor has prescribed medication for your migraines, take the recommended dose at the first sign that a migraine is starting.

- If you use over-the-counter or prescription headache medications too often, they may actually make the headaches more frequent or severe. If this happens, call your doctor for advice.

When to Call a Health Professional

- If you suspect your headaches are migraines. Professional diagnosis and treatment, combined with your self-care, can help decrease the impact of migraines on your life. Discuss relaxation and biofeedback techniques, which help many people prevent migraines.

- Also see "Headache Emergencies" on page 121.

Tension Headaches

More than 90 percent of headaches are tension headaches, which become more frequent and severe during times of physical or emotional stress. A tension headache may be accompanied by tightness or pain in the muscles of the neck, back, and shoulders. A previous neck injury or arthritis in the neck can also cause tension headaches.

A tension headache may cause pain all over the head, pressure, or a feeling of having a band around the head.

Cluster Headaches

Cluster headaches are sudden, very severe, sharp, stabbing headaches that occur on one side of the head, usually in the temple or behind the eye. The eye and nostril on the affected side may be runny.

The pain often begins at night, and may last from 30 minutes to a few hours. The headache may recur several times a day. Attacks may last 4 to 12 weeks, then disappear for months or years.

Cluster headaches are five times more common in men. Many men who get them are heavy smokers and drinkers. Avoid alcohol and cigarettes during an attack.

See your doctor if you think you have cluster headaches or if you have persistent, severe headaches with no apparent cause.

Also see "Headache Emergencies" on page 121.

The head may feel like it is in a vise. Some people feel a dull, pressing, burning sensation above the eyes.

The pain may also affect the jaw, neck, and shoulder muscles. You can rarely pinpoint the centre or source of pain.

Prevention

• Reduce emotional stress. Take time to relax before and after you do something that causes a headache. See page 248 for good ways to cope with stress.

• Reduce physical stress. Change positions often during desk work and stretch for 30 seconds each hour. Make a conscious effort to relax your jaw, neck, shoulder, and upper back muscles.

• Evaluate your neck and shoulder posture at work and make adjustments if needed. See page 58.

• Daily exercise helps relieve tension.

• Treat yourself to a massage. Some people find regular massages very helpful in relieving tension.

• Limit your caffeine intake to one to two cups per day. People who drink a lot of caffeinated beverages often develop a headache several hours after they have their last beverage, or may wake with a headache that is relieved by drinking caffeine. Cut down slowly to avoid caffeine-withdrawal headaches.

Home Treatment

- Stop whatever you are doing and sit quietly for a moment. Close your eyes and inhale and exhale slowly. Try to relax your head and neck muscles.

- Take a stretching break or try a relaxation exercise. See page 248 or Resources 66 and 113 on pages 306 and 308.

- Gently and firmly massage the neck muscles. See page 60 for neck exercises.

- Apply heat with a heating pad, hot water bottle, or a warm shower.

- Lie down in a dark room with a cool cloth on your forehead.

- Aspirin, acetaminophen, or ibuprofen often helps relieve a tension headache. However, using over-the-counter or prescription headache medications too often may make headaches more frequent or severe. If this happens, call your doctor for advice.

When to Call a Health Professional

- If a headache is severe and cannot be relieved with home treatment.

- If a headache occurs with fever of 39.4°C (103°F) or higher and no other symptoms.

- If unexplained headaches continue to occur more than three times a week.

- If headaches become more frequent and severe.

- If headaches awaken you out of a sound sleep or are worse first thing in the morning.

- If you need help discovering or eliminating the source of your tension headaches, talking with a health professional may be helpful.

- Also see "Headache Emergencies" on page 121.

Tracking Your Headaches

If you have recurring headaches, keep a record of your symptoms. This record will help your doctor if medical evaluation is needed.

1. The date and time each headache started and stopped.

2. Any factors that seem to trigger the headache: food, smoke, bright light, stress, activity.

3. The location and nature of the pain: throbbing, aching, stabbing, dull.

4. The severity of the pain.

5. Other physical symptoms: nausea, vomiting, visual disturbances, sensitivity to light or noise.

6. If you are a woman, note any association between headaches and your menstrual cycle or use of birth control pills or hormone replacement therapy.

I have a simple philosophy ... scratch where it itches.
Alice Roosevelt Longworth

Chapter 9

Skin Problems

Skin problems can be a nuisance, but they are rarely life-threatening. Diagnosing skin problems may require a doctor's help, especially the first time you have a particular ailment. Use the chart on the next page and the index to find the skin problem you're interested in. Also see "Childhood Rashes" on page 154.

Acne

Acne is the term for pimples or blackheads that form on the face, chest, upper back, or shoulders. A pimple forms when an oil gland in the skin is blocked and secretions and bacteria build up under the skin. Acne usually starts during the teens, and often persists into adulthood.

Many women get a few pimples just before their menstrual period. Stress and some medications such as oral contraceptives may make acne worse. Fatty foods such as chocolate and nuts are generally no longer considered a cause of acne.

Many cases of acne will respond to home treatment, especially if they are mild. For severe or persistent cases, your doctor can prescribe stronger topical medication, antibiotics, or other drugs.

Prevention

- Wash your face with a mild soap, such as Dove, or one that contains benzoyl peroxide, such as Pan-Oxyl-5 Soap. Wash as often as necessary to keep it clean, but do not scrub.

- While foods are no longer considered a significant cause of acne, avoid any food that seems to cause pimples.

Skin Problems

Skin Symptoms	Possible Causes
Raised, red, itchy welt after an insect bite or taking a drug	See Hives, p. 136; Insect Bites and Stings, p. 138.
Red, painful, swollen bump under the skin	See Boils, p. 130.
Red, flaky, itchy skin	See Dry Skin, p. 132; Eczema, p. 133; Fungal Infections, p. 135; Rashes, p. 141.
Crusty, honey-coloured rash	See Impetigo, p. 137.
Rash that develops after wearing new jewelry or clothing, exposure to poisonous plants, eating a new food, or taking a new drug	See Rashes, p. 141.
Red, itchy blistered rash	Possible poison ivy, oak, sumac. See Rashes, p. 141; Chickenpox, p. 153.
Painful blisters in a band around one side of the body	See Shingles, p. 135.
Change in shape, size, or colour of a mole, or persistently irritated mole	See Skin Cancer, p. 143.
Cracked, blistered, itchy, peeling skin between the toes	See Fungal Infections (athlete's foot), p. 135.
Red, itchy, weeping rash on the groin or thighs	See Fungal Infections (jock itch), p. 135; Impetigo, p. 137.
Scaly, itchy, bald spots on scalp	See Fungal Infections (ringworm), p. 135.
Flaky, silvery patches of skin, especially on knees, elbows, or scalp	See Psoriasis, p. 134.
Sandpapery skin rash with sore throat, "raspberry" tongue	See Scarlet fever, see p. 102.

Home Treatment

- Cleanliness is essential. Wash your face, shoulders, chest, and back with a very gentle soap such as Aveeno or Neutrogena. Avoid drying soaps such as deodorant soaps. Always rinse well.

- Keep long hair off the face and shoulders, and wash it daily.

- Don't pop pimples and blackheads. This can cause infection and scarring.

- Benzoyl peroxide gel or cream, an over-the-counter medication, is one of the best treatments for acne. Start with the lowest strength and apply once a day one-half hour after washing. It may take several weeks to work and may cause mild redness and dryness. Strengths of 10 percent or more require a prescription from your physician.

- Use only non-comedogenic (does not clog skin pores), water-based lotions and cosmetics, and only if they don't aggravate acne.

- Controlling stress may help reduce acne flare-ups. See page 248.

When to Call a Health Professional

- If acne gets worse despite several months of home treatment.

- If you have severe red or purple inflammation, cysts, or nodules under the skin.

- If scars develop as acne heals.

Blisters

Blisters are usually the result of persistent or repeated rubbing against the skin. Some illnesses, such as shingles, cause blister-like rashes (see page 135). Burns can also blister the skin. See page 211.

Prevention

- Avoid shoes that are too tight or rub on your feet.

- Wear gloves to protect your hands when doing heavy chores.

Home Treatment

- If a blister is small and closed, leave it alone. Protect it from further rubbing with a loose bandage, and avoid the activity or shoes that caused it.

- If a small blister is in a weight-bearing area, protect it with a donut-shaped moleskin pad. Leave the area open over the blister.

- If a blister is larger than one inch across, it is usually best to drain it. The following is a safe method:

  ○ Sterilize a needle with rubbing alcohol.

  ○ Gently puncture the blister at the edge.

  ○ Press the fluid in the blister toward the hole you have made to drain it.

- Once you have opened a blister, or if it has torn open, wash the area with soap and water.

- Do not remove the flap of skin covering the blister unless it is very dirty or torn, or if pus is forming under the blister. Gently smooth it flat over the tender skin underneath.

- Apply an antibiotic ointment (Polysporin) and a sterile bandage. Do not use alcohol or iodine. They will delay healing.

- Change the bandage once a day to reduce the chance of infection.

- Remove the bandage at night to let the area dry.

When to Call a Health Professional

- If blisters recur often and you do not know the cause.

- If signs of infection develop:

  ○ Increased pain, swelling, redness or tenderness

  ○ Heat or red streaks extending from the blister

  ○ Discharge of pus

  ○ Fever of 38°C (100°F) or higher with no other cause

- If you have diabetes or peripheral vascular disease.

Boils

A boil is a red, swollen, painful bump under the skin, similar to an overgrown pimple. Boils are often caused by an infected hair follicle. Bacteria from the infection will form an abscess or pocket of pus. The abscess can become larger than a ping-pong ball and be extremely painful.

Boils occur most often in areas where there is hair and chafing. The face, neck, armpits, breasts, groin, and buttocks are common boil sites.

Prevention

- Wash boil-prone areas often with soapy water. An antibacterial soap may help. Dry thoroughly.

- Avoid clothing that is too tight.

Home Treatment

- Do not squeeze, scratch, drain, or lance the boil. Squeezing can push the infection deeper into the skin. Scratching can spread the bacteria and form new boils.

- Wash yourself well with an antibacterial soap to prevent the boil from spreading.

- Use moist heat often. Apply hot, wet washcloths to the boil for 20 to 30 minutes, three to four times a day. Do this as soon as you notice a boil. The heat and moisture can help bring the boil to a head, but it may take five to seven days. A hot water bottle or heating pad applied over a damp towel may also help.

- Continue using warm compresses for three days after the boil opens. Apply a bandage to keep draining material from spreading, and change it daily.

When to Call a Health Professional

If needed, your doctor can drain the boil and treat the infection. Call the doctor:

- If the boil is on your face, near your spine, or in the anal area.

- If signs of worsening infection develop:

  ○ Increased pain, swelling, heat, redness, or tenderness

  ○ Red streaks extending from the boil

  ○ Continued discharge of pus

  ○ Fever of 38°C (100°F) or higher with no other cause

- If any other lumps, particularly painful ones, develop near the infected area.

- If the pain limits your normal activities.

- If you have diabetes.

- If the boil is as large as a ping-pong ball.

- If the boil has not improved after five to seven days of home treatment.

- If many boils develop and persist over several months.

Birthmarks

Birthmarks are common in babies and small children and usually fade as the child grows. Report any changes in birthmarks to your health professional.

Salmon patches ("stork bites") are light pink birthmarks that may appear on the upper lip, eyelids, forehead, and back of the neck. They will fade within a few months.

Strawberry birthmarks are soft, red lumps formed by clusters of blood vessels. They may be present at birth or appear during the first few months. They may grow for up to six months, stabilize for a short time, and then usually begin to recede and fade. Sixty percent are gone by age five; nearly all have disappeared by age nine. No treatment is necessary unless they continue to grow.

Port-wine stains are light pink or wine-colored birthmarks that appear most often on the head and face. They are permanent, and become darker as the child grows.

Birthmarks need to be removed only if they interfere with breathing or vision, or if they disfigure the face. If surgery is desired for cosmetic reasons, it is best to wait until the child is older.

Dandruff

Dandruff occurs when the skin cells of the scalp flake off. This flaking is natural and occurs all over your body. On the scalp, however, flakes can mix with oil and dust to form dandruff. Dandruff cannot be cured, but it can be controlled.

Home Treatment

- Try frequent and energetic shampooing with any shampoo. Wash hair daily if it controls dandruff.

- If dandruff is excessive and itchy, try a dandruff shampoo (Head & Shoulders, Sebulex, T-Gel, Tegrin) three times a week alternating with your regular shampoo. Work the dandruff shampoo into your scalp and leave it on for several minutes before rinsing. Experiment to find the one that works best for you.

When to Call a Health Professional

- If frequent shampooing, or shampooing with a dandruff shampoo, doesn't control dandruff. Your doctor may prescribe a stronger dandruff shampoo.

Relief from Itching

- Keep the itchy area cool and wet. Try a compress soaked in ice water.

- An oatmeal bath may help relieve itching. Wrap one cup of oatmeal in a cotton cloth and boil as you would to cook it. Use this as a sponge and bathe in tepid water without soap. Or try an Aveeno Colloidal Oatmeal bath.

- Calamine lotion is helpful for poison ivy or oak rashes.

- Try an over-the-counter 0.5 percent hydrocortisone cream for small itchy areas. Use very sparingly on the face or genitals. If itching is severe, your doctor may prescribe a stronger cream.

- Try an over-the-counter oral antihistamine (Chlor-Tripolon, Benadryl).

- Cut nails short or wear gloves at night to prevent scratching.

- Wear cotton clothing. Avoid wool and acrylic fabrics next to the skin.

Dry Skin

Dry, itchy, flaky skin is a common problem. It results when the skin loses water (not oil) to the air. Dry indoor air is a common cause, as is excessive bathing with strong soaps and hot water. Dry skin is often worse in the winter due to lower humidity and indoor heat.

Prevention

- Humidify your home, especially the bedroom.

- Avoid hot showers and baths. They strip the skin's natural oil, which helps hold in moisture.

- Avoid strong detergents and deodorant soaps. Limit use of perfumes and perfumed products.

- Avoid overexposure to the sun. See page 144.

Home Treatment

- Follow the prevention guidelines above.

- Bathe every other day instead of every day. Use warm or cool water and a gentle soap (Dove, Oil of Olay). Use little or no soap on dry skin areas. Pat dry with a towel; don't rub skin.

- Apply a moisturizer (Vaseline, Lubriderm, Keri Lotion) immediately after bathing while skin is still damp to seal in moisture. A light layer of petroleum jelly is also an effective and inexpensive moisturizer. Reapply lotion often.

- For very dry hands, try this for a night: Apply a thin layer of petroleum jelly, and wear thin cotton gloves to bed. (May also help dry feet.)

- Avoid scratching, which damages the skin. If itching is a problem, see "Relief from Itching" on page 132.

When to Call a Health Professional

- If you itch all over your body without obvious cause or rash.

- If itching is so bad that you cannot sleep and home treatment is not helping.

- If the skin is badly broken due to scratching.

Eczema

Eczema (atopic dermatitis) is a chronic skin disorder common in people with asthma, hay fever, and other allergies. It causes a very itchy, red, raised rash that may weep or ooze a clear fluid. The rash may develop first as tiny blisters, which break and crust over. The lesions are prone to infection, especially if scratching is not controlled.

In children, eczema appears most often on the face, scalp, buttocks, thighs, and torso. In adults, it usually affects the neck, inside the elbows, and backs of the knees.

Adults whose hands or feet are often exposed to irritating substances may often have eczema on those areas.

Eczema is often worse during infancy and greatly improves by early adulthood. Many children improve by age two.

Home Treatment

Helping the skin retain moisture is important to successful treatment.

- Take brief daily baths or showers with lukewarm (not hot) water. Use a gentle soap (Dove, Oil of Olay, Neutrogena) or non-soap cleanser (Cetaphil or Aveeno). If possible, bathe without soap.

- After bathing, pat skin dry and apply a lubricating cream (Lubriderm, Moisturel). The cream may help keep your skin from drying out. Reapply cream often.

- Use a humidifier in the bedroom.

- An oral antihistamine (Benadryl) may help relieve itching and relax you enough to allow sleep. Avoid antihistamine and antiseptic creams and sprays, as they irritate the skin.

- Avoid contact with any irritants or allergens that cause problems. Wear gloves when working with irritating substances.

- Wash clothes and bedding in mild detergent and rinse at least twice. Do not use fabric softener if it is irritating.

- For more tips on relieving itching, see page 132.

When to Call a Health Professional

- If crusting or weeping sores appear. A bacterial infection may be present.

- If a red patchy rash appears on the face accompanied by joint pain and fever.

- If itching interferes with sleep and home treatment is not working.

Psoriasis

Psoriasis is a chronic skin condition that causes raised red patches topped with silvery, scaling skin on the knees, elbows, scalp, and back. The fingernails, palms, and soles of the feet may also be affected. It is not contagious.

The patches, called plaques, are made up of dead skin cells that accumulate in thick layers. Normal skin cells are replaced every 30 days. In psoriasis, skin cells are replaced every three to four days.

Small patches of psoriasis can often be treated with regular use of hydrocortisone cream.

Tar products (lotions, gels, shampoos) may also be useful, although they may increase sensitivity to the sun. Limited exposure to the sun may also help (protect unaffected skin with sunscreen). If psoriasis affects the scalp, try a dandruff shampoo.

Stress may contribute to psoriasis. Stress reduction may help in some cases. See page 248.

Call your doctor if psoriasis covers much of your body or is very red. More extensive cases often need professional care.

Fungal Infections

Fungal infections of the skin may affect the feet, groin, scalp, or nails. Fungi grow best in warm, moist areas of the skin, such as between the toes, in the groin, and the area beneath the breasts.

Athlete's foot (tinea pedis) is the most common fungal skin infection. Symptoms include cracked, blistered, and peeling areas between the toes, redness and scaling on the soles, and intense itching. It rarely affects children before puberty; if it does, it may resemble eczema. Athlete's foot often recurs and must be treated again each time.

Jock itch (tinea cruris) causes severe itching and moistness on the skin of the groin and upper thighs. There may be red, scaly, raised areas on the skin that weep or ooze pus or clear fluid.

Ringworm is a contagious fungal infection of the scalp or body. It is *not* caused by worms. Its symptoms include round spots that may be scaly and itchy. It may appear on the torso as a small, red, scaly spot that itches and grows until it is about an inch across. It is more common in children than in adults.

Fungal infections of the fingernails and toenails cause discoloration, thickening, and often softening of the nails. They are difficult to treat and often cause permanent damage to the nails.

Thrush is a yeast infection that occurs in the mouth, especially in babies. It causes a white coating inside the mouth, often on the cheeks, that may look like milk but is hard to remove. If a mother is breast-feeding and her baby has thrush, the mother may also require treatment. Contact your doctor if you suspect thrush.

Shingles

Shingles (herpes zoster) is caused by the reactivation of the chicken pox virus in the body years after the initial illness. The virus usually affects one of the large nerves that spread outward from the spine, causing pain and a rash in a band around one side of the chest, abdomen, or face. The rash will blister and scab, then clear up over the course of a few weeks.

No one knows what makes the virus active again. Shingles is more common in older adults and people who have weakened immune systems, but can affect anyone who has had chickenpox.

Shingles itself is not contagious, but exposure to the rash can cause chickenpox in a person who has not had it before.

If you suspect shingles, call your doctor or advice nurse, within a day after the rash starts if possible, to discuss medication that can limit the pain and rash.

Prevention

- Keep the feet clean and dry. Dry well between the toes after swimming or bathing.

- Wear leather shoes or sandals that allow your feet to "breathe," and wear cotton socks to absorb sweat. Use powder on your feet and in your shoes. Give shoes 24 hours to dry between wearings.

- Wear thongs or shower sandals in public pools and showers.

- Keep the groin clean and dry. Wash and dry well, especially after exercise, and apply talcum powder to absorb moisture. Wear cotton underclothes and avoid tight pants and pantyhose.

- Teach children not to play with dogs or cats that have bald or mangy spots on their coats.

- Don't share hats, combs, curling irons, or brushes.

Home Treatment

- Follow the prevention guidelines above.

- For athlete's foot and jock itch, use an over-the-counter antifungal powder or lotion, such as Micatin or Canesten Cream. Use the medication for a week or two after the symptoms clear up to prevent recurrence. Do not use hydrocortisone on a fungal infection.

- Consider wearing cotton socks, and change them twice a day to keep your feet dry. If possible, wear open sandals with cotton socks. When indoors, go in stocking feet.

- Ringworm on the body can be treated with an antifungal.

When to Call a Health Professional

- If signs of infection are present: increased swelling and redness or signs of pus.

- If you have diabetes and develop athlete's foot. People with diabetes are at increased risk of infection and may need professional care.

- If home treatment fails to clear up athlete's foot or jock itch after two weeks.

- If there is a sudden loss of hair associated with flaking, broken hairs, and inflammation of the scalp; or if there are several household members with hair loss.

- If ringworm is severe and spreading, or is present on the scalp. Prescription medicine may be needed.

Hives

Hives (urticaria) are an allergic reaction of the skin. Hives are raised, red, itchy patches of skin (wheals or welts), often fluid-filled, that may appear and disappear at random. They range in size from less than a quarter-inch to an inch or more, and they may last a few minutes or a few days.

Multiple hives often occur in response to a drug, food, or infection. A single hive commonly develops after an insect sting. Other possible causes include plants, inhaled allergens, stress, cosmetics, and exposure to heat, cold, or sunlight. Often a cause cannot be found. If possible, avoid foods, medications, and insects that have previously caused hives.

Home Treatment

- Continue to avoid the substance that causes hives.

- Cool water compresses will help relieve itching. Also see page 132.

- An oral antihistamine (Benadryl, Chlor-Tripolon) may help treat the hives and relieve itching. Once the hives have disappeared, decrease the dose of the medication slowly over five to seven days.

When to Call a Health Professional

- Call *immediately* if hives occur with dizziness, wheezing, difficulty breathing, tightness in the chest, or swelling of the tongue, lips, or face.

- If hives develop soon after taking a new drug.

- If hives persist for several days despite home treatment and avoiding the suspected irritants.

Impetigo

Impetigo is a bacterial infection that is much more common in children than in adults. It often starts when a small cut or scratch becomes infected. Symptoms are oozing, honey-colored, crusty sores that often appear on the face between the upper lip and nose, especially after a cold. Scratching the sores may spread impetigo to other parts of the body. The child should not attend day care or school until the condition is treated.

Prevention

- Wash all scratches and sores with soap and water.

- If your child has a runny nose, keep the area between the upper lip and nose clean to prevent infection.

- Keep fingernails short and clean.

Home Treatment

Small areas of impetigo may respond well to prompt home treatment.

- Remove crusts by soaking the area in warm water (use a warm washcloth for the face) for 15 to 20 minutes, then scrub gently with a washcloth and antibacterial soap such as Betadine or Hibitane. Pat dry gently; do not rub. Repeat several times a day.

- Apply an antibiotic ointment such as Bactroban (see page 291). Cover the area with gauze taped well away from the sores. This will help keep the infection from spreading and prevent scratching.

- To prevent spreading the infection, do not share towels, washcloths, or bath water. Men should shave around the sores, not over them, and use a clean blade daily. Do not use a shaving brush.

When to Call a Health Professional

- If impetigo covers an area larger than two inches in diameter.

- If impetigo is not improving after three to four days of home treatment, or any new infected areas appear. Your doctor may prescribe an antibiotic.

- If the area around the nostrils, lips, or face swells and becomes tender.

- If signs of infection develop:

  ○ Pain, swelling, or tenderness

  ○ Redness or red streaks extending from the area

  ○ Discharge of pus

  ○ Fever of 38°C (100°F) or higher with no other cause

Ingrown Toenails

Ingrown toenails are often caused when an improperly trimmed toenail cuts into the skin at the edge of the nail or by wearing shoes that are too tight. Because the cut can easily become infected, prompt care is needed.

Prevention

- Cut toenails straight across and leave the nails a little longer at the corners so that the sharp ends don't cut into the skin.

- Wear roomy shoes and keep your feet clean and dry.

Cutting toenails

Home Treatment

- Soak your foot in warm water.

- Wedge a small piece of wet cotton under the corner of the nail to cushion the nail and lift it slightly to keep it from cutting the skin.

- Repeat daily until the nail has grown out and can be trimmed.

When to Call a Health Professional

- If signs of infection develop:

  ○ Increased pain, swelling, or tenderness

  ○ Red streaks extending from the area

  ○ Discharge of pus

  ○ Fever of 38°C (100°F) or higher with no other cause

- If you have diabetes or circulatory problems.

Insect Bites and Stings

Insect and spider bites and bee, yellow jacket, and wasp stings usually cause a localized reaction with swelling, redness, and itching. In some people, especially children, the redness and swelling may be worse, and the local reaction may last up to a day. In most cases, bites and stings do not cause reactions all over the body. (In a few areas, mosquitoes may spread illnesses, including encephalitis and malaria.)

Some people have severe skin reactions to insect or spider bites or stings, and a few have allergic (anaphylactic) reactions that affect the whole body. Symptoms may include hives all over the body, shortness of breath and tightness in the chest, dizziness, wheezing, or swelling of the tongue and face. If these symptoms develop, *immediate* medical attention is needed.

Few spiders cause serious bites, although any bite may be serious if the person has an allergic reaction.

Black widow spiders can be up to two inches across (although they are generally much smaller) and are shiny black with a red hourglass mark on their undersides. Their bites may cause chills, fever, nausea, and severe stomach pain. Infants and children will be more affected by a bite than adults.

Brown recluse (fiddler) spiders are smaller with long legs, and brown with a white violin-shaped mark on their back. Their bites cause intense pain and may result in a blister that turns into a larger open sore.

Jellyfish are common on some ocean beaches. If touched, their tentacles release a stinging poison that causes a painful reaction.

Also see Tick Bites on page 145.

Prevention

- To avoid bee stings, wear white or light-colored solid fabrics. Bees are attracted to dark colors and flowered prints.

- Avoid wearing perfumes and colognes when you are outside.

- Apply an insect repellent containing DEET every few hours when in insect- and spider-infested areas. Use a lower-concentration DEET product for small children and pregnant women. Wash DEET off when you come inside. Alpha-Keri bath oil also seems to repel insects.

- Wear gloves and tuck pants into socks when working in woodpiles, sheds, and basements where spiders are found.

Home Treatment

- Remove a bee stinger as quickly as possible by scraping or flicking it out (if the stinger isn't visible, assume there isn't one). Don't squeeze the stinger; you may release more venom into the skin.

- If the bite is from a black widow or brown recluse spider, apply ice to the bite and call your doctor.

- Apply a cold pack or ice cube to the bite or sting. Some people also find that a paste of baking soda, meat tenderizer, or activated charcoal mixed with a little water helps relieve pain and decrease the reaction.

- An oral antihistamine (Benadryl, Chlor-Tripolon) may help relieve pain and swelling, and relieve itching if there are many bites. Calamine lotion, hydrocortisone cream, or a local anaesthetic containing benzocaine (Solarcaine) may also help.

- Anyone who has had a severe systemic allergic reaction to insect venom should carry an emergency kit containing a syringe and adrenalin (epinephrine). Ask your doctor or pharmacist how to use the kit.

- Trim fingernails to prevent scratching, which can lead to infection.

For jellyfish stings:

- Rinse the area immediately with saltwater. Do not use fresh water and do not rub; it will release more poison.

- Splash vinegar, alcohol, or meat tenderizer dissolved in saltwater on the area to neutralize the poison.

- Remove any attached tentacles carefully. Protect your hand with a towel and apply a paste of sand or baking soda and saltwater to the area. Scrape the tentacles off with the towel or the edge of a credit card.

- Apply calamine lotion to relieve pain and itching.

- If you are stung by a Portuguese man-of-war jellyfish, scrape the stinging tentacles off with sand and seek medical care immediately.

When to Call a Health Professional

- Call *immediately* if signs of a severe allergic reaction develop soon after being stung by an insect:

  ○ Wheezing, difficulty breathing

  ○ Swelling around the lips, tongue, or face, or significant swelling around the site of the insect sting (e.g., entire arm or leg is swollen)

  ○ Skin rash, itching, feeling of warmth, or hives

- If a blister appears at the site of a spider bite, or if the surrounding skin becomes discolored.

- To talk with your doctor about adrenalin kits or allergy shots (immunotherapy) for insect venom if you have had a serious allergic reaction.

Bald Spots

Bald spots are not the same as baldness. Some men have a natural tendency toward baldness. This natural hair loss is largely hereditary. It poses no major health risks other than sunburn (wear a hat and use sunscreen).

Bald spots may be caused by repeated pulling of the hair, such as tight braids or habitual tugging or twisting. Ringworm is a fungal infection that causes scaly bald spots. See page 135.

Bald spots that appear on a normal scalp may indicate a more significant problem. If hair loss is sudden, or if it develops after beginning a new medication, call your doctor.

Lice and Scabies

Lice are tiny, white, wingless insects that may live on the skin, hair, or clothing. They feed by biting the skin and sucking blood. The bites itch. Lice lay tiny eggs, called nits, which can often be seen on the hair. Head lice live in the hair on the head; body lice live on clothing; and pubic lice (also called crabs) live in the groin, underarms, and eyelashes. Lice are spread by close physical contact or contact with the clothing, bedding, brushes, or combs of an infected person. Pubic lice can be spread by sexual contact.

Scabies are tiny mites that burrow under the skin and lay eggs. This burrowing causes an allergic reaction with a rash that itches intensely. They are often found between folds of skin on the fingers and toes, wrists, underarms, and groin. Itching may last for several weeks after treatment.

Prevention

- Be alert for signs of lice: itching and signs of lice or nits along the hair shafts of the head. Prompt treatment can help prevent spreading them to others.

Home Treatment

- Contact your pharmacist or local health unit/public health office for more information on treatment and preventing reinfestation. The school should be notified. Some school districts have established specific policies around students staying away from school until they are free of lice.

- Over-the-counter medications are available for the treatment of lice. Follow the manufacturer's directions for use. Treat the entire family. For head lice, comb the hair well with a fine-toothed comb after treatment to remove all nits.

- On the day you start treatment, wash all clothing worn in the last week, bedding, and towels in hot water to help get rid of lice, nits, and mites. Iron things that cannot be washed.

When to Call a Health Professional

- If treatment with over-the-counter medication is not successful.

- If you suspect scabies.

Rashes

A rash (dermatitis) is any irritation or inflammation of the skin. Rashes can be caused by illness, allergy, or heat, and sometimes by emotional stress.

Poison ivy and other plant rashes are often red, blistered, and itchy, and appear in lines where the leaves brushed against the skin.

When you first get a rash, ask yourself these questions to help determine the cause (also see pages 128 and 154):

- Did a localized rash follow contact with anything new that could have irritated your skin: poison ivy, oak, or sumac; soaps, detergents, shampoos, perfumes, cosmetics, or lotions; jewelry or fabrics; new tools, appliances, latex gloves, or other objects? The location of the rash is often a clue to the cause.

- Have you eaten anything new that you may be allergic to?

- Are you taking any new medications, either prescription or over-the-counter?

- Have you been unusually stressed or upset recently?

- Is there joint pain or fever with the rash?

- Is the rash spreading?

- Does the rash itch?

Prevention

- If you are exposed to poison ivy, oak, or sumac, wash the skin with dish soap and water within 30 minutes to get the irritating oil off the skin. This may help prevent or reduce the rash. Also wash your clothes, your dog, and anything that may have come in contact with the plant.

- Avoid products that cause the rash: detergents, cosmetics, lotions, clothing, jewelry, etc.

- Use fragrance- and preservative-free or hypoallergenic detergents, lotions, and cosmetics if you have frequent rashes.

Home Treatment

- Wash affected areas with water. Soap can be irritating. Pat dry thoroughly.

- Apply cold, wet compresses to reduce itching. Repeat frequently. Also see page 132.

- Leave the rash exposed to the air. Baby powder can help keep it dry. Avoid lotions and ointments until the rash heals. However, calamine lotion is helpful for plant rashes. Use it three to four times a day.

- 0.5 percent hydrocortisone cream can provide temporary relief of itching. Use very sparingly on facial rashes.

- Rashes on the feet or groin may be due to fungal infections. See page 135.

When to Call a Health Professional

- If signs of infection develop:

  ○ Pain, swelling, or tenderness

  ○ Heat and redness, or red streaks extending from the area

  ○ Discharge of pus

  ○ Fever of 38°C (100°F) or higher with no other cause

- If you suspect a medication reaction caused the rash.

- If rash occurs with fever and joint pain.

- If rash occurs with sore throat. See page 102.

- If a rash appears and you aren't sure what is causing it.

- If rash continues after two to three weeks of home treatment.

Skin Cancer

Skin cancer is the most common type of cancer. Fortunately, many types of skin cancer are easy to cure.

Most skin cancer is caused by sun damage. Ninety percent of skin problems occur on the face, neck, and arms, where sun exposure is greatest. Light-skinned, blue-eyed people are more likely to develop skin cancer. Dark-skinned people have less risk.

Most skin cancers are generally slow-growing, easy to recognize, and easy to treat in a doctor's office. A small percentage of skin cancers are more serious.

Basal cell and **squamous cell skin cancers** tend to develop in sun-exposed areas. They differ from noncancerous growths in several important ways.

Skin cancers:

- Tend to bleed more and are often open sores that do not heal.

- Tend to be slow-growing.

Most moles are harmless. However, **malignant melanomas** (one type of cancerous mole) can be fatal and should be promptly treated.

Prevention

Most skin cancers can be prevented by avoiding excessive exposure to the sun. Much damaging sun exposure has occurred by age 20, so keep your children protected (see page 144). Cumulative exposure to sun is a major factor in some types of skin cancers.

Home Treatment

Examine your skin with a mirror or another person's help. Look for unusual moles, spots, or bumps. Pay special attention to areas that get a lot of sun exposure: hands, arms, chest, neck (especially the back of the neck), face, ears, etc. Report any changes to your doctor.

Size of a pencil eraser

Mole

| Asymmetrical shape | Border irregular | Color varied | Diameter larger than a pencil eraser |

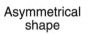

Watch for these mole changes

When to Call a Health Professional

If your moles do not change over time, there is little cause for concern. If you have a family history of malignant melanoma, let your doctor know. You may be at higher risk. Call your doctor if you notice any of the following changes:

- Asymmetrical shape: One half does not match the other half.

- Border irregularity: The edges are ragged, notched, or blurred.

- Color: The color is not uniform. Watch for shades of red and black, or a red, white, and blue mottled appearance.

- Diameter: Larger than a pencil eraser (harmless moles are usually smaller than this.)

- Scaliness, oozing, bleeding, or spreading of pigment into surrounding skin.

- Appearance of a bump or nodule on the mole, or any change in appearance of the mole.

- Itching, tenderness, or pain.

- Unusual skin changes or growths, especially if they bleed and keep growing.

Sunburn

A sunburn is usually a first-degree burn that involves just the outer surface of the skin. Sunburns are uncomfortable, but are usually not dangerous unless they are extensive. Severe sunburns can be serious in infants and small children.

Repeated sun exposure and sunburns increase the risk of skin cancer.

Prevention

If you are going to be in the sun for more than 15 minutes, take the following precautions:

- Use a sunscreen with a sun protection factor (SPF) of at least 15.

- Apply the sunscreen 15 minutes before exposure. Reapply every two hours and after swimming or as directed.

- If you are allergic to PABA, the active ingredient in many sunscreens, ask your pharmacist about non-PABA alternatives.

- Wear light-colored, loose-fitting, long-sleeved clothes and a broad-brimmed hat to shade your face.

- Drink lots of water. Sweating helps cool the skin.

- Avoid the sun between 10 a.m. and 2 p.m., when the burning rays are strongest.

- Don't forget the kids. Sun exposure may be very hard on their tender skin. Teach your young children safe sun habits—hats and sunscreen—early.

Home Treatment

- Watch sunburned infants or children for signs of dehydration. See page 33. Also watch for signs of heat exhaustion. See page 223. Drink lots of water.

- Cool baths or compresses can be very soothing. Take acetaminophen or aspirin for pain. Don't give aspirin to children.

- A mild fever and headache can accompany a sunburn. Lie down in a cool, quiet room to relieve headache.

- There is nothing you can do to prevent peeling; it is part of the healing process. Lotion can help relieve itching.

When to Call a Health Professional

- If signs of heat stroke develop (dry, flushed skin, confusion). See page 223.

- If there is severe blistering (over half of the affected body part) with fever or you feel very ill.

- If there is fever of 38.9°C (102°F) or higher.

- If dizziness or vision problems persist after you have cooled off.

Tick Bites

A tick is a small insect that fastens itself to the body. A tick should be removed as soon as you discover it.

Lyme disease is a bacterial infection spread by deer ticks. Deer ticks are tiny, about the size of the period at the end of this sentence. Therefore, if the tick is large enough to be seen easily, it is probably not a deer tick.

Early symptoms of Lyme disease include a red "bulls-eye" rash with a white centre around the bite. The rash develops four days to three weeks after the bite. Flu-like symptoms such as fever, fatigue, headache, muscle aches, and joint pain may also occur. Lyme disease can be treated with antibiotics to prevent later symptoms, such as arthritis and heart problems.

Prevention

- Wear hats and light-colored clothing, and tuck pant legs into socks.

- Apply an insect repellent containing DEET to exposed areas of skin or to clothing when in tick-infested areas. Apply carefully around eyes and mouth.

  ○ Use a lower-concentration product on children. Consult a physician or pharmacist for insect repellent if you are pregnant.

  ○ Don't put repellent on small children's hands, as they often put their hands in their mouths.

  ○ After returning indoors, wash the repellent off with soap and water.

Home Treatment

- Check regularly for ticks when you are out in the woods and thoroughly examine your skin and scalp when you return home. Check your pets, too. The sooner ticks are removed, the less likely they are to spread bacteria.

- Remove a tick by gently pulling with tweezers, as close to the skin as possible. Pull straight out and try not to crush the body. Save the tick in a jar for tests if symptoms of Lyme disease develop.

- Wash the area and apply an antiseptic.

When to Call a Health Professional

- If you are unable to remove the entire tick.

- In areas where Lyme disease is common, see a doctor if a tick has been attached for more than 24 hours.

- If a red "bulls-eye" rash, fever, fatigue, or flu-like symptoms develop up to three weeks after a tick bite.

Warts

Warts are skin growths that are caused by a virus. They can appear anywhere on the body. Warts are not dangerous, but can be bothersome.

Little is known about warts. Most types are only slightly contagious. They can spread to other areas on the same person but rarely to other people. Genital and anal warts are an exception; they are easily transmitted through sexual contact and may increase the risk of cervical cancer. See page 198.

Plantar warts appear on the soles of the feet. Most of the wart lies under the skin surface, and may make you feel like you are walking on a pebble.

Because warts seem to come and go for little reason, it's possible they are sensitive to slight changes in the immune system. Although there is no scientific explanation why it works, in some cases, you can "think" them away.

When necessary, your doctor can remove warts. Unfortunately, they often come back.

Home Treatment

- Warts appear and disappear spontaneously. They can last a week, a month, or even years. To get rid of your warts, it helps to believe in the treatment. If something works for you, stick with it.

- If the wart bleeds a little, cover it with a bandage and apply light pressure to stop the bleeding.

• If the wart is in the way, use a pumice stone or an over-the-counter salicylic acid ointment. This drug can be irritating in high concentrations; you may need to use a milder form for a longer period of time. Do not use salicylic acid if you have diabetes or peripheral vascular disease.

• If you use a pumice stone, both the debris from the wart and the area of the pumice stone that touched the wart can be infectious. Do not handle this material. Discard both the wart debris and pumice stone promptly.

• For plantar warts, apply a donut-shaped pad to cushion the wart and relieve pain. Apply salicylic acid solution to the wart at night, and rub the whitened skin off in the morning.

• Try the least expensive method of treating warts. You may save a trip to your doctor.

• Don't cut or burn off a wart.

When to Call a Health Professional

• If a wart looks infected after being irritated or knocked off.

• If a plantar wart is painful when you walk and foam pads do not help.

• If you have warts in the anal or genital area. See page 198.

• If the wart causes continual discomfort.

• If a wart develops on the face and is a cosmetic concern.

Calluses and Corns

Calluses are hard, thickened skin on parts of the foot exposed to friction. Corns are caused by pressure on the skin from the inside, such as a bone.

Soak your feet in warm water and rub the callus or corn with a pumice stone. You may need to do this for several days until the thickened skin is gone.

Do not try to cut or burn off corns or calluses. If you have diabetes or peripheral vascular disease, talk with your doctor about removing troublesome corns or calluses.

My mother had a great deal of trouble with me,
but I think she enjoyed it.
Mark Twain

Chapter 10

Infant and Child Health

When your child gets sick or hurt, you are usually the first person to provide care. Your calmness, confidence, and competence in caring for your children's health problems will help them enjoy healthy childhoods and learn the importance of self-care for their own use as they mature.

Virtually every health problem in this book may affect children. However, a few are almost exclusively childhood concerns. For convenience, we have grouped these problems into this chapter. If the problem you are looking for is not in this chapter, please look for it in the index.

Facts About Infants and Young Children

The following brief notes are of particular concern to parents. This information may help dispel some unnecessary fears and give you some guidance.

For more information on child health, see Resources 39 to 48 on pages 304 and 305.

Umbilical Cords and Bellybuttons

After each diaper change, clean the bellybutton (navel) gently but firmly around the base of the cord with a cotton swab soaked in rubbing alcohol. Fold diapers below the cord and shirts above the cord to promote drying.

The umbilical cord will drop off and the navel will heal in one to three weeks. After the cord comes off, there may be a moist or bloody oozing for a few days, between diaper changes. This does not need special treatment.

Call your doctor if there is redness or swelling around the navel, or a large amount of foul-smelling discharge from the navel.

The appearance of the bellybutton is not affected by the way the cord is tied off. A small nodule of tissue sometimes remains after the cord falls off. If it is small, no treatment is usually needed. If it is larger or persists longer than two weeks, call your doctor.

Breast-Feeding

Breast milk is the best milk for babies. The World Health Organization recommends that infants be breast-fed exclusively for the first six months. After that time breast-feeding continues with complementary foods until at least two years of age. Up until age four to six months, infants should be fed only breast milk or formula. Do not give unpasteurized milk.

Child Car Seats

Infant and child car seats save lives. In Canada, car seats are required by law and must meet Canadian Motor Vehicle Safety Standards (CMVSS). A car seat is used until your child weighs 18 kilos (40 pounds) and is about 100 cm (40 inches) tall. Children who are not in car seats can be seriously injured or killed during crashes or even abrupt stops at low speeds. Children should always travel in the rear seat; passenger-side airbags can seriously harm or kill children. For maximum safety, follow the manufacturer's recommendations for car seat use. Contact your local health unit/public health office about loaner programs for newborn car seats that may be available in your area.

Infants under 20 pounds: Use an infant car seat that reclines and faces the rear. You must put the car seat in the back. Check the manufacturer's instructions.

Infants and children over 20 pounds: Use a toddler seat that faces the front and has a shield or harness.

Some infant seats can be converted into toddler seats. All front-facing car seats must be tethered. NOTE: An infant who is over 20 pounds but does not sit well (until about nine months) should be in a rear-facing position in a convertible seat. Once the baby can sit well alone, the seat can be turned around to a front-facing position.

Children over age four and over 40 pounds: Use a booster seat that raises the child so he can see out of the window. Use regular lap and shoulder straps. Attach a locking clip to hold the booster seat firmly in position if your vehicle has a continuous shoulder belt with a free-sliding seat belt clip. Adjust the shoulder belt to fit across the shoulder, not the neck. In order to avoid neck injuries, the child should be taken out of the booster seat once the middle of his ears is above the top of the car seat.

Set a good example for your children by always wearing your own seat belt, and always insist that they buckle up.

Breast-feeding has many advantages for both baby and mother. Breast milk contains antibodies and other disease-preventing substances. It protects against allergies and asthma, and also is easier to digest than formula. Breast-fed babies have fewer colds, ear infections, diarrhea, and vomiting.

Some instruction helps ensure that you can breast-feed successfully. Try to take a breast-feeding class. Also see Resources 126 and 127 on page 309. The La Leche League and your health unit/public health office are good sources of information, advice, and support.

Nursing mothers should eat a healthy diet with a variety of foods from the four food groups similar to what they ate during their pregnancy. Although you don't need to drink milk to make milk, extra calcium and protein are important, and your doctor may pre-scribe a vitamin supplement. Avoid smoking and drinking alcohol, and limit caffeine to one or two beverages per day. Do not take any medication while breast-feeding unless it was prescribed by a health professional.

Although breast-feeding is best, babies can also get good nutrition from formula.

Circumcision

Circumcision is the removal of the foreskin from the top of the penis. The Canadian Pediatric Society states that routine circumcision should not be recommended for newborns. There are risks from circumcision. Compli-cations include local infection, bleeding, and blockage of the urinary tract. Local anaesthetics may be used to reduce the pain of circumcision. After circumcision, a petroleum dressing is applied to the head of the penis. The dressing will fall off in one or two days, but if not, soak it with warm water. After the dressing is off, wash the penis with warm water and pat dry gently.

If the circumcision site is red, apply an antibiotic ointment (Baciguent or Polysporin). Call your doctor if the redness extends down the shaft of the penis.

If your son is not circumcised, the foreskin is usually retractable by age three or four years, but may not be fully retractable until puberty. Do not forcibly retract the foreskin. Teach your son to wash his penis well at every bath and to gently retract the foreskin and clean beneath it.

Toilet Training

Every child has a unique timetable for becoming toilet trained. Most children are ready to begin toilet training between age 18 and 36 months. Look for these other signs of readiness in your child:

- Understands words referring to bowel movements and urination.

- Recognizes the sensation of a full bladder and the urge to have a bowel movement.

- Knows what the toilet is for and has watched others use it.

- Prefers clean, dry diapers to soiled ones.

- Understands that using the potty means having a dry diaper.

If you think your child is ready to begin toilet training, the following tips may make it go more smoothly:

• Get the child a potty chair. Make sure the child's feet can rest on the floor or on a footrest. Encourage the child to sit on the chair at least once a day at about the same time each day. Let the child use the chair for looking at books or watching TV.

• After she has had a bowel movement in a diaper, put her on the chair, and put the contents of the diaper in the pot.

• Once she is interested, let her play for short periods without a diaper and have the chair nearby. Encourage her to use the chair if she needs to "go potty."

• Reward every success with hugs and words of praise. Relapses are common in the first few weeks, but don't scold or punish when she forgets. Keep a casual attitude.

• Bladder control may take longer than bowel control. Praise her for success and give gentle encouragement when she wets her pants.

Don't worry if there are relapses following toilet training. For example, following the birth of a new baby or other stressful events it is not uncommon for toddlers to relapse.

Sleep Habits

Babies have both deep and light sleep cycles. In each four-hour sleep cycle, there are 60 minutes of light sleep, 60 to 90 minutes of deep sleep, and another 30 minutes of light sleep. At the end of this cycle, the baby is semi-alert and can be wakened easily.

Parents can help the baby sleep through the night by helping him learn to soothe himself back to sleep during the light sleep cycles.

For infants (birth to 2 months):

• Put the baby in the crib when he is drowsy but awake.

• Make middle-of-the night feedings short and boring.

• As the baby gets older, delay the middle-of-the-night feeding, and discontinue it sometime after age four months.

• When you position the baby to sleep place them on either their side or back.

• Also see Resource 44 on page 305.

Bed-Wetting

Bed-wetting (enuresis) in children who have never been dry is common, and most children will outgrow it by about age six to eight. In almost all cases, it is really not a disease, but rather a normal variation. In some cases, a child who has been dry for several months or longer may begin bed-wetting again. This may be without a clear cause, or possibly due to a urinary tract infection or to emotional problems.

Home Treatment

There are a number of ways to deal with bedwetting that don't require medication. Ask your doctor for advice in managing bedwetting until your child outgrows it.

- Do not punish, embarrass, or blame the child.

- Remind the child to get up during the night to urinate. Providing a bedside potty chair and night light may help.

- Let children over age five take control of the problem. Help them learn to wake themselves at night to go to the bathroom. Set an alarm for three to four hours after bedtime, and make sure the child has to get out of bed to turn it off.

- Do not force a child to wear diapers at night. However, some children may be more comfortable wearing adult diapers such as Attends or Depends. Waterproof, extra-absorbent underwear or thick pads to protect the mattress may also help avoid daily bed changes. Wash them with one-half cup of vinegar to eliminate odor.

When to Call a Health Professional

Your doctor can rule out or treat any physical causes of bedwetting and help you and your child manage the problem.

- If bed-wetting occurs with painful or burning urination, or other signs of urinary tract infection. See page 181.

- If prevention and home treatment are not successful after four to six weeks in a child older than six.

- If bed-wetting becomes more frequent or severe.

- If bed-wetting occurs in a child who had previously been dry for several months.

- If bed-wetting occurs with soiling of the underwear with bowel movements after age three.

- If a child over age three has daytime bladder control problems.

Chickenpox

Chickenpox (varicella) is a relatively minor illness. Almost all children will get it. The first couple of days, your child will be in generally ill health, with a cold, cough, fever, and abdominal pain, then a rash of red, pimple-like spots appears. A child may have just one or two spots or the rash may cover the entire body, including the throat, mouth, ears, groin, and scalp.

The spots turn into clear blisters that become cloudy, break open, and crust over. This rash itches a lot. Spots continue to appear for one to five days, and subside over a week or two.

Chickenpox is very contagious. After exposure, symptoms occur in ten days to three weeks. It is contagious for one to two days before the rash appears, and for up to five days after the spots appear. Children can generally return to school or day care when all the spots have scabbed, or on the sixth day after the rash appeared. Encephalitis (see page 96) is a rare complication of chickenpox.

Prevention

Adults should avoid exposure to children who have chickenpox and people who have shingles (see page 135).

Pregnant women who have never had chickenpox and have not been vaccinated should also avoid exposure to children who have chickenpox or adults who have shingles, since the illness can harm the developing fetus.

Childhood Rashes

Rashes that come with childhood illnesses are hard to tell apart. Review all symptoms before deciding what to do. Also see page 141.

Description	Possible Illness
Red, pimple-like spots that turn to blisters; fever	Chickenpox, p.153
Rash in diaper area only	Diaper Rash, p. 158
Red rash on face that looks like slapped cheeks; pink rash on torso that comes and goes; possible fever	Fifth Disease, p. 166
Red or pink dots on head, neck, shoulders; more common in infants	Prickly Heat, p. 165
Sudden high fever for 2–3 days followed by rose-pink rash on torso, arms, neck after fever goes down	Roseola, p. 166
Fine pink rash; starts on face and covers whole body; swollen glands behind ears	Rubella (rare), p. 165
Fever, runny nose, hacking cough; red eyes 2–3 days before spotty red rash covers whole body	Rubeola (measles) (rare), p. 165
High fever, sore throat, sandpapery rash, and raspberry-textured tongue	Scarlet fever, p. 102

Home Treatment

- Use acetaminophen to relieve fever. Do *not* give aspirin to children and teens under age 20 who may have chickenpox because aspirin use is related to Reye's Syndrome.

- Control the itching (see page 132). Oral Benadryl and warm baths with some baking soda or Aveeno Colloidal oatmeal added to the water will help.

- Cut the child's fingernails to prevent scratching. If scabs are scratched off too early, they may become infected.

When to Call a Health Professional

- If your child is at risk of complications from chickenpox (is taking steroid medications or cancer chemotherapy, or has immuno-deficiency problems).

- If a child age three months to three years has a fever of 39.4°C (103°F) or higher for 24 hours. See Fever on page 161.

- If severe itching cannot be controlled by Benadryl and warm baths.

- If bruising appears without injury.

- If sores appear in the eyes.

- If you notice signs of encephalitis (see page 96):
  - Fever, severe headache, and stiff neck
  - Unusual sleepiness or lethargy
  - Persistent vomiting

Colic

Colic is a group of symptoms that cause otherwise healthy babies to cry inconsolably, usually in the evening and at night. Doctors aren't sure what causes colic. The leading theory is that colic is caused by abdominal pain due to intestinal gas. Generally, breast-fed babies experience colic less frequently.

All babies cry, so how do you know if your baby has colic? Colic usually follows the "rule of three": crying starts in the first three months after birth, continues more than three hours a day, more than three days a week.

Fortunately, colic goes away as the baby matures, almost always by the end of the third or fourth month, sooner for many babies. Although no one method always works to relieve colicky babies, there are a number of things you can try. Unfortunately, what works one time may not work the next. Be creative and persistent.

Home Treatment

- Most important: stay calm and try to relax. If you start to lose control, take a minute to calm down. *Never* shake a baby; it can cause permanent brain damage.

- Make sure the baby is getting enough to eat and not too much. The problem may be hunger, not colic.

- Make sure the baby isn't swallowing too much air while eating. Feed the baby slowly, holding him almost upright. Burp the baby periodically. Prop the baby up for 15 minutes after feeding.

- If the baby is bottle-fed, use nipples with holes large enough to drip cold formula at least one drop per second. Babies will swallow more air from around the nipple if the hole is too small.

- Keep a regular routine for meals, naps, and playtime. Breast-feeding time should be quiet and undisturbed by bright lights and loud noises.

- If you are using formula, warm it to body temperature. Don't overheat.

- Make sure the baby's diaper is clean, that the baby isn't too hot or cold, and isn't bored.

- Try rocking or walking the baby or carrying her in a sling. Putting her stomach-down over your knee or forearm may be helpful.

- Calm the baby with a car ride or a walk outside. Placing the baby near the hum of a clothes dryer, dishwasher, or bubbling aquarium may help soothe him.

- Don't worry about spoiling a baby during the first three months; comforting a baby makes both of you feel better.

- Ask a friend or neighbor to baby-sit some evening while you go to dinner and a movie!

- If nothing seems to work, don't feel guilty but remember the baby needs your comfort and that holding her is one of the best ways to do that. Try shutting the bedroom door and turning up the stereo once in a while; if it will help you to relax, it will help

the baby. However, don't let your baby cry alone for more than 5 to 10 minutes. After 10 minutes, try the above suggestions again.

When to Call a Health Professional

Colic generally does not require professional treatment unless it is accompanied by vomiting, diarrhea, or other signs of more serious illness. If the baby looks healthy and acts normally between crying episodes, and if your emotions can stand the noise for the first three months, you have little cause for worry.

However, if colic lasts more than four hours a day, or if you feel like you need help, contact your doctor for advice.

In rare cases, colic may be so severe that you and your doctor may consider a medication. Ask about side effects.

Cradle Cap

Cradle cap is a crusting on an infant's scalp. It is caused by a buildup of normal oils on the skin. Cradle cap is common in babies and is easily treated.

Home Treatment

- Wash the baby's head with non-perfumed shampoo once a day. Rinse well.

- You can also rub mineral oil or vegetable oil on the scalp one hour before shampooing to loosen the scales.

- If the cradle cap does not improve, call your public health nurse or physician.

Croup

Croup is a respiratory problem most common in children ages two to four years. It may accompany a viral infection, such as a cold. The main symptom is a harsh cough that sounds like a seal's bark. A fever of 100° to 101° is common. The child may become very frightened. Croup usually gets worse at night and may last one to seven days.

Home Treatment

- Stay calm. The child is already frightened and needs reassurance.

- Get moisture into the air to make it easier for the child to breathe. Take the child into the bathroom, turn on all hot-water faucets, then sit on the floor in the steamy room and read a story together.

- Bundle up and take the child outside for a walk in the cool fresh air. Cool moist air is best.

- Set up a vaporizer or croup tent in the child's bedroom. Put a vaporizer under the crib and drape a blanket over the head of the crib to trap the moisture near the child's head. If the child is older and no longer in a crib, drape the blanket over an umbrella

or card table. Stay with your child to be sure the blanket doesn't fall. With a cold-mist vaporizer, the air will be quite cold. Dress the child in warm pajamas, and place a sheet over the blankets to catch moisture. Don't worry about your child getting chilled. The cool, moist air is the important part.

- If the child starts crying, this may be a positive sign that he is breathing more normally.

When to Call a Health Professional

- If the child stops breathing or begins to turn blue, call 911 or emergency services. Give rescue breathing (see page 204) until help arrives.

- Medical care is needed *immediately* if these signs of respiratory distress appear and persist despite home treatment:

  ○ Squeaky or raspy sound as child inhales (stridor)

  ○ Sucking in or retraction between ribs as child inhales

  ○ Flaring nostrils

- If the child is so short of breath that she can't walk or talk.

- If the child drools or is breathing with the chin jutting out and the mouth open.

- If 20 minutes of steam inhalation or cold outdoor air do not relax the child enough to allow sleep.

- If the child has a fever of 39.4°C (103°F) or higher.

- If you or your child get hysterical and cannot calm down.

- If it is the first case of croup in your family and you need reassurance.

- If croup lasts longer than three nights.

Diaper Rash

Diaper rash is a skin reaction, usually to the moisture and bacteria in babies' urine and stools, or to the soap used to wash diapers. While it is uncomfortable, diaper rash is usually not dangerous.

Symptoms of the rash are a red bottom and thighs. It will be easier for you to recognize after you have seen it the first time.

Prevention

Wash your hands before and after changing your baby.

- Change diapers as soon as possible after they have been soiled or wet.

- Leave the skin open to the air for 5 to 10 minutes after each diaper change as often as possible.

- Wash diapers with mild detergent and rinse twice. Do not use bleach.

- If your baby has frequent problems, avoid using plastic pants for a while. They trap moisture against the baby's skin.

- Protect the diaper area with zinc oxide or another ointment when your baby has diarrhea. If the problem is due to frequent diarrhea, see Diarrhea on page 159.

Home Treatment

- Change diapers frequently. Rinse and dry the skin in the diaper area at every diaper change. Use a washcloth with water and allow the diaper area to air dry if possible. Wash with a mild soap once a day.

- Try protecting the skin with Desitin, A & D Ointment, or zinc oxide. Apply cream only to dry skin. Discontinue creams if a rash develops as they slow healing.

- Try another brand or type of diaper. Some babies tolerate one kind better than another.

- Avoid bulky or multilayered diapers.

- Stop using plastic pants when the rash appears.

- Try changing detergents if the rash does not clear.

When to Call a Health Professional

- If the diaper rash becomes very red, raw, or sore looking, or if it has blisters, pus, peeling areas, or crusty patches.

- If the rash is mainly in the skin creases, which may indicate a yeast infection.

- If the rash does not clear up in a few days, check with your physician.

Diarrhea and Vomiting

Diarrhea and vomiting may be caused by viral stomach flu, by food poisoning, or even by eating unusual kinds or amounts of foods. An infant's developing digestive system sometimes will not tolerate large amounts of juice, fruit, or even milk. Breast-fed babies are less likely to develop diarrhea.

Stomach flu often starts with vomiting that is followed in a few hours (sometimes 8 to 12 hours or longer) by diarrhea. Sometimes there is no diarrhea.

Infants and children under age four, and especially under six months, need special attention when they have diarrhea or are vomiting, as they can quickly become dehydrated. Careful observation of the child's appearance and fluid intake can help prevent problems. For children age four and older, see Diarrhea on page 35 and Vomiting on page 41.

Home Treatment

Infants age 3 months to 2 years:

• If the baby is breast-fed, continue breast-feeding. If the diarrhea gets worse (larger, more frequent stools), or if the child is vomiting, supplement feedings with a children's oral rehydration drink (Pedialyte or store brand).

• If the baby is formula-fed, switch to an oral rehydration drink. Gradually add back formula feedings within 6 to 24 hours. Keep giving the oral hydration solution until the diarrhea is less frequent. Then offer the baby's usual diet in small, frequent feedings. Return to the usual amount of formula within another day.

• Give 120 to 240 ml (4 to 8 ounces) of fluid (breast milk or rehydration drink) for each large loose stool.

• Do not use sports drinks, fruit juice, or soda. These drinks contain too much sugar and not enough of the electrolytes that are being lost.

• Do not use rehydration drinks as the sole source of fluid for more than 12 to 24 hours.

• After 24 to 48 hours most children can resume their normal diet. Allow the child to eat what he prefers; the particular food is not important. Avoid high-fibre foods (such as beans) and foods with a lot of sugar, such as juice and ice cream.

• Protect the diaper area with zinc oxide or another cream. Diaper rash is common after diarrhea.

Children age 2 years and older:

• Give 120 to 240 ml (4 to 8 ounces) of a children's oral rehydration drink each hour. Give smaller amounts more often if the child is vomiting.

• Offer easily digestible foods (cooked cereal, toast, crackers) in addition to the rehydration drink. Resume a regular diet within a day or so. Do not use a rehydration drink as the sole source of fluids and nutrients for more than 24 hours.

As the child gets better, the stools will become smaller and less frequent. Some types of diarrhea may cause four to six days of watery diarrhea. Watch for signs of dehydration (see below). You can treat the illness at home as long as the child is taking in enough fluids and nutrients, is urinating normal amounts, and seems to be improving.

When to Call a Health Professional

• If the diarrhea is bloody, tarry, or dark red.

• If the urine becomes bloody or cola colored.

• If there is blood in the vomit.

• If vomiting occurs with severe headache, sleepiness, lethargy (child cannot be awakened easily) or a stiff neck (child may cry out when the neck is moved). See page 96.

• If signs of dehydration appear (also see page 33):

  ◦ No urine output for 12 hours or less than 3 urinations in 24 hours

  ◦ Sunken eyes

  ◦ Child cries without tears

  ◦ Grayish skin

  ◦ Extreme thirst

  ◦ Rapid breathing

  ◦ Sleepiness

  ◦ Sunken fontanelle (soft spot)

  ◦ Dry mouth, skin, or tongue

  ◦ Sticky saliva

• If a child with diarrhea or vomiting refuses to drink or cannot take in enough liquid to replace lost fluids.

• If severe vomiting (vomiting most or all clear liquids and feedings) occurs in an infant under age three months. In older children, call if severe vomiting continues:

  ◦ Two to four hours in an infant age three to six months

  ◦ One day in a child age six months to three years

• If occasional vomiting occurs without other symptoms and the child is able to keep fluids down between vomiting episodes, call if it continues longer than:

  ◦ One to two days in an infant under three months

  ◦ Two to four days in an infant age three to six months

  ◦ One to two weeks in a child age six months to three years

• If severe diarrhea (large loose stools every one to two hours) continues for longer than:

  ◦ Four hours in an infant under three months

  ◦ Eight hours in an infant age three to six months

  ◦ One to two days in a child age six months to four years

- If mild to moderate diarrhea continues without obvious cause or other symptoms for longer than:

  ○ 24 hours in an infant under three months

  ○ One to two days in an infant age three to six months

  ○ Four to seven days in a child age six months to four years

- If the child has a fever of 39.4°C (103°F) or higher, or a lower fever with diarrhea for more than two days.

- If the child has severe stomach pain.

- If stomach pain is persistent and there is frequent vomiting for more than 12 hours with little or no diarrhea.

- If stomach pain starts several hours before the vomiting and seems like more than stomach cramps.

- If stomach pain is not located near the bellybutton, especially if it seems to be in the lower right abdomen. This can be difficult to determine in small children.

Fever

Fever is usually defined as a rectal temperature above 38.2°C (100.6°F) or an oral temperature above 37.5°C (99.6°F). Rectal temperatures are not recommended for children. Body temperature can also rise above normal when an infant is overdressed or in a room that is too warm.

In most, but not all, cases, fever indicates that an illness is present. By itself, a fever is not harmful; in fact, it may help the body fight infections more effectively.

In children, viral infections, such as colds, flu, and chickenpox can cause high fevers. Flu (see page 41) can cause a high fever for five days or longer, along with body aches, headache, and cold-like symptoms. Bacterial infections, such as strep throat and ear infections, also cause fevers. Teething may cause a low-grade fever up to 37.8°C (100°F).

Children tend to run higher fevers than adults. Although high fevers are uncomfortable, they do not often cause medical problems. Convulsions from fever (febrile convulsions) occur only occasionally. See page 163.

For information on taking accurate temperatures in infants and children, see page 22. All temperatures in this section are oral.

There is no medical evidence that prolonged high fevers from infection can cause brain damage. The body limits a temperature from going above 42°C (106°F). However, when heat from external sources (like a car parked in the sun) raises the body temperature above 43°C (107°F), brain damage can occur.

Home Treatment

It can be hard to know when to call your doctor when your child has a fever, especially during the cold and flu season.

The degree of the fever is not always related to the severity of the infection. How your child looks and acts is a better guide than the thermometer.

Most children will be less active when they have a fever. However, if there are periods during the day when your child is more active, cheerful and playing, and is taking fluids well, it is a good sign.

Generally, if a child over three is comfortable, eating well, and playing as usual, leave the fever alone. It will do more good than harm.

• Dress the child lightly, and do not wrap him in blankets.

• Encourage him to drink extra liquids or suck on ice chips or popsicles.

If the fever is over 38.9°C (102°F) and the child is uncomfortable:

• Give acetaminophen. See page 296 for dose information. Do *not* give aspirin to children or teens under age 20.

• Sponge the child with lukewarm water for 20 minutes. Do not use cold water, ice, or rubbing alcohol. Stop sponging if shivering occurs. Check the temperature frequently. It may take up to an hour to reduce the fever.

• Keep encouraging the child to drink extra fluids.

When to Call a Health Professional

• Call a health professional *immediately* if fever is accompanied by these symptoms:

○ Stiff neck, headache or confusion, or bulging soft spot on an infant's head

○ Headache, nausea, vomiting, and excessive sleepiness or lethargy

○ Rapid, difficult breathing

○ Drooling or inability to swallow

○ Purple rash that does not lighten when you press on it

• If your child suffers a convulsion (see page 163).

• If an infant under three months has a fever.

• If a child has a fever of 40°C (104°F) or higher that does not come down after four to six hours of home treatment.

• If a child age three months to three years has a fever of 39.4°C (103°F) or higher for 24 hours.

• If a fever of 37.8° to 39.4°C (100° to 103°F) has lasted more than three days.

• If a child with a fever seems sicker than you would expect with a viral illness such as a cold or flu.

• If fever occurs with pain that isn't relieved by home treatment.

• If a child becomes delirious or has hallucinations.

• Call a health professional within 24 hours if fever is accompanied by:

○ Vomiting, diarrhea, and stomach pain

○ Signs of dehydration (see page 160)

○ Unexplained skin rash (see page 154 for common childhood illnesses that cause rash)

- Ear pain (babies often pull at painful ears)

- Painful urination

- Joint pain

- Any unusual or significant pain

Fever Convulsions

Fever (febrile) convulsions or "fits" are involuntary muscle spasms that sometimes occur in children who have had a rapid increase in temperature (often before you have realized that your child has a fever). Once a high fever has developed, the risk of a convulsion is probably gone.

A child having a convulsion stiffens up and clenches his arms, legs, and teeth. His eyes may roll back, and he may also stop breathing for a few seconds, vomit, urinate, or pass stools. Convulsions usually last one to five minutes.

Although frightening, fever convulsions in children age six months to four years are seldom serious and do not cause any harm. Only one percent of children at this age are prone to fever convulsions. About 30 percent of children who have a fever convulsion will have another one, usually within two years.

Home Treatment

During a convulsion:

- Protect the child from injury. Ease the child to the floor, or hold a very small child face down on your lap. Do not restrain the child.

- Turn the head to the side and clear the mouth of any vomit or saliva so the child can breathe.

- Do not put anything in the child's mouth, including your fingers, to prevent tongue biting. This may injure the child.

- Try to stay calm, which will help calm the child.

- Time the length of the convulsion, if possible.

After a convulsion:

- Check for injuries.

- Reduce fever with acetaminophen or ibuprofen and lukewarm sponge baths. See page 161.

- Put the child in a cool room to sleep. Drowsiness is common following a convulsion.

When to Call a Health Professional

- Call 911 or emergency services:

  - If the child stops breathing for longer than 30 to 60 seconds. Begin rescue breathing (see page 204).

  - If a convulsion lasts longer than five minutes, or a second convulsion occurs.

- If a convulsion occurs without fever.

- If it is the child's first convulsion, or if you haven't discussed with your doctor what to do if there is another one.

- If the child is under six months old, is five years or older, or if an adult has a convulsion.

- If you are unable to reduce fever to 38.9°C (102°F) after a convulsion.

- If a high fever occurs with severe headache, vomiting, stiff neck, or a bulging soft spot on an infant's head. See "Encephalitis and Meningitis" on page 96.

Pinworms

Pinworms are tiny, thread-like worms that infect the digestive tracts of young children. Pinworms are most common in four- to six-year-olds, although anyone may be infected. The worms live in the upper end of the large intestine, near the appendix, and travel to the outside of the anus to lay their eggs.

The egg-laying almost always occurs at night and usually causes the child to scratch the anal area.

When the child later sucks a thumb or licks a finger, the eggs are ingested and the cycle begins again. The eggs are very sticky, and can survive on clothing and bedding for days, where they can be picked up by other family members.

Rectal itching, especially at night, is the most common symptom of pinworm infection. If the infection is severe, there may also be abdominal pain and loss of appetite.

Pinworms are common and affect many families. If you suspect pinworms, it's easy to find out for sure in your own home and at no cost. Go into your child's darkened bedroom several hours after bedtime and shine a flashlight on the child's anus. The light will make the worms move back into the anus. If you don't see the worms after checking for two or three nights, it is unlikely that the child is infected.

Prevention

Teach children to wash their hands after using the toilet and before meals.

Home Treatment

- Ask your pharmacist for an over-the-counter medication for pinworms.

- Treat every child in the house between the ages of 2 and 10. If infection recurs, consider treating everyone in the family over age two.

- On the first day of treatment, wash all underwear, nightclothes, bedding, and towels in hot water to get rid of any eggs and prevent reinfection. Sanitize toilet and sleeping areas with a strong disinfectant.

- Trim and keep all fingernails short.

- Require frequent hand washing, morning showers, and daily changes of pajamas and underwear.

When to Call a Health Professional

- If any drug produces reactions such as vomiting or pain.

- If you suspect pinworms but the nighttime checks reveal nothing.

- If you continue to see worms at night after three days of home treatment. Prescription drugs are available.

Prickly Heat (Sweat Rash)

Prickly heat, also called heat rash, sweat rash, or miliaria, is a rash of red or pink dots that appears over an infant's head, neck, and shoulders. The dots look like tiny pimples.

Prickly heat is often caused by well-meaning parents who dress their baby too warmly, but it can happen to any baby in really hot weather. An infant should be dressed just as lightly as an adult and will be comfortable at the same temperature. Babies' hands and feet feel cold to your touch because most of their blood is near the stomach helping digestion.

Prevention

Do not overdress your baby. Place your hand between the baby's shoulder blades. If the skin is hot or moist, the baby is too warm.

Home Treatment

- Dress the baby in as few clothes as possible during hot weather.
- Keep the skin cool and dry.
- Keep the baby's sleeping area cool.
- Hydrocortisone cream (0.5 percent) can help heal the rash.

When to Call a Health Professional

- If the rash looks infected or persists over three to four days.
- If the infant looks sick.

Measles, Mumps, and Rubella

Measles (rubeola), mumps, and rubella (German measles) were once common childhood illnesses. Today, they are quite rare, thanks to the measles, mumps, and rubella (MMR) vaccine. Two shots, one given at 12 months of age and a second at either 18 months of age or at school entry, provide lifelong protection. Adults born after 1956 who have not been immunized or not had the illnesses will need one shot.

Local outbreaks of measles, mumps, or rubella can occur where immunization rates are low.

Measles symptoms:

- Fever, runny nose, hacking cough
- Reddened eyes
- Spotty red rash on entire body

Mumps symptoms:

- Swelling along the jawline
- Fever and vomiting

Rubella symptom:

- Fine pink rash starting on face and covering entire body

Contact your health unit/public health office for up-to-date information on ages at which immunizations are recommended. Contact your health professional if you suspect your child has measles, mumps, or rubella.

- If sweat rash is accompanied by a fever of 38.3°C (101°F) that doesn't come down after you remove extra clothing.

Roseola

Roseola (roseola infantum) is a mild viral illness that often starts with a sudden high fever (39° to 42°C or 103° to 105°F) and irritability. The fever lasts two to three days. As the fever drops, a rosy-pink rash appears on the torso, neck, and arms. It may last one to two days. Since the fever is quite high and may come on quickly, fever convulsions may occur (see page 163). Roseola is most common in children six months to two years of age. It is rare after age four.

Home Treatment

- If the child is uncomfortable, reduce the fever. See page 161.

- Give lots of liquids.

- If a convulsion occurs, see page 163.

When to Call a Health Professional

- See When to Call a Health Professional under Fever on page 162.

Fifth Disease

Another common childhood illness that causes a rash is erythema infectiosum, or "fifth disease." The main symptom is a red rash on the face that looks like slapped cheeks, and a lacy pink rash on the backs of the arms and legs, torso, and buttocks. There may be a low fever. The rash may come and go for several weeks in response to changes in temperature and sunlight.

This illness is most contagious the week before the rash appears. Once the rash has developed, the child is no longer contagious.

Home treatment for fifth disease is simply to keep the child comfortable and watch for signs that a more serious illness is present (fever over 38.9°C or102°F; child seems very sick).

Fifth disease is harmless in children, but it poses a slight risk to developing fetuses. Pregnant women should avoid exposure if possible. If you are pregnant and are exposed to a child with fifth disease, or if you develop a fifth disease-like rash, contact your obstetrician.

Behind every successful woman is herself.
New American Proverb

Chapter 11

Women's Health

From puberty to menopause, women cope with unique health problems. This chapter covers some health problems that are of special interest to women. Important health issues that affect both men and women are covered in other chapters.

Healthy Lifestyles

Good health habits are the best way to reduce your risk of the five most common causes of death for women ages 25 to 44. For older women and for men, heart disease and cancer are leading causes of death.

1. Cancer

• Quit smoking to reduce your risk of lung cancer (page 105).

• Have regular mammograms and Pap tests (pages 170 and 172).

2. Accidents (especially motor vehicle accidents)

• Buckle up. Seatbelts save lives and prevent serious injury.

• Don't drink and drive.

3. Heart Disease

• Quit smoking to reduce your risk of heart disease and stroke.

• Limit dietary fat and cholesterol, especially if your cholesterol is high (page 258).

• Maintain a healthy weight and get regular exercise.

• Take prescribed high blood pressure medications as directed.

4. Suicide

• Learn the warning signs of depression and seek help if you have them (page 276).

5. Homicide

• If you are in an abusive personal relationship, take steps to protect yourself (page 282).

Specific tips for controlling cholesterol, blood pressure, and weight, for getting enough exercise, quitting smoking, and managing stress are

167

included in other chapters. Check the page numbers above and the index for help in getting started.

Breast Health

Breast cancer is the leading cause of cancer deaths in women ages 40 to 55. The good news is that breast cancer is highly treatable if detected early. There are three methods of early detection: breast self-exam, clinical breast exam, and mammogram.

One of the most important risk factors for breast cancer is age. The risk goes up significantly after age 40. Women younger than 40 are at relatively low risk of breast cancer (about 1 in 200). However, if your mother or a sister had breast cancer before menopause, talk with your doctor about starting breast self-exams and other screenings before age 40.

Breast Self-Exam

Most breast lumps are discovered by women themselves, often quite by accident. The breast self-exam is a simple technique to help you learn what is normal for you and how to recognize any changes.

Many organizations recommend monthly breast self-exams for all women starting at age 18 to 20. Other organizations feel there is not enough information on the benefits of breast self-exams to make a recommendation about when to start. You may wish to talk with your doctor and decide for yourself when to begin doing monthly breast self-exams.

Establish a regular time each month to examine your breasts. Seven to ten days after the start of your period when your breasts are not swollen or tender is a good time. Women who do not menstruate (after menopause and hysterectomies) can examine their breasts the first day of each month.

Most women's breast tissue has some lumps or thickening. When in doubt about a particular lump, check the other breast. If you find a similar lump in the same area on the other breast, both breasts are probably normal. Be on the lookout for a lump that feels much harder than the rest of the breast.

Have any areas of concern checked by your health professional. The important thing is to learn what is normal for you and to report changes to your doctor.

The breast self-exam takes place in two stages.

Stage 1: In front of the mirror

Examine your breasts visually in a mirror. Few women have breasts that match exactly. It is normal for one breast to be slightly larger than the other. Learn what is normal for you.

Stand and look at your breasts in four positions:

• With your arms at your sides

• With your hands on your hips

• With your arms raised overhead

• While bending forward

In each position, look for changes in the contour and shape of your breasts, the color and texture of the skin and nipples, and any discharge from the nipples.

Squeeze the nipple of each breast gently between your thumb and index finger. A discharge is a common finding and may rarely be significant.

Stage 2: Lying down

To examine your right breast, place a pillow or folded towel under your right shoulder. If your breasts are large, lie on your left side and turn your right shoulder back flat to spread the breast tissue more evenly over your chest wall.

Use the pads of the three middle fingers of your left hand to examine your right breast. Move your fingers in small, dime-sized circles. Use light to medium pressure in each spot to feel the full thickness of the breast tissue. Don't lift your fingers away from the skin. You are feeling for lumps, thickening, or changes of any kind.

Stage 1

Stage 2

Examine your entire breast using a vertical strip pattern (see illustration). Examine all tissue from the collarbone to the armpit and from the bra line to the breastbone. Start in the armpit and work down to the bottom of the bra line. Move one finger width toward the middle and work up to the collarbone. Repeat until you have covered all the breast tissue.

Another method is to imagine that your breast is a clock. Start on the outside of the breast at 12:00, move slowly to 1:00 and then around the clock back to 12:00. Then move one inch in toward the nipple and go around the clock again.

Move the pillow or towel to the left shoulder and repeat this procedure for the left breast.

If you discover any unusual lumps, thickening, or changes of any kind, or if there is a discharge from the nipple when you are not squeezing it, report them to your doctor immediately. Most lumps are not malignant, but your doctor needs to make a diagnosis.

If you examine your breasts monthly, you will learn what is normal for you and quickly recognize if something changes. The breast self-exam takes some practice. Ask your doctor for help in learning the technique.

Clinical Breast Exam

The second component for early detection of breast problems is your health professional's physical exam. This exam is very similar to the self-exam. A clinical breast exam is recommended every two years starting at age 50.

Mammogram

A screening mammogram is a safe, low-dose X-ray of the breast that produces a clear image of the inner structure of the breast. The technique is the most accurate and effective method of detecting breast cancers in women who have no signs suggestive of breast cancer, such as lumps or bleeding. Since small lumps often cannot be felt by breast self-examination, a screening mammogram for early detection of breast cancer benefits most women.

If you are a woman 50 years of age or older, it is recommended that you have an annual clinical breast exam and a screening mammogram every two years. Women under 50 who have high-risk factors for developing breast cancer, such as a strong history of breast cancer in immediate family members (mother, sister, or daughter), may also benefit from a screening mammogram.

Where possible, have your mammogram performed at a screening mammography centre, where quality control and monitoring are ensured and additional information is available to you. Your doctor or public health unit can direct you to the screening mammography centre in your area.

Scheduling an Exam

- Schedule your mammogram one to two weeks after your period.

- Do not wear deodorant, perfume, powder, or lotion, which can affect the quality of the X-ray.

- Wear clothing that allows you to remove only your top.

Breast Health Tips

- Do your breast self-exam every month. Most breast lumps are discovered by women themselves. If detected early, breast cancer usually can be successfully treated.

- Have a clinical breast exam every one to two years starting at age 40.

- Have a mammogram every one to two years after age 50.

- Limit alcohol to one drink per day. Heavy drinking increases the risk of breast cancer.

Gynecological Health

Regular pelvic exams and Pap smears are a vital component of women's health. These exams can give you early indications of any abnormalities in your reproductive organs. It is better to catch any disease in its early stages, when it is much easier to treat.

Self-Exam

Self-exams will help you better understand your own body and what is normal for you. A female's genitals include two sets of lips: the inner (labia minora) and the outer (labia majora). These lips form around the urinary opening, the vaginal opening, and the clitoris.

Periodically examine your entire genital area for any sores, warts, red swollen areas, or unusual discharge. A normal vaginal discharge may be white to yellowish-white and smell slightly like vinegar. It can be either thick or thin and present in large or small amounts; every woman is different. During ovulation (14 days before the next period) there is often a large amount of clear, slippery mucus. If your discharge seems unusual in amount, smell, or texture, see Vaginitis on page 183.

There should be no pain or straining on urination, and the urine should come out in a fairly steady stream. The urine should be pale yellow and it should not have a strong ammonia smell. If you experience pain or burning on urination, see Urinary Tract Infections on page 181 or Vaginitis on page 183.

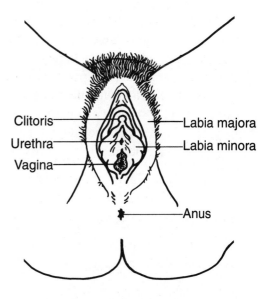

Female genitals

The Pelvic Exam and Pap Test

A pelvic exam given by a health care professional will generally consist of an external genital exam, a Pap test, and a manual exam.

The Pap test is the screening exam for cancer of the cervix. Pap smears detect 90 to 95 percent of cervical cancers, making it a reliable and important test. The clinician will insert a speculum into your vagina and gather some cells from your cervix and vagina. There may be some discomfort. Tell the clinician if you feel any pain. The speculum can be adjusted to ease the discomfort.

The cells are put on a slide and sent to a lab for classification. If abnormal cells are found, your doctor will ask you to return for more testing. In any case, your doctor should let you know the results of your Pap test. Ask for an explanation of your results.

For a manual exam, the clinician inserts two gloved and lubricated fingers into your vagina and presses on your lower abdomen with the other hand to feel the ovaries and uterus. An STD screen should be added for women who are not in a long-term monogamous relationship (see page 198).

Scheduling an Exam

The first Pap test is recommended only after a female becomes sexually active. Therefore, a 16-year-old female who has been sexually active should have an exam.

Pap smears are recommended every one to three years, depending on your risk factors. Women with a single sexual partner and several consecutive normal Pap smears need less frequent exams (every two to three years).

Women with multiple sexual partners, other risk factors such as smoking, or a history of abnormal exams need yearly exams. Discuss this with your doctor.

Schedule the exam one to two weeks after your period. Do not douche, have intercourse, or use feminine hygiene products for 24 hours before the exam as they can alter the results.

For more information on women's health, see Resources 123 to 131 on page 309.

Pregnancy: How to Make a Healthy Baby

You can increase the chances that your baby will be healthy. The following guidelines will help.

Before Conception

Your health, before and during the first weeks after conception, is particularly important for your baby's health. Start helping your baby even before you become pregnant.

• Before you start trying to get pregnant, have a blood test to check your rubella immunity. If you test negative, you will want to receive your immunization and then use some form of birth control for at least three months.

• If you have diabetes, high blood pressure, seizure disorders, heart disease, kidney disease, anemia, or any inherited diseases, talk with your doctor before getting pregnant. Your doctor may want to modify your treatment and may be able to prescribe medicine that is safer for the developing baby.

- If you have symptoms of sexually transmitted diseases or are unsure of your partner's sexual history, read pages 198 to 202 and arrange for an examination and testing with your doctor.

- Eat well. Make sure your diet includes plenty of green leafy vegetables and legumes, and take a folic acid supplement containing 0.4 mg of folate. Folic acid helps prevent certain birth defects, such as spina bifida. Other good sources of folic acid include fortified cereal and whole-wheat bread.

- Stop smoking (see page 105) and stop drinking alcohol. This includes hard liquor, beer, wine, and coolers.

- Avoid drugs and medications of any kind unless you take them with your doctor's knowledge.

Home Pregnancy Tests

If you become pregnant, it is important that you know right away. The quickest way is with a home pregnancy test. Home pregnancy tests are inexpensive and very reliable when done correctly. Some tests can show positive results within a few days of the first missed period. Select a test that has simple instructions and follow them *exactly*. Mistakes can lead to false results.

If the test is positive, schedule an appointment with your doctor to confirm it. Even if the test is negative, treat yourself as if you are pregnant until you are sure.

- If you are anxious or depressed, get help. See pages 274 to 278.

- Buy a good book on pregnancy and begin reading. See Resources 104 to 107 on page 308.

Early Pregnancy (First Trimester)

- Continue to avoid smoking, alcohol, and drugs.

- Get regular prenatal care from your family doctor or obstetrician.

- Call your local health unit or public health office and ask about enrolling in prenatal classes and about special programs such as nutritional counselling.

- Continue to eat a healthy diet and check with your doctor about taking a vitamin supplement. Call your health unit/public health office to find out if you are eligible for food supplements available in some communites.

- Take part in a regular exercise program appropriate to your level of fitness. Check with your health professional if you are uncertain about the exercise program right for you.

- Continue taking 0.4 mg folic acid daily (daily dosage should not exceed 1.0 mg). As long as you are eating a well-balanced diet, most obstetricians no longer recommend vitamin supplements. In fact, there is some evidence that vitamin supplements may cause more morning sickness early in the pregnancy.

- Avoid touching cat feces and litter boxes. Also, cook all meats well before eating. Cat feces and undercooked or raw meat can carry toxoplasmosis, an infection that can cause brain damage in the fetus or miscarriage.

- Avoid all chemical vapors, paint fumes, and poisons.

- If you drink coffee or soda with caffeine, limit yourself to two cups a day.

Middle Pregnancy (Second Trimester)

- Continue with the safeguards described above.

- Reduce the risk of injury and falls:

  ○ Always wear a seat belt. It should be low and fitted snugly across the upper thighs, not over the abdomen. The shoulder belt should also be worn.

  ○ Wear sensible shoes.

  ○ Continue moderate levels of your regular exercises so you don't become exhausted or short of breath.

  ○ Avoid sports with a high risk of falls or impact.

- Continue eating a healthy diet. If you are unable to eat the recommended amounts or have special needs, call your public health nurse or nutritionist. Increase your calcium intake by drinking more milk (a litre of skim or low-fat milk a day) or through other sources of calcium. See page 261.

Late Pregnancy (Third Trimester)

- Maintain all of the other guidelines listed above.

- Get plenty of rest.

- If you have not already done so, check with your local health unit or public health office about taking childbirth/prenatal classes.

Morning Sickness

For many women, the first few months of pregnancy bring morning sickness, which can happen at any time of the day. This is a normal result of the body's adjustment to pregnancy and is caused by hormonal action, tension, and/or fatigue. The following home treatment can help:

- Eat five or six small meals a day to avoid an empty stomach. Include some protein in each of these meals.

- Eat crackers or dry toast before getting up in the morning.

- Increase your intake of vitamin B_6 by eating more whole grains and cereals, wheat germ, nuts, seeds, and legumes. Talk with your doctor before taking vitamin supplements during early pregnancy. They may cause nausea.

- Keep a positive attitude. Morning sickness lasts about 8 to 12 weeks only, but may persist longer. Notify your doctor if vomiting persists and you become concerned.

- If appropriate, have your other children take a class to help them adjust to the new baby.

- Practice the relaxation exercises on page 248. They will be helpful during labor.

- Develop a written birth plan with your doctor that outlines your wishes and expectations throughout the labor and delivery.

- Maintain a good sense of humor.

Cesarean Deliveries

Most babies are delivered vaginally, just as nature intended. However, when the health of the baby or mother is at risk, doctors can deliver the baby through an incision in the abdomen. This is called a cesarean delivery or a C-section.

There are three main concerns with cesarean deliveries:

- More risk. Mothers who have C-sections have a greater risk of developing infections or bleeding that requires additional medications or treatment.

- Longer recovery. You can usually go home within two days after a vaginal birth. Hospital stays after cesarean deliveries may be two to three days. After a cesarean, you must limit your activity over the next four to six weeks to allow the incision to heal.

- Less involvement. The mother and other family members can be more involved with a vaginal delivery. Cesarean delivery is a surgery, which may limit family involvement.

C-sections are often performed when either the baby or the mother is in danger. A cesarean should not be done just because it is easier to schedule or because you have previously had a C-section delivery. Ask your doctor, public health nurse, midwife, or childbirth educator what you can do to help avoid the need for a cesarean delivery.

Breast-Feeding

Breast milk is the best food for your baby. Consider taking a breast-feeding class before your baby is born. See page 150.

Bleeding Between Periods

Many women experience bleeding or spotting between periods. It does not necessarily mean a serious condition is present. Use of an intrauterine device (IUD) may increase your chances of spotting. Some minor bleeding is common during ovulation and during the first three months of using birth control pills. It is also common to spot or bleed regularly while breast-feeding.

If the bleeding is not heavy and occurs only occasionally, it is probably not a cause for concern.

Use tampons as directed or pads, and avoid aspirin, which may prolong the bleeding.

When to Call a Health Professional

- If bleeding is accompanied by unusual pain, cramping, or fever.

- If the bleeding is heavy (changing a maxi pad or super tampon every hour for more than six hours).

- If bleeding between periods lasts more than 10 days in a row or occurs three months in a row.

- If bleeding occurs after intercourse.

- If you are over age 35 and have any bleeding between periods or prolonged bleeding with periods.

Menopause

For most women, menopause occurs between the ages of 45 and 55, when the production of female hormones (estrogen and progesterone) begins to decline. These hormonal changes will cause irregular menstrual periods before they stop altogether. You may also experience hot flashes, vaginal dryness, and mood changes. Osteoporosis is also directly linked to the decrease in estrogen that comes with menopause. See page 71.

Irregular periods may mean lighter or heavier menstrual flows, either shorter or longer intervals between flows, or spotting. Some women have irregular periods for years during menopause. Others have regular periods until they suddenly stop. Each woman is unique and will experience menopause differently.

Hot flashes are sudden periods of intense heat, sweating, and flushing. A hot flash usually begins in the chest and spreads out to the neck, face, and arms. Seventy-five to 80 percent of women going through menopause will have hot flashes. They may occur as frequently as once an hour and last as long as three to four minutes. If they occur at night, they may disrupt your sleep. Most hot flashes cease within one or two years, but may persist for several years.

Vaginal dryness, the loss of lubrication and moisture in the vagina, may lead to soreness during and after intercourse. These vaginal changes may also increase the risk of infections. See Vaginitis on page 183.

Birth Control During Menopause

Some women may continue to ovulate during menopause, which means there is a slight chance that they could become pregnant, even though they are no longer menstruating regularly.

Women who have their last period *before* age 50 and who do not want to become pregnant should continue using contraceptives (other than birth control pills) for two years. Birth control pills may be used with medical supervision.

Women who have their last period *after* age 50 generally need to use contraceptives only for one year.

Mood changes are caused by the hormonal and physical changes of menopause. Symptoms such as nervousness, lethargy, insomnia, moodiness, or depression are common.

With menopause, many women fear emotional upheaval and the loss of sexuality. On the other hand, many women look forward to the freedom that menopause brings, particularly freedom from menstrual cycle discomfort and freedom from contraception.

Understanding what is happening to you and using home care techniques to relieve any discomfort will help you through menopause.

Home Treatment

Irregular periods:

• Keep a written record of your periods in case you need to discuss them with a health professional.

Hot flashes:

• Keep your home and work place cool.

• Wear layers of loose clothing that can be easily removed.

• Drink lots of water and juices. Avoid caffeine and alcohol if they bring on hot flashes.

• Exercise regularly. This will help to stabilize hormones and prevent insomnia.

Vaginal dryness:

• Use a water-soluble vaginal lubricant such as K-Y Jelly or Surgilube to relieve painful intercourse. Do not use a petroleum-based product such as Vaseline.

Mood changes:

• The best thing you can do for yourself is to realize you are not alone. Discuss your symptoms with other women. Give yourself, and ask others for, abundant amounts of love, caring, and understanding.

When to Call a Health Professional

• If you have prolonged irregular bleeding, particularly if you are overweight.

• If you are considering hormone replacement therapy.

• If mood changes are causing problems, and home treatment isn't helping.

Hormone Therapy

Hormone therapy helps relieve the short-term symptoms of menopause and reduces some long-term risks associated with lower estrogen levels. There are two types of hormone therapy. **Estrogen replacement therapy** (ERT) is estrogen alone. **Hormone replacement therapy** (HRT) combines estrogen with progestin, another hormone.

ERT is usually prescribed only for women who have had a hysterectomy, since it increases the risk of endometrial cancer. HRT is usually prescribed only for women who have a uterus. Women with a uterus who take ERT need regular checkups for uterine lining changes.

Hormone therapy reduces some health risks and increases others. Consider the following factors in your decision.

Osteoporosis

Both ERT and HRT reduce the risk of osteoporosis and slow the rate of bone loss that occurs after menopause, which helps reduce the risk of fractures. See page 71 for information on preventing osteoporosis.

Heart Disease

ERT reduces a woman's risk of heart disease by increasing high-density lipoprotein (HDL or "good") cholesterol. Studies of HRT suggest it also has a significant "heart-protective" effect.

Because the risk of heart disease is much greater than other health risks for postmenopausal women, the "heart-protective" effect of ERT may make it a wise choice for many women.

Breast Cancer

It is not clear whether hormone therapy increases the risk of breast cancer. Some studies find that it may increase the risk slightly; others find no increase in risk. However, women who currently have breast cancer should not take ERT or HRT. Some women who have had breast cancer in the past but have been cancer-free for at least two to three years may be able to take HRT. Discuss this with your doctor.

Endometrial Cancer

Estrogen alone (ERT) increases the risk of endometrial (uterine) cancer (although the risk is still very low). Estrogen combined with progestin (HRT) protects against this increased risk.

Gallbladder Disease

Both ERT and HRT increase the risk of gallbladder disease.

Considerations

Hormone therapy reduces the discomfort caused by menopausal symptoms. However, HRT also has side effects that may be unacceptable to some women. They include periodic vaginal bleeding, bloating, cramping, nausea, and breast tenderness. Your doctor may be able to ease these side effects by adjusting the dose.

To gain the long-term benefits of hormone therapy, the medications must be taken for many years. Women on long-term hormone therapy need regular visits to a health professional.

Should You Take Hormones?

Hormone therapy is not usually recommended for women who have had breast cancer, trouble with blood clots, liver disease, or undiagnosed vaginal bleeding.

Discuss the risks and benefits of hormone therapy with your doctor. Few risks appear to be associated with short-term (up to one year) hormone therapy to relieve menopause symptoms. If you are considering longer-term therapy, keep the following in mind:

• If your risk of osteoporosis and heart disease is already low, long-term hormone therapy may not give you enough additional benefits to justify the added risk and inconvenience.

• If your risk of osteoporosis and heart disease is high, the benefits of long-term therapy may outweigh the added risk and inconvenience.

Menstrual Cramps

Many women suffer from painful menstrual cramps (dysmenorrhea). Symptoms include mild to severe cramping in the lower abdomen, back, or thighs, headaches, diarrhea, constipation, nausea, dizziness, and fainting.

During the menstrual cycle, the lining of the uterus produces a hormone called prostaglandin. This hormone causes the uterus to contract, often painfully. Women with severe cramps may produce higher than normal amounts of prostaglandin, or may be more sensitive to its effects.

Home Treatment

• Exercise. Regular workouts decrease the severity of cramps. See Chapter 16.

• Ibuprofen inhibits the production of prostaglandins and generally helps ease cramps better than aspirin or acetaminophen. Take it the day before your period starts, or at the first sign of pain. Take ibuprofen with milk or food, as it can upset your stomach.

• Use heat (hot water bottles, heating pads, or hot baths) to relax tense muscles and relieve cramping.

• Herbal teas, such as chamomile, mint, raspberry, and blackberry may help soothe tense muscles and anxious moods.

• Try using sanitary napkins instead of tampons.

• If you have symptoms other than cramping, such as weight gain, headache, and tension, see Premenstrual Syndrome on page 180.

When to Call a Health Professional

• If sudden, severe pelvic pain occurs, with or without menstrual bleeding.

• If your period is accompanied by sudden high fever, diarrhea, or skin rash.

• If menstrual bleeding is very heavy (changing more than one maxi pad or super tampon an hour for more than six hours) or lasts longer than 10 days.

• If periods come closer than 21 days apart.

• If you suspect that your intrauterine device (IUD) is causing cramps.

• If painful cramping suddenly occurs after years of less painful periods.

• If cramps begin five to seven days before your period begins, or if cramps do not cease when menstrual flow stops.

• If pelvic pain seems unrelated to your menstrual cycle.

• If cramps fail to respond to home treatment.

Missed or Irregular Periods

Missed or irregular periods have a variety of causes. Pregnancy is usually the first cause to be considered, but other common causes include:

• Stress, weight loss or gain, increased exercise (missed periods are common in endurance athletes), and travel.

• Use of birth control pills, which may cause lighter, less frequent, or skipped periods.

• Menopause or menarche (starting of menstrual periods). For the first few years of menstruation, periods may be irregular.

• Medications, including steriods, tranquilizers, and diet pills.

• Hormone imbalance or problems in the reproductive system.

If you've skipped a period, try to relax. Restoring your life to emotional and physical balance will help. Many women miss periods now and then. Unless you are pregnant, chances are your cycle will return to normal next month. If you could be pregnant, treat yourself as if you are until you know for sure.

Home Treatment

• If you had intercourse during the previous month, do a home pregnancy test. See page 173.

• Avoid fad diets that greatly restrict calories and food variety, and avoid rapid weight loss. To maintain a healthy weight, focus on eating a variety of low-fat foods. See page 257.

• Increase exercise gradually. If you are an endurance athlete, cut back on training or talk with a doctor about hormone and calcium supplements to protect against bone loss.

• Learn and practice relaxation exercises to reduce and cope with stress. See Chapter 16.

• If you are age 45 or older, you may be starting menopause. See page 176.

When to Call a Health Professional

• If pregnancy is possible, see a doctor to confirm your home pregnancy test and begin pregnancy counseling and/or prenatal care.

• If you have missed two regular periods, are not pregnant, are not approaching menopause, and are not dieting or exercising a lot, or under psychological stress.

• If you are an endurance athlete who is unable to cut back on training. You may need hormones or calcium supplements.

• If you miss two or three periods while taking birth control pills, and you have not skipped any pills.

Premenstrual Syndrome

Premenstrual syndrome (PMS) occurs 7 to 10 days before the menstrual period begins. It is estimated that 90 percent of women have had some of the symptoms associated with PMS. Only about 10 percent of women have severe problems with PMS. Symptoms generally improve when menstrual bleeding starts.

Over 150 physical and psychological symptoms are associated with PMS. Physical symptoms include: headaches, backaches, weight gain, breast tenderness, water retention and bloating, food cravings and increased appetite, diarrhea or constipation, dizziness or fainting, and clumsiness.

Emotional symptoms include: irritability and anger, mood swings, anxiety, sudden bouts of crying, sadness, fatigue, poor concentration, diminished sex drive, and aggression.

A self-test to determine if you have PMS:

• Do the same symptoms occur each month?

• Do symptoms improve or disappear when bleeding begins?

• Do you have at least one symptom-free week per month?

Keep a diary charting your premenstrual symptoms, their timing, and severity. If symptoms appear fairly consistent over several months, chances are you have PMS.

Home Treatment

• Eat smaller meals every three to four hours with plenty of whole grains, fruit, and vegetables. Limit fats and sweets, and reduce salt to help limit bloating.

• Eliminating tobacco, alcohol, and caffeine may help relieve some symptoms.

• Get some exercise. Regular exercise will help minimize PMS symptoms.

• Try an over-the-counter PMS medication, such as Midol or Pamprin. Many products contain a combination of drugs to help relieve symptoms of cramps, bloating, and headache.

• Taking 50 mg of vitamin B_6 twice a day is often helpful. Do not take more than 100 mg per day.

• Be good to yourself. Reduce your stress level as much as possible. Try relaxation techniques such as yoga and deep breathing. See Chapter 16.

• Talk with others. Your PMS also affects those with whom you live and work. Join a PMS self-help group. You can ask for information and referrals from your local hospital.

When to Call a Health Professional

• If physical or emotional symptoms are severe and home treatment does not help.

• If symptoms do not stop when menstrual bleeding starts.

Urinary Tract Infections

Urinary tract infections (UTIs), also called bladder infections or cystitis, are a common health problem for women, young girls, and some infant boys. They may also occur in men.

Early symptoms may include burning or pain during urination and itching or pain in the urethra (the tube that carries urine from the bladder). There may be discomfort in the lower abdomen and a frequent urge to urinate without being able to pass much urine. Men with these symptoms may have an infection of the prostate gland. See page 191.

Urinary infections are generally caused by *E. coli* bacteria, which are normally present in the digestive system. Because women have shorter urethras, they are much more susceptible to the infection than men.

Other causes of irritation to the genital area that may be associated with bladder infection include intercourse, diaphragms, wearing tight jeans or pants, bike riding, infrequent urination, perfumed soaps and powders, even spicy food.

Prevention

- Drink more fluids; water is best.

- Urinate frequently.

- Women should wipe from front to back after going to the toilet to reduce the spread of bacteria from the anus to the urethra. Teach young girls this habit during toilet training.

- Avoid douching, and do not use vaginal deodorants or perfumed feminine hygiene products.

- Wash the genital area once a day with plain water or mild soap. Rinse well and dry thoroughly.

- If you are susceptible to urinary infections, drink extra water before intercourse and urinate promptly afterwards.

- Wear cotton underwear, cotton-lined pantyhose, and loose clothing.

- Drinking cranberry juice may protect against infection, especially in women after menopause.

Home Treatment

Apply home care at the first sign of irritation or painful urination. A day or so of home treatment may eliminate minor symptoms. However, if your symptoms last longer than a day or worsen despite home care, call your doctor. Because the organs of the urinary tract are connected, untreated bladder infections can spread and can lead to kidney infections and other serious problems.

- Drink as much water as you can (think in terms of gallons) as soon as you notice the symptoms and for the next 24 hours. This will help flush bacteria out of the bladder.

- Avoid alcohol and caffeine.

- A hot bath may help relieve pain and itching. Avoid using bubble bath.

Blood in the Urine

A blow to the kidneys, excessive running, or an infection can cause blood in the urine. Blood in the urine can be a sign of a serious illness in both women and men and should *always* be discussed with a health professional.

Eating foods such as beets, blackberries, and those containing red artificial food colorings can temporarily color the urine pink or red.

- Check your temperature and examine the genital area twice daily. Fever may indicate a more serious infection is present.

- Avoid intercourse until symptoms improve.

- If abdominal pain or vaginal burning and redness occur in a young girl, consider the possibility of an allergy to bubble bath or soap.

When to Call a Health Professional

- If painful urination occurs with any of the following symptoms:

  ○ Fever over 38.3°C (101°F) and chills

  ○ Inability to urinate when you feel the urge

  ○ Lower back pain just below rib cage

  ○ Blood or pus in the urine

  ○ Unusual vaginal discharge

  ○ Nausea or vomiting

- If symptoms do not improve after 24 hours of home treatment.

- If you are pregnant or have diabetes, and have symptoms of a urinary tract infection.

- If you suspect a child has a urinary tract infection.

Vaginitis

Vaginitis is any vaginal infection, inflammation, or irritation that causes a change in normal vaginal discharge. General symptoms include a change in the amount, color, odor, or consistency of the discharge, itching, painful urination, and pain during intercourse. Common types of vaginitis include yeast infection (see page 184) and bacterial vaginosis. Some types of sexually transmitted diseases can cause an unusual vaginal discharge. See page 198. If you have burning and pain on urination and feel the need to urinate often, see Urinary Tract Infections on page 181.

Symptoms of bacterial vaginosis often include a thin, grayish-white, "fishy-smelling" vaginal discharge. The odor is often worse after intercourse.

Bacterial vaginosis is commonly associated with using tampons, an intrauterine device or diaphragm, and multiple sex partners. In addition, irritation caused by frequent douching, tight clothing, or use of strong soaps or perfumed feminine hygiene products may contribute to vaginal irritation or infection.

Prevention

- Limit the number of your sexual partners and use condoms during intercourse. Multiple sexual partners may increase the risk of bacterial vaginosis by changing the normal environment of the vagina.

- If you think frequent vaginal infections are related to diaphragm or IUD use, discuss other birth control options with your doctor.

- Wipe from *front to back* after using the toilet to avoid spreading bacteria from the anus to the vagina.

- Wash the genital area once a day with plain water or a mild, non-perfumed soap. Rinse well and dry thoroughly. Avoid douching.

- Avoid using feminine deodorant sprays and other perfumed products. They irritate tender skin.

- Change tampons at least three times a day or alternate tampons with pads. Be sure to remove the last tampon used during your period.

Home Treatment

Bacterial vaginosis may clear up without treatment in three or four days. If symptoms persist, call your doctor.

- Avoid intercourse for two weeks to give irritated vaginal tissues time to heal.

- Avoid scratching. Relieve itching with a cold water compress.

- Make sure that the cause of the vaginitis is not a forgotten tampon or other foreign object.

When to Call a Health Professional

- If you have pelvic or lower abdominal pain, fever, and unusual vaginal discharge.

- If you have an unusual, foul-smelling vaginal discharge that is especially noticeable after intercourse.

- If the discharge and other symptoms are very uncomfortable.

- If you think you've been exposed to a sexually transmitted disease (see page 198). Your partner may need to be treated as well.

- If you have pain with intercourse that is not eased by use of a vaginal lubricant, such as K-Y Jelly.

- If any unusual discharge lasts more than two weeks.

If you plan to see a health professional, do not douche, use vaginal creams, or have intercourse for 48 hours before your appointment, since they may make diagnosis difficult.

Yeast Infections

A yeast infection is an excess growth of yeast organisms in the vagina due to an imbalance among the normal vaginal microorganisms. Yeast infections are common in women of childbearing age. They can cause severe discomfort but rarely cause serious problems.

Common symptoms of yeast infection include itching (often severe) in the genital area, white, curdy, usually odorless vaginal discharge, painful urination, and pain during intercourse. The skin around the vagina (labia) may be red and irritated. If you have burning and pain on urination and feel the need to urinate often, see Urinary Tract Infections on page 181.

Yeast infections are not sexually transmitted. However, some doctors feel that treating your male sexual partner may help prevent chronic, recurrent infections.

Yeast infections (candidiasis) are commonly associated with antibiotic or steriod use, pregnancy, diabetes, and illnesses that impair the immune system. In addition, irritation caused by frequent douching, tight clothing, or use of strong soaps or perfumed feminine hygiene products may contribute to vaginal irritation or infection.

Prevention

- Eat a cup of yogurt that contains live Lactobacillus organisms each day.

- Wear cotton or cotton-lined underwear. Avoid tight-fitting pants and undergarments. They increase body heat, which may allow yeast to grow more easily in your vagina.

- Avoid feminine sprays, talcs, or perfumes in your vaginal area, which may affect the balance among the microorganisms in your vagina. Do not douche unless told to by your health professional.

- Wipe your vaginal area from front to back after using the toilet and when bathing.

- It is not clear that a high-sugar diet causes yeast infections, but limiting sugar may help.

Home Treatment

Left untreated, vaginal yeast infections often clear up on their own, usually when menstruation begins. Be sure your symptoms indicate a yeast infection before self treatment.

- Use an over-the-counter antifungal medication for yeast infections (Canesten, Monistat 7) as directed.

- Drink acidophilus milk or eat yogurt with live Lactobacillus cultures regularly.

- Avoid excessive cleaning of the vaginal area. Wash once a day with plain water or a mild, non-perfumed soap.

- Consider using condoms while being treated to avoid (possibly) being reinfected by your sexual partner. If intercourse is painful, use a water-soluble lubricant (K-Y Jelly) to reduce irritation.

When to Call a Health Professional

- If you have pelvic or lower abdominal pain, fever, and unusual vaginal discharge.

- If you think you have a yeast infection for the first time, or if you aren't sure whether your symptoms are due to a yeast infection.

- If home treatment with an OTC product fails to clear up a yeast infection within three or four days, or if you are using antifungal creams repeatedly.

- If you have pain with intercourse that is not eased by use of a vaginal lubricant.

- If any unusual discharge lasts more than two weeks.

If you plan to see a health professional, do not douche, use vaginal creams, or have intercourse for 48 hours before your appointment, since they may make the diagnosis difficult.

The man who says it cannot be done should not interrupt the man doing it.
Old Chinese Proverb

Chapter 12

Men's Health

This chapter focuses on several health problems that are unique to men. However, it doesn't address basic lifestyle habits, which are the most important health issues for men and also for women.

Healthy Lifestyles

Good health habits are the best way to reduce your risk of the five most common causes of death for men ages 25 to 44. For older men and for women, heart disease and cancer are the leading causes of death.

1. Accidents

• Buckle up, even if your vehicle has airbags. Seatbelts save lives and prevent serious injury.

• Don't drink and drive.

2. HIV Infection

• Always use condoms with new sex partners and any partner whose sexual history may not be risk free (see page 201).

3. Heart Disease

• Limit dietary fat and cholesterol, especially if your cholesterol is high (page 258).

• Quit smoking to reduce your risk of heart attack and stroke (page 105).

• Maintain a healthy weight and get regular exercise.

• Take prescribed high blood pressure medications as directed.

4. Cancer

• Quit smoking. Lung cancer is the most common type of cancer among both men and women.

5. Suicide

• Learn the warning signs of depression and seek help if you have them (page 276).

If your health is already good, these habits will help you stay healthy and active as you get older. If you have some health problems, good habits are even more important. Specific tips for controlling cholesterol, blood pressure, and weight, for getting enough exercise, quitting smoking, and managing stress are included in other chapters. Check the page numbers above and the index for help in getting started.

Genital Health

Daily cleaning of the penis, particularly under the foreskin of an uncircumcised penis, can prevent bacterial infection. Daily washing also reduces the already low risk of penile cancer. Boys should be taught by age three or four how to retract the foreskin, wash the penis, and replace the foreskin over the head of the penis after cleaning. The foreskin may not be fully retractable until puberty. Do not forcibly retract a child's foreskin if it is painful or difficult to do so.

Testicular Self-Exam

Teen males and young men who are at increased risk of testicular cancer (who have had undescended testicles or a family history of testicular cancer) are encouraged to examine their testes once a month. Testicular cancer is very rare and highly curable when detected early.

The best time to do the exam is after a warm bath or shower when the scrotal skin is relaxed.

- Stand and place your right leg on an elevated surface. A tub side or toilet seat works fine.

- Examine the surface of the right testicle by gently rolling it between the thumb and fingers of both hands. Feel for any hard lumps or nodules. The testicle should feel round and smooth.

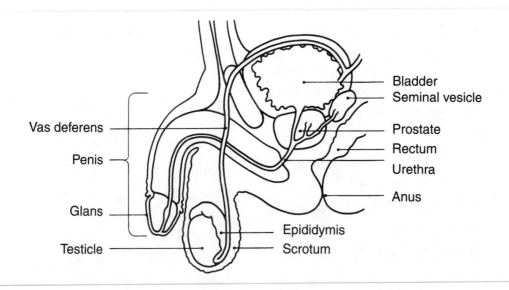

Male genitals

- Notice any enlargement of the testicle or a change in its consistency. It is normal for one testicle to be slightly larger than the other. Report any major size differences to a health professional.

- Repeat, lifting your left leg and examining your left testicle.

Call your health professional for an immediate appointment if you notice any of the following:

- Unusual lumps or nodules in the testes

- Unexplained pain or swelling in the testes or scrotum

- If you notice any penile discharge or sores on your penis, see page 198 and discuss it with your doctor.

Erection Problems

Erection problems are common and can often be solved with self-care. By definition, an erection problem is difficulty in raising or maintaining an erection capable of intercourse.

Erection problems are often due to stress at work, tension in relationships, depression, fatigue, lack of privacy, physical injury, or side effects of medications. These causes are generally temporary and will usually resolve with home treatment. Other less reversible causes include diabetes, a long history of smoking, or vascular disease.

While the ease of gaining and sustaining erections generally decreases with age, with the right foreplay and environment, there is no age limit to the ability of healthy men to have erections.

Prevention

Most erection problems can be resolved by taking a more relaxed approach to lovemaking and watching for possible side effects from medications or illnesses.

Home Treatment

- Rule out medications first. Many drugs have side effects that can cause erection problems, especially blood pressure medicines, diuretics, and mood-altering drugs. Ask your doctor or pharmacist to check your medications for possible side effects on sexual function, or look it up yourself. See Resource 2 on page 302.

- Avoid alcohol and smoking, which make erection problems worse.

- Cope with stress (see Chapter 16). Tension in your life can distract you and make erections difficult. Regular exercise and other stress-relieving activities may help ease tension.

- Take time for more foreplay. Let your partner know that you would enjoy some stroking. Slow down, then slow down some more.

- Make sure you're ready. If you have experienced a recent loss or change in a relationship, you may not yet be emotionally ready for erections. Generally, the stress will subside and the erection problem will disappear after a few weeks. Do what you can to relax.

- Find out if you can have erections at other times. If you can have an erection during masturbation or on awakening, the problem is probably stress-related or due to an emotional problem.

When to Call a Health Professional

- If you think that a medication may be causing the problem. Substitutes may be available.

- If you are unable to have an erection at all, or think that your problem may be a physical one.

- If you are still having problems after a few months of self-care, consider talking with a psychological therapist.

- After all other options have been tried for several months without success, you may wish to talk with your doctor about erection-producing injections, a vacuum device, or penile implant.

Hernia

A hernia occurs when tissue from inside the abdomen bulges out through a weak spot in the abdominal wall. Hernias are more common in men than in women. They commonly occur in the groin and may bulge into the scrotum. An inguinal hernia is one that occurs in the inguinal canal, which leads from the abdomen to the scrotum.

Hernias are often caused by increased abdominal pressure resulting from lifting heavy weights, coughing, or straining during a bowel movement. Sometimes, a weak spot in the abdominal wall is present at birth.

The symptoms of a hernia may come on gradually or suddenly. There may be a feeling that something has given way and varying degrees of pain.

Symptoms may include:

- Feeling of weakness, pressure, burning, or pain in the groin or scrotum.

- A bulge or lump in the groin or scrotum. These bulges may be easier to see when the person coughs, and may disappear when the person lies down.

- Pain in the groin when straining, lifting, or coughing.

A hernia is called reducible if it can be pushed back into place in the abdomen; irreducible if it cannot.

A hernia becomes incarcerated when the tissue becomes trapped outside the abdominal wall. If the blood supply is cut off, the hernia is said to be strangulated. When this occurs, the tissue swells and dies. The dead tissue quickly becomes infected, requiring immediate medical attention. Rapidly increasing pain in the groin or scrotum is a sign that the hernia has become strangulated.

Prevention

- Use proper lifting techniques (see page 51), and avoid lifting weights that are too heavy for you.

- Avoid constipation and do not strain during bowel movements and urination.

- Stop smoking, especially if you have a chronic cough.

When to Call a Health Professional

If you have been diagnosed with a hernia, call a health professional immediately:

• If you experience sudden, severe, or increasing pain in the area of the hernia, scrotum, or groin.

• If the hernia cannot be reduced with gentle pressure when lying down.

• If you have sudden swelling in the groin that pulsates (possible aneurysm).

Call a health professional:

• If you suspect a hernia, to confirm the diagnosis and discuss treatment options.

• If mild groin pain or an unexplained groin bump or swelling continues for more than one week.

Prostate Problems

The prostate is a doughnut-shaped cluster of glands located at the bottom of the bladder about halfway between the rectum and the base of the penis. It encircles the urethra, the tube that carries urine from the bladder out through the penis. This walnut-sized gland produces most of the fluid in semen.

The three most common prostate problems are: infection (prostatitis), prostate enlargement (benign prostatic hypertrophy), and prostate cancer.

Prostate Infection (Prostatitis)

There are two types of prostate infection, acute and chronic. Acute infections come on suddenly and have some or all of the following symptoms:

• Fever and chills

• Pain and burning on urination and ejaculation

• Strong and frequent urge to urinate while passing only small amounts of urine

• Lower back or abdominal pain

• Blood in the urine (occasionally)

Symptoms of chronic prostatitis are usually milder than those of an acute infection, and fever and chills are usually not present. Either infection may occur with a urinary tract infection. See page 181.

Prostate infections usually respond well to home care and antibiotics. If the infection recurs, long-term antibiotic treatment may be needed.

Sometimes, men will have painful urinary symptoms without infection. This condition, called prostatodynia, is often related to stress or anxiety.

Prevention

• Increase your fluid intake to as much as 8 to 12 glasses per day, until you are urinating more often than usual. Extra fluids help flush the urinary tract clean.

- Avoid alcohol and caffeine. Caffeine can cause a strong and frequent urge to urinate. Remember that colas as well as coffee and tea contain caffeine.

- Keep stress under control. Stress is closely associated with prostatodynia.

- Drink as much water as you can tolerate.

Home Treatment

- Eliminate all alcohol and caffeine from your diet.

- Hot baths help soothe pain and reduce stress.

- Aspirin or ibuprofen may help ease painful urinary symptoms.

When to Call a Health Professional

- If urinary symptoms occur with fever, chills, vomiting, or pain in the back or abdomen.

- If urine is red or pink with no dietary reason (see page 182). Always call your doctor if you have blood in your urine.

- If symptoms continue for five days despite home care.

- If there is a sudden change or worsening of symptoms.

- If you have pain on urination or ejaculation and a discharge from the penis. See page 198.

Prostate Enlargement (Benign Prostatic Hypertrophy)

As men age, the prostate may enlarge. This seems to be a natural process and is not really a disease. However, as the gland gets bigger, it tends to squeeze the urethra and cause urinary problems, such as:

- Difficulty getting urine started and completely stopped (dribbling)

- Urge to urinate frequently, or being wakened by the need to urinate

- Painful urination

- Decreased force of the urine stream

- Incomplete bladder emptying

An enlarged prostate gland is not a serious problem unless urination becomes extremely difficult, or backed-up urine causes bladder infections or kidney damage. Some dribbling after urination is very common and not necessarily a sign of prostate problems.

Surgery is usually not necessary for an enlarged prostate. Although surgery used to be a common treatment, recent research shows that most cases of prostate enlargement do not get worse over time as previously thought. Many men find that their symptoms are stable and some even clear up on their own. In these cases, the best treatment may be no treatment at all. Drugs are available that may help improve symptoms in some men. Your doctor can advise you on the various treatment options.

Prevention

Since the prostate produces seminal fluid, there is a long-standing belief that regular ejaculations (two to three times per week) will help prevent an enlarged prostate. There is no scientific proof of this, but it is risk-free.

Home Treatment

- Avoid antihistamines and decongestants, which can make urinary problems worse.

- If you are bothered by a frequent urge to urinate at night, cut down on beverages before bedtime, especially alcohol and caffeine.

- Don't postpone urinating, and take plenty of time. Try sitting on the toilet instead of standing.

- If dribbling after urination is a problem, wash your penis once a day to prevent infection.

- Also see Urinary Incontinence on page 45.

When to Call a Health Professional

- If fever, chills, or back or abdominal pain develop.

- Diuretics, tranquilizers, antihistamines, decongestants, antidepressants, and drugs that lower blood pressure can aggravate urinary problems. If you take these drugs, ask your doctor if there are other medications that do not cause these side effects.

- If the symptoms of an enlarged prostate last longer than two weeks. Early examination enables you to confirm the diagnosis and consider treatment options.

Prostate Cancer

Prostate cancer is the most common cancer and the second leading cause of cancer deaths in men. It is usually a small and slow-growing cancer. When detected early, before it has spread to other organs, the cancer may be curable. Risk increases with age, and most cases are in men over 65. Since it is more common in older men, it usually does not shorten life. However, when it is large, advanced, or appears at a younger age, it can be very serious.

There are no specific symptoms of prostate cancer. Most men have no symptoms at all. In some cases, it can cause urinary symptoms very similar to those of prostate enlargement. In advanced cases, other symptoms may be caused by spread of the cancer to other organs such as bone.

Prostate cancer sometimes runs in families, is more common in African-American men, and tends to be more common in men who eat a high-fat diet.

Prevention

Maintaining a low-fat diet is the only known way to reduce the risk of prostate cancer.

Home Treatment

Prostate cancer treatment is tailored to each individual. Work together with your doctor to be sure that you will receive long-term benefit from treatment.

Learn all you can about the available treatment options, which may include watchful waiting, so that you and your doctor can select the one best suited for you.

Your age, overall health, other medical conditions, and the characteristics of the cancer are all important factors to consider in making treatment decisions.

When to Call a Health Professional

There is a great deal of controversy about the value of using rectal exams and the prostate-specific antigen (PSA) blood test to screen men who do not have any symptoms of prostate cancer. Using these tests to detect early prostate cancer has not been shown to improve the quality of life or to prolong life. Therefore, many experts are uncertain whether routine rectal exams or PSA tests are appropriate for all men.

Talk with your doctor for more information about screening.

I wasn't kissing her, I was whispering in her mouth.
Groucho Marx

Chapter 13

Sexual Health

Sexuality is an important aspect of our health. It influences how we love, how we show affection, how we value ourselves, and how we bond with and befriend each other. Sexuality is based on deep personal values we learn from our parents, our culture, our religion, and who we are.

Sexuality can be confusing; there are myths and misunderstandings about it. Parents have a special obligation to help guide their children as they develop sexual values. Talk with your children about their sexuality and give them good information. Help them learn to make responsible and safe decisions about sex and sexuality.

This chapter covers specific health issues of concern to people who are sexually active, from birth control to sexually transmitted diseases, including AIDS.

Birth Control

Birth control can help prevent unplanned pregnancies. However, no birth control method (except abstinence) is 100 percent effective and without risks. Each method has different risks and effectiveness. The text below and the chart on page 196 briefly describes the most common birth control methods. Review each method with your partner before deciding which one meets your needs. Your health professional can help you better understand the effectiveness and risks of each method. Contact your local health unit or public health office about good pamphlets in this area.

Use all birth control methods *exactly* as your doctor or the package instructions recommend. Proper use helps ensure the most effectiveness.

Birth Control

Method	Pregnancies*	Comments
Sterilization Tubal ligation (women) Vasectomy (men)	Less than 1	Consider it permanent.
Hormonal Methods Oral contraceptives	3 (less than 1 with proper use)	Increased risk of circulatory disorders and high blood pressure in smokers.
Norplant (implant) or Depo-Provera (shot)	Less than 1	Either may cause irregular menstrual bleeding.
Intrauterine Device (IUD)	Less than 1	May cause bleeding and cramping. May be expelled without being noticed. Increased risk of pelvic infection.
Barrier Methods Condom alone	12	Use properly for best protection.
Condom with spermicide	5	Provides the most reliable protection against STDs.
Diaphragm (with spermicide)	18	
Cervical cap	18	
Spermicides Jelly, cream, foam, suppositories	21	Use with a condom for best protection.
Used with condom	5	
Periodic Abstinence (natural family planning: basal body temperature, mucous, or rhythm/calendar method)	20	
Withdrawal	18	
No method (chance)	85	

*Typical number of accidental pregnancies per 100 women in one year. When birth control methods are used exactly as directed, pregnancy rates are lower

Adapted from: R. Hatcher, et al., *Contraceptive Technology, 1994-1996.*

Hormonal methods of birth control for women require a doctor's prescription. Hormones prevent the ovaries from releasing an egg each month (ovulation). *They do not protect against sexually transmitted diseases and are not recommended for women in non-monogamous relationships.*

Oral contraceptives are pills taken daily. Norplant is a set of small cylinders inserted under the skin that release hormones continuously for up to five years. They can be removed whenever you decide you want to get pregnant. Depo-Provera is an injection given once every three months.

The intrauterine device (IUD) is a plastic or metal device that is inserted into the uterus by a doctor. It isn't clear how it prevents pregnancy. The IUD does not provide any protection against STDs.

Barrier methods of birth control keep sperm from reaching the egg.

Condoms are a thin covering of latex or other material that fits tightly over the man's erect penis to catch the ejaculated semen.

Spermicides are foams, jellies, and suppositories that contain chemicals that kill sperm. Look for spermicides that contain nonoxynol-9.

Condoms used with spermicides provide the most reliable, but not total, protection against sexually transmitted diseases, including HIV. You can buy both condoms and spermicides without a doctor's prescription.

The diaphragm and cervical cap are small rubber caps that are filled with spermicide and inserted into the vagina to cover the cervix (opening to the uterus). They are left in place for six to eight hours after intercourse. Both require a doctor's prescription.

These barrier methods provide minimal protection against STDs and HIV.

Surgical methods are the most effective forms of birth control.

During a vasectomy, the tubes (vas deferens) that carry a man's sperm from the testes are cut and tied off, thus preventing pregnancy. A tubal ligation (having your "tubes tied") closes or blocks a woman's fallopian tubes to keep eggs from moving from the ovaries into the uterus.

Both procedures should be considered permanent but may be successfully surgically reversed in some cases.

"Morning-after" (emergency) contraception can be used within 72 hours of unprotected sex if you did not use birth control, or had unplanned sex; a condom broke or slipped off; you forgot to take two or more birth control pills; or you were forced to have sex. Ask about morning-after contraception at your doctor's office, walk-in clinics, or health unit/public health office.

Natural family planning (fertility awareness) methods help a couple estimate when the woman is most likely to become pregnant (during ovulation) and avoid intercourse during that time. To estimate when ovulation occurs, a woman records her temperature, examines her vaginal mucus discharge, and tracks her menstrual periods.

Sexually Transmitted Diseases

Sexually transmitted diseases (STDs) or venereal diseases (VD) are infections passed from person to person through sexual intercourse or genital contact. Chlamydia, genital herpes, genital warts, gonorrhea, hepatitis B, and syphilis are among the most common STDs. AIDS (acquired immune deficiency syndrome), the most virulent and deadly of all STDs, is discussed on page 200.

Chlamydia (kla-mid-ee-uh) is a bacterial infection that affects millions of men and women. It may be difficult to detect chlamydia, and in many cases there may be no symptoms. If symptoms do show up, it is two to six weeks after exposure. In women, symptoms may include vaginal discharge or irregular menstrual bleeding, painful urination, genital itching, or lower abdominal pain. In men, there may be a penile discharge, genital itching, and painful urination.

Chlamydia is easily treated with antibiotics. If undetected and untreated, chlamydia can cause pelvic inflammatory disease (infection in the ovaries and fallopian tubes), which may lead to sterility.

Genital herpes is caused by the herpes simplex virus, which also causes cold sores (see page 234). Genital herpes is easily spread through sexual and other direct skin contact.

Symptoms occur 2 to 30 days after contact with an infected person. It is also possible to be infected with herpes and have no symptoms.

The first case of genital herpes may be quite severe, with many painful sores or blisters. Fever, swollen glands, and headache or muscle aches may also occur. If the sores develop inside the urethra or vagina, there may be pain on urination or a vaginal discharge. The sores will crust and disappear in one to three weeks' time. Sometimes, the first episode is so mild it is unnoticed. It is possible to transmit herpes even when no sores are present, as the virus may still be living on the skin.

Herpes can be very dangerous to babies if they are born when a mother has an outbreak. A cesarean section can prevent transmission, so always tell your health care provider about any history of herpes when planning a family.

There is no known cure for herpes. Once infected, you may have recurrent outbreaks, which are usually shorter and less severe than the first one. Itching, burning, or tingling may occur at the place where the sores will later appear. Medication may be helpful if you have very frequent and severe outbreaks.

Genital warts are caused by the human papillomavirus (HPV), which is spread by sexual contact. They generally appear as small fleshy bumps or flat white patches on the labia (the lips around the vagina), inside the vagina, on the penis or scrotum, or around the anus. The warts may be too small to be seen. HPV seems to increase the risk of cervical cancer in women. If warts are bothersome or develop on the cervix, they can be removed by a health professional. In many cases, the warts may recur.

Gonorrhea, also known as clap, drip, or GC, is a bacterial infection spread through sexual contact.

Symptoms include painful urination, vaginal discharge, irregular menstrual bleeding, or a thick discharge from the penis. Many people who have the bacteria have no symptoms. If untreated, gonorrhea in women may lead to pelvic inflammatory disease and sterility. It can sometimes spread to the joints and cause arthritis, or perhaps even lead to serious complications such as swelling of the linings of the heart and brain.

Hepatitis B is a viral infection spread through sexual contact or contact with infected blood. An infected pregnant woman can also transmit the virus to her baby. Symptoms appear two to five months after exposure, and include vomiting, abdominal pain, loss of appetite, and yellow tint to the eyes and skin (jaundice). About one-third of infected people have no symptoms, and 10 percent of infected people become chronic carriers. This means that, although they are not actively ill with the virus, they can continue to pass the virus on to others for years. Long-term effects of the disease include life-threatening liver damage. The hepatitis B vaccine is provided for adolescents and recommended for all others in higher-risk groups.

Syphilis is a bacterial infection spread through sexual contact or by sharing contaminated needles. Symptoms may occur two weeks to three months after contact. The first symptom is a chancre, a small red blister, ulcer, or sore that appears on the genitals, rectal area, or mouth. This sore is painless and may go unnoticed. The lymph nodes in the groin may also swell.

If syphilis is not treated early, it can proceed to a second phase in 4 to 10 weeks. Symptoms of the second phase include skin rash, patchy hair loss, fever, swollen lymph glands, and flu-like symptoms, which are easily confused with other illnesses.

Syphilis can be treated with antibiotics. If untreated, syphilis will cause serious problems and premature death.

Prevention

Preventing a sexually transmitted disease is easier than treating an infection once it occurs. Only sexual activity with one uninfected partner or sexual abstinence completely eliminates the risk.

- Avoid sexual contact while you or your partner is being treated for a sexually transmitted disease.

- If you or your partner has herpes, avoid sexual contact when a blister or any open ulcer or sore is present, and use condoms at all other times.

- The same behaviors that reduce your risk of HIV infection also reduce your risk of getting other STDs. See page 201 for additional prevention guidelines, including condom use.

When to Call a Health Professional

If you notice any unusual vaginal or penile discharge, sores, redness, or growths on the genitals, or if you suspect that you have been exposed to an STD, make an appointment as soon as possible.

STDs need to be diagnosed and treated by a health professional. Your doctor or a health department can diagnose and treat STD. Your sexual partner must also be treated, even if he or she has no symptoms. Your partner may reinfect you or develop serious complications.

HIV Infection and AIDS

AIDS (acquired immune deficiency syndrome) is caused by the human immunodeficiency virus (HIV). HIV destroys the immune system, which makes it impossible for the body to fight off disease or even minor illnesses. AIDS is the last phase in HIV disease, when the body is unable to fight a disease or infection.

A person is said to be HIV-positive if antibodies to the virus are detected in his or her blood. It may take up to six months after infection for the antibodies to appear. Someone who is HIV-positive may appear to be healthy for 10 years or longer before the symptoms of AIDS develop.

HIV is *not* spread by mosquitoes, toilet seats, being coughed on by an infected person, casual contact with someone who is HIV-positive or who has AIDS, or by donating blood.

Because all blood has been tested for HIV since 1985, the risk of getting the virus from blood or blood products is extremely low.

HIV is spread only when blood, semen, or vaginal fluids from an infected person enter someone else's body. HIV can also be spread through amniotic fluid. The specific behaviors that spread HIV include:

1. Sharing injection needles and syringes with someone who is HIV-positive.

2. Unprotected (without a condom) rectal entry intercourse (anal sex) with someone who is HIV-positive. Anal sex often tears the rectal blood vessels, allowing the virus to enter the body.

3. Unprotected vaginal intercourse or oral sexual activity with someone who is HIV-positive.

4. Sharing toothbrushes with an HIV-positive person.

Babies born to or breast-fed by women who are HIV-positive are also at high risk of contracting the virus.

Being touched, hugged, or lightly kissed by someone who is HIV-positive will not transfer the virus to you. As long as you practise the prevention behaviors on page 201, you have virtually no risk of contracting the virus.

A simple, confidential blood test, available from your doctor or a local health unit/public health office, can determine if you are HIV-positive. Remember that it can take up to six months after infection for HIV antibodies to develop, and the virus can be transmitted even before antibodies have developed.

Therefore, if your behavior puts you at risk for HIV infection, have a blood test six months after the risky behaviour. Early diagnosis and treatment of HIV is important even before symptoms develop.

Researchers believe that most people who are HIV-positive will eventually develop AIDS. Although there are treatments for some of the symptoms of AIDS, there is currently no cure, and it is apparently always fatal.

Symptoms of HIV Infection and AIDS

The early symptoms of HIV infection are like flu symptoms that won't go away. Common symptoms are:

• Rapid unexplained weight loss

• Persistent unexplained fever and night sweats

• Persistent severe fatigue

• Persistent diarrhea

• Swelling of glands in neck, armpits, or groin

As the immune system deteriorates, a variety of other symptoms may appear, including:

• Unusual sores on the skin or in the mouth; white patches in the mouth

• Increased outbreaks of cold sores

• Unexplained shortness of breath and dry cough

• Severe numbness or pain in the hands and feet

• Personality change or mental deterioration

• Unusual cancers and infections

These symptoms are caused by many illnesses other than HIV infection or AIDS. However, if any symptom develops or persists without a good explanation, especially if your behavior puts you at risk of HIV infection, call your doctor.

Prevention

Only having sexual activity with one uninfected partner or sexual abstinence completely eliminates the risk of HIV and other sexually transmitted diseases. The following actions will *reduce* your risk:

• If you are beginning a sexual relationship, take time before having sex to talk about HIV and other STDs. Find out if your partner has ever been exposed or infected or if your partner's behavior puts him or her at risk of HIV infection. Remember that it is possible to be infected without knowing it.

• Use condoms with any new partner until you are certain that person does not have any sexually transmitted diseases and that neither of you will have unprotected sexual contact with anyone else while your relationship lasts.

• Remember that it can take up to six months before HIV can be detected in the blood. If you plan to use HIV testing to decide whether condoms are needed, wait six months after any unprotected sexual contact or other high-risk behavior. During this time, both you and your partner need to avoid unprotected sexual contact and use condoms every time you have sexual contact.

- Avoid unprotected sexual contact with anyone who has symptoms of or who has been exposed to an STD, or whose behaviour puts them at risk of HIV infection. Keep in mind that a person may have no symptoms but still be able to transmit the diseases.

- Avoid unprotected vaginal and anal intercourse and oral sex with anyone whose sexual history may not be risk-free. Use latex condoms from the beginning to the end of sexual contact. "Natural" or lambskin condoms do not protect against HIV infection. For even greater protection, use a spermicide containing nonoxynol-9 in addition to condoms. Apply the spermicide directly into the vagina, not into the condom.

- Do not rely on spermicides or the diaphragm to protect against STDs. They add some protection to condoms, but do not provide adequate protection when used alone. They do not protect against HIV.

In addition to the guidelines above, taking the following precautions will reduce your risk of getting HIV and hepatitis B:

- Avoid the activities on page 202 that spread HIV. Safer activities include closed-mouth kissing, hugging, massage, and other pleasurable touching.

- Never share needles, syringes, toothbrushes, or other personal items that could be contaminated with blood. Even needles that have been boiled can remain contaminated.

For more information, contact your local health unit/public health office or check your phone book for the AIDS and Sexually Transmitted Disease Information toll-free number in your area.

It is by the presence of mind in untried emergencies
that the native metal of a man (or woman) *is tested.*
James Russell Lowell

Chapter 14

First Aid and Emergencies

This chapter covers both serious medical emergencies and minor first aid situations. Review this chapter before you need it. Then, when you are faced with an emergency or injury, you will know where to turn. Your confidence in dealing with both major and minor emergencies will be reassuring to an injured person. Also see Resources 62 to 64 on page 306.

Medical emergencies covered in this chapter include:

- Bleeding, page 216.

- Cardiopulmonary Resuscitation (CPR), page 204.

- Head Injuries, page 221.

- Poisoning, page 228.

- Shock, page 231.

- Unconsciousness, page 232.

Dealing With Emergencies

Take a deep breath. Count to 10. Tell yourself you can handle this situation.

Assess the danger. Protect yourself and the injured person from fire, explosions, or other hazards. If you suspect a spinal injury, do not move the person unless the danger is great.

If the person is unconscious or unresponsive, check the ABCs: Airway, Breathing, Circulation. If the person is not breathing, see Rescue Breathing and CPR on page 204.

Identify and prioritize the injuries. Treat the most life-threatening problems (bleeding, shock) first. Check for broken bones and other injuries. If you need emergency assistance, call 911 or emergency services.

Legal Protection

If you are needed in an emergency, give what help you can. Most provinces have a Good Samaritan law to protect people who help in an emergency. You cannot be sued for giving first aid unless it can be shown that you are guilty of gross negligence.

Rescue Breathing and CPR

Warning: Improper CPR or CPR performed on a person whose heart is still beating can cause *serious* injury. *Never* perform CPR unless:

1. Breathing has stopped.

2. There is no heartbeat.

3. No one with more training in CPR is present.

Be prepared: Take a CPR course from the Canadian Red Cross, St. John's Ambulance, or the provincial Health and Stroke Foundation.

For basic life support, think **ABC:** **A**irway, **B**reathing, and **C**irculation, in this order. You must establish an open airway to start breathing, and you must give rescue breathing before you can begin the chest compressions needed if the victim's heart has stopped.

Step 1: Check for consciousness.

Tap or gently shake the victim and shout, "Are you okay?" If he does not respond, roll him onto his back, *unless* there is a possible spinal injury. If he may have suffered a spinal injury, gently roll the head, neck, and shoulders together as a unit until he is on his back.

When a victim does not respond:

- **Adults and children age 9 and older:** Call 911 or emergency services immediately. Then give rescue breathing (and CPR if there is no pulse).

- **Children age 8 and younger:** Give one full minute of rescue breathing (and CPR if there is no pulse), then call 911 or emergency services.

Step 2: Open the airway.

- Kneel next to the victim. Clear any foreign material from the mouth with your fingers.

- Place one hand on the victim's forehead and tilt the head back gently.

- Place the fingers of your other hand under the chin and lift to pull it forward. See Illustration A. **For an infant:** Use care not to tilt the head back too far. **For suspected spinal injury:** Do not tilt the head back; stabilize the head with one hand and lift the lower jaw upward with the other to open the airway.

- Look to see if the victim's chest is rising and falling. Listen and feel for air moving out of the mouth.

- Sometimes, just opening the airway will allow the victim to breathe. If the victim does not start breathing, begin rescue breathing immediately.

Step 3: Begin rescue breathing.

- Pinch the victim's nostrils shut with your thumb and forefinger (of the hand on the forehead). With your other hand, continue tilting the chin forward to keep the airway open.

A. Head tilt, chin lift

B. Blow air in slowly

• Take a deep breath and place your mouth over the victim's, making a tight seal. See Illustration B.

For an infant: Place your mouth over the baby's mouth and nose.

• Slowly blow air in until the victim's chest rises. Take 1½ to 2 seconds to give each breath. Remove your mouth from the victim's and take a deep breath between rescue breaths. Allow the victim's chest to fall and feel the air escape.

• Give 2 full breaths, then check for circulation.

Step 4: Check for circulation.

Locate the carotid artery in the neck:

• Find the voice box or Adam's apple. Slide the tips of your index and middle fingers into the groove beside it.

• Feel for a pulse for 5 to 10 seconds.

If there is no pulse: Begin chest compressions. See Step 5.

If there is a pulse: Continue rescue breathing until help arrives or the victim starts to breathe on his own. If he begins breathing again, he still needs to be seen by a health professional.

Give rescue breaths:

• Adult (age 9 and older): 1 breath every 5 seconds

• Children age 1 to 8: 1 breath every 3 seconds

• Infant under 1 year: 1 breath every 3 seconds

Step 5: Begin chest compressions.

Infants and children: see page 207.

- **For adults:** Kneel next to the victim. Use your fingers to locate the end of the breastbone (sternum), where the ribs come together. Place 2 fingers at the tip of the breastbone. Place the heel of one hand directly above your fingers. See Illustration C.

- Place your other hand on top of the one that is in position. Do not allow your fingers to touch the chest as that may damage the ribs. See Illustration D.

- Straighten your arms, lock your elbows, and centre your shoulders directly over your hands. See Illustration E.

- Press down in a steady rhythm, using your body weight and keeping your elbows locked. The force from each thrust should go straight down onto the sternum, compressing it 1½ to 2 inches. It may help to count "one and two and three and four...," up to 15 compressions. Give one downward thrust each time you say a number. Lift your weight, but not your hands, from the victim's chest on the upstroke.

- After 15 compressions, open the airway with the head tilt/chin lift, and give 2 full, slow breaths, taking one breath in between.

- Repeat the 15 compressions-2 breaths cycle 4 times. Check the pulse again. If there is still no pulse, continue the rescue breathing and chest compressions until help arrives, or the victim's pulse and breathing return.

Collarbone
Sternum
(breastbone)
Rib cage

C. Location of sternum

D. Correct hand position
to avoid rib damage

E. Shoulders over sternum

- **For an infant:** Place 2 fingers on the sternum, about one finger width below an imaginary line connecting the nipples. Press with gentle force, compressing the sternum about ½ inch.

- **For a child:** Using the heel of one hand, press with less force, compressing the sternum 1 to 1½ inches.

- **For infants and children:** Give 5 chest compressions, then 1 breath. Repeat 20 times (one minute) and check the pulse again. If the rescuer is alone, call 911 or emergency services. If there is still no pulse, continue rescue breathing and chest compressions until help arrives, or until the pulse and breathing are restored.

- **For pregnant women:** Call 911 or emergency services immediately; then start CPR as soon as possible. Put a pillow or some other wedge-shaped object under the right side of the woman's abdomen to shift the uterus to the left side. This will help blood return to the heart.

CPR Ready Reference

	Adults	Children	Infants
If the victim has a pulse, give one rescue breath every:	5 seconds	3 seconds	3 seconds
If the victim has no pulse, locate the chest compression landmark:	Trace ribs into notch; place 2 fingers on sternum	Same as adult	1 finger width below nipple line
Do chest compressions with:	2 hands stacked; heel of 1 hand on sternum	Heel of 1 hand on sternum	2 or 3 fingers on sternum
Rate of compressions per minute:	80 to 100	100	100
Compression depth:	3.75 to 5 cm (1½ to 2")	2.5 to 3.75 cm (1 to 1½")	1.25 to 2.5 cm (½ to 1")
Ratio of compressions to breaths:			
1 rescuer	15:2	5:1	5:1
2 rescuers	5:1	5:1	N/A

Guidelines from the Heart and Stroke Foundation of Canada

Accidental Tooth Loss

If a permanent tooth is knocked out, a dentist may be able to reimplant it in the mouth. Baby teeth need to come out anyway, so are not usually reimplanted.

Home Treatment

- Call your dentist immediately for an emergency visit. Teeth reimplanted within 30 minutes have the best chance of success. After two hours, it is unlikely the procedure will be successful.
- Clean the tooth and replace it in the socket, or between the gum and cheek (use care not to swallow the tooth), or in a small container of milk. Do not transport the tooth in tap water.

When to Call a Health Professional

- If a permanent tooth is knocked out.
- If a baby tooth is knocked out, schedule an appointment within two weeks to determine if a spacer is needed until permanent teeth come in.

Animal Bites

When bitten by an animal, most people want to know if they need a rabies shot. The main wild animal carriers of rabies are raccoons, skunks, foxes, and bats. Pet dogs and cats that have been vaccinated rarely have rabies. However, many stray animals have not been vaccinated. Rabies is quite rare, but is fatal if not treated. The treatment is no more painful than a typical injection. Report all wild animal bites to your doctor or local health unit/public health office.

Bites that break the skin can cause bacterial infections. Cat and human bites are particularly prone to infection. Tetanus can occur if shots are not up to date. See page 18.

Prevention

- Vaccinate all pets against rabies. Do not keep wild animals as pets.
- Do not disturb animals while they are eating, even your family pet.
- Teach children not to approach or play with stray dogs or cats.
- Do not touch wild animals or provoke them to attack. Do not handle sick or injured animals.

Home Treatment

- Scrub the bite immediately with soap and water. Treat it as a puncture wound. See page 229.
- If you are bitten by a pet dog or cat, find out whether it has been vaccinated for rabies.
- A healthy pet that has bitten someone should be confined and observed for 10 days to see if it develops symptoms of rabies. If the owner cannot be located or relied on to confine and watch the animal, contact the local health unit/public health office.

• If you are bitten by a wild animal, contact the local health unit/public health office. They can tell you whether that animal is a rabies carrier in your area, and whether treatment is needed.

When to Call a Health Professional

• If the bite is from a wild animal.

• If the bite is from a dog or cat that is acting strangely, foaming at the mouth, or if it attacked for no apparent reason.

• If the bite is from a pet whose owner cannot confirm that it has been vaccinated for rabies.

• If the bite is severe and may need stitches, or if it is on the hand, face, or genitals.

• If signs of infection develop:

  ○ Increased pain, swelling, redness, or tenderness

  ○ Heat or red streaks extending from the bite

  ○ Discharge of pus

  ○ Fever of 100° or higher with no other cause

Blood Under a Nail

Fingernails and toenails often get crunched, bashed, or smashed. These injuries usually aren't too serious, but if there is bleeding under the nail, the pressure can be very painful.

The only way to relieve the throbbing and pain is by making a hole in the nail to drain the blood. You may feel squeamish about trying this at home, but it is the same thing a health professional would do.

Draining is helpful only if there is severe, throbbing pain (you can feel the pulse beating under the nail) that is bad enough to keep you from sleeping.

Home Treatment

• Apply ice and elevate the injured area as soon as possible after the injury to minimize swelling and relieve pain. Acetaminophen will also ease discomfort.

• To make a hole in the nail and relieve throbbing, follow these steps:

  ○ Straighten a paper clip and heat the tip in a flame until it is red hot.

  ○ Place the tip of the paper clip on the nail and let it melt through. You do not need to push. This will not be painful as the nail has no nerves. A thick nail may take several tries.

  ○ As soon as the hole is complete, blood will escape and the pain will be relieved.

Relieve pressure

- Soak the finger three times a day in a half-and-half mixture of hydrogen peroxide and warm water.

- If the pressure builds up again in a few days, repeat the procedure, using the same hole.

When to Call a Health Professional

- If the person is uncooperative and won't let you try the procedure.

- If signs of infection appear:

  ○ Increased pain, swelling, redness or tenderness

  ○ Heat or red streaks extending away from the area

  ○ Discharge of pus

  ○ Fever of 38.3°C (100°F) or higher with no other cause

Blunt Abdominal Wounds

Blunt abdominal wounds caused by a blow to the stomach can cause severe bruising of the abdominal wall and bleeding from the internal organs. Such injuries are often caused by automobile, bicycle, tobogganing, or skiing accidents, where the victim is thrown into something or to the ground.

The symptoms of abdominal injury are similar to those of shock: rapid pulse, low blood pressure, and cold, clammy skin. The abdomen may become rigid or tender. The injured person may become confused and unable to remember or describe the injury.

Home Treatment

- Monitor the injured person's pulse, blood pressure, and breathing. A rapid, weak pulse, falling blood pressure, or very rapid or very slow breathing may indicate internal bleeding. If these signs develop, call 911 or take the patient to the emergency room.

- Have the injured person lie down with the feet elevated above the heart. Loosen his clothing and cover him with a blanket to keep him warm. Do not give him anything to eat or drink, even though he may be thirsty.

- Watch for signs of shock: faintness, weakness, drowsiness, or confusion; sweating, and cool, clammy skin.

When to Call a Health Professional

Call 911 or take the patient to the emergency room:

- If signs of shock or internal bleeding (see above) develop up to 48 hours after an abdominal injury.

- If there is bleeding from the rectum, urethra, or unexpected vaginal bleeding following a blow to the abdomen.

- If the injury causes nausea, vomiting, heartburn, or loss of appetite.

- If the abdomen is swollen and hard, or if pressing on the abdomen causes severe pain.

- Call a health professional if you have any concerns about the symptoms you observe.

Bruises

Bruises (contusions) are usually caused by a bump or fall, which ruptures small blood vessels under the skin. Blood seeps into the surrounding tissues, causing the black and blue color of a bruise.

People who take aspirin or blood thinners (anticoagulants) may bruise easily. A bruise may also develop after blood is drawn.

A black eye is a type of bruise. Apply home treatment for a bruise and inspect the eye.

Home Treatment

- Apply ice or cold packs for 15-minute intervals during the first 48 hours to help vessels constrict and to reduce swelling. The sooner you apply ice, the less bleeding will result.

- If possible, elevate the bruised area. Blood will leave the area and there will be less swelling.

- Rest the limb so you don't injure it further.

- If the area is still painful after 48 hours, apply heat with warm towels, a hot water bottle, or a heating pad.

When to Call a Health Professional

- If signs of infection develop:

  ○ Increased pain, swelling, redness, or tenderness

  ○ Heat or red streaks extending away from the area

  ○ Discharge of pus

  ○ Fever of 38.3°C (100°F) or higher with no other cause

- If a blow to the eye causes:

  ○ Severe bleeding in the white of the eye, or blood in the colored part of the eye

  ○ Impaired or double vision

  ○ Inability to move the eye normally in all directions

  ○ Severe pain in the eyeball rather than in the eye socket

- If you suddenly begin to bruise easily, or if you have unexplained recurrent or multiple bruises.

Burns

Burns are classified as first, second, or third degree depending on their depth, not on the amount of pain or the extent of the burn. A first-degree burn involves only the outer layer of skin. The skin is dry, painful, and sensitive to touch. A mild sunburn is an example.

A second-degree burn involves several layers of skin. The skin becomes swollen, puffy, weepy, or blistered.

A third-degree burn involves all layers of skin and any underlying tissue or organs. The skin is dry, pale white or charred black, swollen, and sometimes breaks open. Nerves are destroyed or damaged, so there may be little pain except on the edge where there may be a second-degree burn.

Prevention

- Install smoke detectors on each story of your home. Check and replace batteries regularly.

- Keep a fire extinguisher near the kitchen. Have it inspected yearly.

- Set your water heater at 50°C (120°F) or lower to avoid burns.

- Don't smoke in bed.

If your clothing catches fire:

- Do not run, as it will fan the flames. Stop, drop, and roll on the ground to smother the flames.

- Smother the flames with a blanket, rug, or coat.

- Use water to douse the fire and cool the skin.

To avoid kitchen burns:

- Use caution when handling hot foods.

- Turn pot handles toward the back of the stove.

- Smother burning food or grease with a lid or pot.

- Supervise children closely.

Home Treatment

- For home treatment of sunburn, see page 144.

- Run cold tap water over the burn for 10 to 15 minutes. Cold water is the best immediate treatment for minor burns. The cold lowers the skin temperature and lessens the severity of the burn. Do not use ice, as it may further damage the injured skin.

- Remove rings, bracelets, watches, or shoes from the burned limb. Swelling may make them difficult to remove later.

For first-degree burns and second-degree burns with intact blisters:

- Leave the burn alone for 24 hours. Don't cover the burn unless clothing rubs on it. If it rubs, cover it with a gauze pad taped well away from the burn. Do not encircle a hand, arm, or leg with tape. Change the bandage after 24 hours, and then every two days.

- Do not put salve, butter, grease, oil, or ointment on a burn. They increase the risk of infection and don't help heal the burn.

- After two to three days of healing, the juice from an aloe leaf can soothe minor burns.

- For second-degree burns: Do not break blisters. If the blisters break, clean the area by running tap water over it. Apply an antibiotic ointment, such as Polysporin or Baciguent, and cover the burn with a sterile dressing. Don't touch the wound with your hands or any unsterile objects. Remove the dressing every day, clean the wound and cover it again.

- Aspirin or ibuprofen can help relieve pain from minor burns.

Third-degree burns require immediate medical treatment. Call a health professional and apply home treatment:

- Make sure the source of the burn has been extinguished.

- Have the person lie down to prevent shock.

- Cover the burned area with a clean sheet soaked in cool water.

- Do not apply any salve or medication to the burn.

When to Call a Health Professional

• For all third-degree burns.

• If in doubt as to the extent of a burn, or in doubt if it is a second- or third-degree burn.

• If a second-degree burn involves the face, hands, feet, genitals, or a joint.

• If the burn encircles an arm or leg, or covers more than one-quarter of the body part involved.

• If it is an electrical burn, which are often more extensive than they appear.

• If the pain lasts longer than 48 hours.

• If signs of infection develop:

  ○ Increased pain, swelling, redness, or tenderness

  ○ Heat or red streaks extending from the area

  ○ Discharge of pus

  ○ Fever of 38.3°C (100°F) or higher with no other cause

• If an infant, older adult, or person with diabetes is burned.

• If the person is immunosuppressed, e.g., HIV-positive, receiving chemotherapy, radiation, or recent transplant.

Chemical Burns to the Eye

Chemical burns to the eye occur when something caustic is splashed into it, such as a cleaning product, gasoline, or turpentine. The vapors or fumes of strong chemicals can also burn or irritate the eyes. The eye becomes red, watery, and may be sensitive to light. If the damage is severe, the eye appears whitish.

Home Treatment

• Immediately flush the eye with water. Fill a sink or dishpan with water, immerse the face in the water, and open and close the eyelids to force the water to all parts of the eye. You may need to to open and close the eyelids with the fingers. Or, flush the eye under a running faucet or shower.

• Continue flushing for 15 to 20 minutes, or until the eye stops hurting, whichever takes longer.

• After flushing the eye, cover it with a clean bandage or cloth.

When to Call a Health Professional

• If there is major exposure to a strong acid, such as battery acid, or to a caustic substance, such as lye or Drano, flush the eye and go immediately to an emergency centre.

• Whenever a chemical is splashed into the eye which required you to flush the eye.

• If the eye still hurts after 20 minutes of home treatment.

- If the eye appears to be damaged. Symptoms include:
  - ◦ Persistent redness
  - ◦ Discharge or watering
  - ◦ Any visual impairment, such as double vision, blurring, or sensitivity to light
  - ◦ Colored part of the eye (iris) appears white

Choking

Choking is usually caused by food or an object stuck in the windpipe. A person who is choking cannot cough, talk, or breathe, and may turn blue or dusky. The **Heimlich Maneuver**, described at right, can help pop out the food or object.

Prevention

- Don't drink too much alcohol before eating. It may dull your senses and you might not chew food properly or might try to swallow too large a portion of food.
- Take small bites. Cut meat into small pieces. Chew your food thoroughly.
- Do not give popcorn, peanuts, hard candy, wieners, hard raw vegetables (e.g., carrots, cauliflower), or hard fruit to children under age three, and supervise older children when they eat these foods.
- Do not allow children under age three to play with toys that have very small parts that could be swallowed.

When to Call a Health Professional

- If you are unable to dislodge the object or the person loses consciousness, call 911 and attempt rescue breathing. See page 204.
- Call even if the food has been dislodged. The throat could be damaged by the object or there could be abdominal damage from the maneuver.

Choking Rescue Procedure (Heimlich Maneuver)

WARNING: Do *not* begin the choking rescue procedure unless the person *cannot breathe* or is turning blue and cannot speak, and you are *certain* they are choking.

Adults and Children Over One Year

If victim is standing or sitting:

- Ask, "Are you choking?"
- Stand behind the victim and wrap your arms around their waist. If the victim is pregnant or obese: Wrap your arms around their chest.
- Make a fist with one hand. Place the thumb side of your fist against their abdomen, just above the navel but well below the breastbone. See Illustration A. If the victim is pregnant or obese: Position your fist against the sternum as outlined for CPR. See page 206, Illustration C, D, or E.
- Grasp your fist with the other hand. Give a quick upward thrust into the victim's abdomen. This may cause the object to pop out. Use less force for young children. See Illustration B.

- Repeat until the object pops out or the victim loses consciousness.

- If the victim becomes unconscious, begin rescue breathing. See pages 204 to 207.

- If you choke while alone, do abdominal thrusts on yourself, or lean hard over the back of a chair to pop out the food.

If victim is on the floor:

- Determine the level of consciousness and assess ABC's. See pages 204 to 205, steps 1 to 3.

- Turn the victim face up and straddle him on your knees next to his hips.

- Place the heel of one hand against the victim's abdomen, just above the navel but well below the breastbone. Place your other hand directly over the first. See Illustration C. If the victim is pregnant or obese: Position yourself as for CPR. See page 206, Illustrations C, D, or E.

- Give a quick upward thrust into the victim's abdomen. Use less force for children. Repeat until the object pops out.

Infant Under One Year

- Hold infant as in Illustration D (page 216).

- Use the heel of one hand to jar the child between the shoulder blades in an attempt to dislodge the object. Repeat five times.

- If the airways remains blocked, support the infant's head and turn him over on your thigh with his head down.

Illustrations A and B

Illustration C

- Place two or three fingers just below a line between the nipples, and give up to five upward thrusts until the object pops out.

- Repeat these steps until object pops out or victim loses consciousness.

- If the victim becomes unconscious, begin rescue breathing. See pages 204 to 207.

Illustration D

Stopping Severe Bleeding

- Have the person lie down and elevate the site that is bleeding.

- Remove any loose visible objects. Do not attempt to clean the wound or try to remove any object that penetrates into the wound. Removal of the object may increase blood loss.

- Press firmly on the wound with a clean cloth or the cleanest material available. If the edges of the wound gape, hold them together. If there is an object in the wound, apply pressure around the cut, not directly over it.

- Apply steady pressure for 15 minutes. If blood soaks through the cloth, apply another one without lifting the first.

- If direct pressure does not immediately slow the bleeding, press firmly on a pressure point. If direct pressure does not completely stop all bleeding within 15 minutes, press firmly on a pressure point. Select a pressure point between the wound and the heart (see below). Continuous pressure on these points can stop the bleeding with less risk than a tourniquet. Tourniquets should be used *only* as a last resort.

- Watch for shock. See page 231.

- Call 911 or go to the emergency room if the bleeding has not been controlled after 15 minutes or if there are any signs of shock.

Pressure points

Cuts

When you see a cut, the first steps are to stop the bleeding and determine whether or not stitches are needed.

If the cut is bleeding heavily or spurting blood, see "Stopping Severe Bleeding" at left.

Bleeding from minor cuts will usually stop on its own or with a little direct pressure. To decide whether stitches are needed, see "Are Sutures Necessary?" on page 218. If stitches are needed, apply home treatment and seek medical care as soon as possible, certainly within eight hours.

If stitches are not needed, you can clean and bandage the cut at home.

Home Treatment

• Wash the cut well with soap and water. Treat an animal bite like a puncture wound. See page 229.

• Stop any bleeding by applying direct pressure over the wound for 10 to 15 minutes.

• Leave small cuts unbandaged, unless they will become irritated. They heal best when exposed to the air.

• If a cut needs bandaging, apply antibiotic ointment (Polysporin or Baciguent). The ointment will keep the cut from sticking to the bandage. Do not use rubbing alcohol, hydrogen peroxide, iodine, or mercurochrome, which can harm tissue and slow healing.

• Use an adhesive bandage (Band-Aid) to continue the pressure. Always put an adhesive strip across a cut rather than lengthwise. A butterfly bandage (made at home or purchased) can help hold cut skin edges together:

○ Cut a strip from a roll of one-inch adhesive tape and fold it sticky side out. Cut notches into the tape as shown in A.

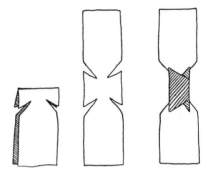

A   Butterfly   B
bandage

○ Unfold the tape, then fold the notched pieces together sticky side in as in B. The centre of the tape will be non-sticky. Keep the part clean that will be over the cut.

○ Place one end of the tape on the skin, then pull the other end to close the wound tightly as in C.

○ If the cut is long, use more than one bandage.

C

Are Sutures Necessary?

For best results, cuts that need stitches should be sutured within eight hours. Wash the cut well and stop the bleeding, then pinch the sides of the cut together. If it looks better, you may want to consider stitches. If stitches are needed, avoid using an antibiotic ointment until after a health professional has examined the cut.

Sutures may be needed for:

• Deep cuts (more than ¼ inch deep) that have jagged edges or gape open.

• Deep cuts on a joint: elbow, knuckle, knee.

• Deep cuts on the palm side of the hand or fingers.

• Cuts on the face, eyelids, or lips.

• Cuts in an area where you are worried about scarring, especially the face.

• Cuts that go down to the muscle or bone.

• Cuts that continue to bleed after 15 minutes of direct pressure.

Cuts like these that are sutured usually heal with less scarring than those that are not.

Sutures may not be needed for:

• Cuts with smooth edges that tend to stay together during normal movement of the affected body part.

• Shallow cuts less than ¼ inch deep that are less than one inch long.

• Apply a clean bandage at least once a day, or when it gets wet. Leave the bandage off whenever possible.

When to Call a Health Professional

• If the cut needs stitches. They need to be done within eight hours.

• If a cut continues to bleed through bandages after 15 minutes of direct pressure.

• If the person goes into shock, even if bleeding has stopped. See Shock on page 231.

• If blood or clear fluid drains from the ears or nose following a blow to the head (not due to a cut or direct blow to the nose).

• If there is blue, white, or cold skin, numbness, tingling, or loss of feeling, or if the person is unable to move a limb below the wound.

• If your tetanus shots are not up to date. See page 18.

• If the cut contains, or might contain, foreign objects such as wood, glass, or gravel.

• If signs of infection develop:

  ○ Increased pain, swelling, or tenderness

  ○ Heat and redness or red streaks extending away from the cut

  ○ Discharge of pus

  ○ Fever of 37.8°C (100°F) or higher with no other cause

Fishhook Removal

In the excitement of fishing, sometimes fingers are hooked instead of fish. It is useful to know how to remove a fishhook, especially if you are far from medical help.

Home Treatment

Remove the hook as follows:

• Use ice, cold water, or hard pressure to provide temporary numbing.

• **Step A:** Tie a piece of fishing line to the hook near the skin surface.

• **Step B:** Grasp the eye of the hook with one hand and press down about 1/8 inch to disengage the barb.

• **Step C:** While still pressing the hook down (barb disengaged), jerk the line parallel to the skin surface so that the hook shaft leads the barb out of the skin.

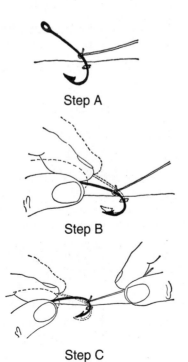

Step A

Step B

Step C

• If the fishhook is deeply embedded, another option is to push the hook the rest of the way through the skin, snip off the barb, and remove the hook.

• Wash the wound thoroughly with soap if possible. Treat as you would a puncture wound. See page 229.

• Do not try to remove a fishhook from the eye.

When to Call a Health Professional

• If you cannot remove the hook.

• If your tetanus shots are not up to date. See page 18.

• If the hook is in the eye.

• If signs of infection develop:

  ○ Increased pain, swelling, redness, or tenderness

  ○ Heat or red streaks extending from the area

  ○ Discharge of pus

  ○ Fever of 38.3°C (100°F) or higher with no other cause

Freeing Trapped Limbs

Fingers, arms, or legs sometimes get caught in objects such as bottles, jars, or pipes, or, in the case of children, between crib or chair posts. Stay calm; panic will only make the situation worse.

Home Treatment

- Don't force the limb, which will make it swell and become more difficult to remove.

- Try to relax the limb. Relaxation alone will sometimes enable you to free the limb.

- If possible, elevate the limb.

- Apply ice around the exposed limb. This may reduce any swelling and allow it to be released.

- If ice doesn't work, dribble soapy water or cooking oil on the limb. Turn the limb or the object so you "unscrew" it rather than pulling it out directly.

Frostbite

Frostbite is freezing of the skin or underlying tissues that occurs as a result of prolonged exposure to cold.

Frostbitten skin is pale or blue, stiff or rubbery to touch, and feels cold and numb. There may be loss of function in the frozen area. The severity is divided into three degrees:

First degree: Frostnip. Numbness and whitening of the skin with little likelihood of blistering if rewarmed promptly.

Second degree: Superficial frostbite. Outer skin feels hard and frozen but tissue underneath has normal resilience. Blistering is likely.

Third degree: Deep frostbite. Skin is white or blotchy and blue. Skin and tissue underneath is hard and very cold.

Prevention

Stay dry and out of the wind in extreme cold and cover areas of exposed skin. Keep the body's core temperature up:

- Wear layers of clothing. Wool and polypropylene are good insulators. Wear wind- and waterproof outer layers. Wear wool socks and well-fitting, waterproof boots.

- Wear a hat to prevent heat loss from your head. Wear mittens rather than gloves.

- Keep protective clothing and blankets in your car in case of a breakdown in an isolated area.

- Don't drink alcohol or smoke when out in extreme cold.

Home Treatment

- Get inside or take shelter from the wind.

- Check for signs of hypothermia (see page 224) and treat it before treating frostbite.

- Don't rewarm the area if refreezing is possible. Wait until you reach shelter.

- Warm small areas (ears, face, nose, fingers, toes) with warm breath or by tucking hands or feet inside warm clothing next to bare skin. Protect the frozen body part from further exposure. If possible, immerse it in warm water to rewarm it. It's best to use water that is 40° to 42°C (104° to 108°F); however, it may hurt less to start with water that is 38°C (100°F). Add warmer water gradually. Never let the water temperature get below 38°C (100°F) or over 42°C (108°F). Keep the part immersed until it is warm to the touch (usually 30 to 60 minutes).

• Don't rub or massage the frozen area, as it would further damage tissues. Avoid walking on frostbitten feet if possible.

• Keep the frostbitten part warm and elevated. Wrap with blankets or soft material to prevent bruising.

• Blisters may appear as the skin warms. Do not break them. The skin may turn red, burn, tingle, or be very painful. Aspirin or acetaminophen may help.

When to Call a Health Professional

• Immediately if skin is white or blue, hard, and cold (third-degree frostbite). Careful rewarming and antibiotic treatment are needed to prevent infection and permanent tissue damage.

• If blisters develop during rewarming (second- or third-degree frostbite). Do not break blisters. The risk of infection is very high.

• If signs of infection develop:

  ◦ Increased pain, swelling, redness, or tenderness

  ◦ Heat or red streaks extending from the area

  ◦ Discharge of pus

  ◦ Fever of 37.8°C (100°F) or higher with no other cause

Head Injuries

Most bumps on the head are minor and heal as easily as bumps anywhere else. Head injuries that cause cuts often bleed heavily because the blood vessels of the scalp are close to the surface. This bleeding is alarming, but does not always mean the injury is severe.

However, head injuries that do not cause visible external bleeding may have caused life-threatening bleeding and swelling inside the skull. Anyone who has experienced a head injury should be watched very carefully for 24 hours for any signs of a severe head injury.

Prevention

• Wear your seat belt when in a motor vehicle. Use child car seats.

• Wear a helmet while biking, motorcycling, and skating.

• Don't dive into shallow or unfamiliar water.

Home Treatment

• If the victim is unconscious, make sure there is no spinal injury before moving him (see page 231). Check for other injuries.

• If there is bleeding, apply firm pressure directly over the wound with a clean cloth or bandage for 15 minutes. If the blood soaks through, apply additional cloths over the first one. See page 216.

• Apply ice or cold packs to reduce the swelling. A "goose egg" may appear anyway, but ice will help ease the pain.

- Watch for the following signs of a severe head injury immediately afterwards and then every two hours for the next 24 hours. If there are any signs of a severe head injury, go to an emergency room immediately:

  ○ Confusion. Ask the person his name, address, age, the date, etc.

  ○ Inability to move arms and legs on one side of the body, or slower movement on one side than the other.

  ○ Lethargy, abnormally deep sleep, or difficulty waking up.

  ○ Vomiting that continues after the first two hours.

Automobile Seat Restraints

Wearing seat belts saves lives and prevents injuries. No one is strong enough to brace against a sudden impact, even at very low speeds. Seat belts reduce the risk of serious injury and death.

- Wear your seat belt every time you are in a vehicle. Keep the belt snug and close to your body. Always use both the lap and shoulder belts.

- Seat belts are necessary even if your car is equipped with air bags. Air bags inflate from the steering wheel or dashboard of your car in the event of sudden impact. They are very effective in protecting front-seat riders, but must be used with seat belts.

- Use child car seats for infants, children under four, and those weighing under 18 kg (40 pounds). See page 150.

- Continue observing the person every two hours during the night. Wake him up and check for any unusual symptoms. Call 911 or go to an emergency room *immediately* if you cannot wake him or if he has any of the above symptoms.

- Check for injuries to other parts of the body, especially if the person has fallen. The alarm from seeing a head injury may cause you to overlook other injuries that need attention.

When to Call a Health Professional

- If there are any signs of a severe head injury (confusion, inability to move arms and legs on one side of the body, lethargy, abnormally long sleep, difficulty waking up, or vomiting that continues after the first two hours), go to an emergency room immediately.

- If bleeding cannot be stopped or the wound needs stitches. See page 218.

- If the person loses consciousness anytime after the injury.

- If blood or clear fluid drains from the ears or nose following a blow to the head (not due to a cut or direct blow to the nose).

- If the person is confused or has any loss of memory after the first few minutes.

- If double vision or speech difficulty occurs after the first minute.

- If a severe headache develops: "The worst headache I've ever had."

- If there are seizures or convulsions.

- If weakness or numbness occur on one side.

- If vomiting occurs after the first two hours or violent vomiting persists after the first 15 minutes. Mild nausea or vomiting at first is usually not serious.

Heat Exhaustion and Heat Stroke

Heat exhaustion occurs when your body cannot sweat enough to cool you off. It generally happens when you are working or exercising in hot weather. Symptoms include:

- Fatigue, weakness, dizziness, or nausea

- Cool, clammy, pale, red, or flushed skin

Heat exhaustion can sometimes lead to **heat stroke**, which requires emergency treatment. Heat stroke happens when your body stops sweating but the body temperature continues to rise, often to 41°C (105°F) or higher. Symptoms include:

- Confusion, delirium, or unconsciousness

- Hot, dry, red or flushed skin, even under the armpits

Prevention

- Avoid strenuous outdoor physical activity during the hottest part of the day.

- Wear light-colored, loose-fitting clothing to reflect the sun.

- Avoid sudden changes of temperature. Air out a hot car before getting into it.

- If you take diuretics, ask your doctor about taking a lower dose during hot weather.

- Drink up to 2 litres (8 to 10 glasses) of water per day. Drink even more if you are working or exercising in hot weather.

- If you exercise strenuously in hot weather, drink more liquid than your thirst seems to require. For example, runners should drink about ¼ litre (1 cup) of water 10 to 15 minutes before running and another ¼ litre of water every two miles or so.

Home Treatment

- Get out of the sun to a cool spot and drink lots of cool water, a little at a time. If you are nauseated or dizzy, lie down.

- Sponge the body with cool water.

- If the body temperature reaches 41°C (105°F), immediate cooling is essential. Use cold, wet cloths all over the body or a cool water bath.

- If the temperature is lowered to 38.9°C (102°F), use care to avoid over-cooling.

When to Call a Health Professional

Call 911 or go to the emergency room if signs of heat stroke develop. Work fast to lower the temperature and seek immediate help if:

- The skin is dry, even under the armpits, and bright red or flushed.

- The body temperature reaches 40°C (104°F) and keeps rising.

- The person is delirious, disoriented, or unconscious.

- Breathe in and out of a paper bag held over the nose and mouth. This will help bring the amount of CO_2 in the blood back to normal. Continue this treatment intermittently for 5 to 15 minutes.

Hyperventilation

When you breathe very fast and deep (hyperventilate), the carbon dioxide (CO_2) level in your blood can drop too low. Symptoms that may occur with hyperventilation include:

- Numbness or tingling in the hands, feet, or around the mouth

- Pounding, racing heartbeat and anxiety

- Feeling you can't get enough air

- Lightheadedness

- Chest pain

In a severe case, you may lose consciousness.

Prevention

If you have hyperventilated before:

- Ask people to mention it if you start to breathe too fast.

- As soon as you notice fast breathing or other symptoms, slow your breathing to one breath every five seconds, or slow enough that symptoms subside.

Home Treatment

- Sit down and concentrate on slowing your breathing.

- Practise a relaxation technique. See page 248.

When to Call a Health Professional

- If hyperventilation occurs in a person who doesn't appear tense or anxious. See page 274 to help determine if a person is anxious.

- If anxiety and hyperventilation are frequent and interfere with your daily activities.

Hypothermia

Hypothermia occurs when the body temperature drops below normal. It occurs when the body loses heat faster than heat can be produced by muscle contractions and shivering.

Early symptoms include:

- Shivering

- Cold, pale skin

- Apathy

- Impaired judgment

Later symptoms include:

- Cold abdomen

- Slow pulse and breathing

- Weakness or drowsiness

- Confusion

Shivering may stop if body temperature drops below 35.5°C (96°F).

Hypothermia is an emergency. It can quickly lead to unconsciousness and death if the heat loss continues. Hypothermia can happen at temperatures of 7°C (45°F), or even higher in wet and windy weather. Frail and inactive people can develop hypothermia indoors if they are not dressed warmly.

Early recognition is very important in the treatment of hypothermia. Often a hiker or skier will lose heat to a critical degree before others notice anything is wrong. If someone begins to shiver violently, stumble, or respond incoherently to questions, suspect hypothermia and warm them quickly.

Prevention

Whenever you plan to be outdoors for several hours in cold weather, take the following precautions:

• Dress warmly and wear wind- and waterproof clothing. Wear fabric that remains warm even when wet, such as wool or polypropylene.

• Wear a warm hat. An unprotected head loses a great deal of the body's total heat production.

• Head for shelter if you get wet or cold.

• Eat well before going out and carry extra food.

• Don't drink alcohol while in the cold. It makes the body lose heat faster.

• Older or less active people can prevent indoor hypothermia by dressing warmly and keeping temperatures above 18°C (65°F).

Home Treatment

The goal of home or "in-the-field" treatment is to stop additional heat loss and *slowly* rewarm the person.

• For mild cases, get the person out of the cold and wind, give him dry or wool clothing, and warm fluids to drink.

• For moderate cases, remove cold, wet clothes first, then warm the person with your own body heat by wrapping a blanket or sleeping bag around both of you.

• Give warm liquids to drink and high-energy foods, such as candy. Do not give food or drink if the person is disoriented or unconscious. Do not give alcoholic beverages.

• Rewarming the person in warm water can cause shock or heart attack. However, in emergency situations when help is not available and other home treatments are not working, you can use a warm water bath (37.8° to 40.6°C or 100° to 105°F) as a last resort.

When to Call a Health Professional

• If the person loses consciousness or seems confused.

• If the victim is a child or older adult. It's a good idea to call regardless of the severity of the symptoms.

• If the body temperature does not return to normal after four hours of warming.

Nosebleeds

Nosebleeds are inconvenient and messy, but they can usually be stopped with home treatment. Some common causes of nosebleeds are low humidity, colds and allergies, blows to the nose, medications (especially aspirin and other anticoagulants), high altitudes, and blowing or picking the nose.

Prevention

- Low humidity is a common cause of nosebleeds. Humidify your home, especially the bedrooms, and keep the heat low (15.5° to 17.7°C or 60° to 64°F) in sleeping areas.

- If your nose becomes very dry, breathe moist air for awhile (e.g., from a shower) and then put a little petroleum jelly on the inside to help prevent bleeding. A saline nasal spray may also help.

- Limit your use of aspirin, which can contribute to nosebleeds.

Home Treatment

- Sit up straight and tip your head slightly forward. Tilting the head back may cause blood to run down the throat.

- Blow all the clots out of the nose. Pinch the nostrils shut between your thumb and forefinger or apply firm pressure against the bleeding nostril for *10 full minutes*. Resist the urge to peek after a few minutes to see if it has stopped bleeding.

- After 10 minutes, check to see if the nose is still bleeding. If it is, hold it for 10 more minutes. Most nosebleeds will stop after 10 to 30 minutes of direct pressure.

- Stay quiet for a few hours and do not blow the nose for at least 12 hours after the bleeding has stopped.

When to Call a Health Professional

- If the bleeding hasn't stopped after 30 minutes of direct pressure.

- If blood runs down the back of your throat even when the nose is pinched.

- If the nose is deformed after an injury and may be broken.

- If nosebleeds recur often.

Objects in the Ear

Children sometimes put small objects in their ears, or an insect may crawl into the ear. It may be hard to know if an insect is in the ear. Your child may say, "My ear is bumping around."

Home Treatment

- Don't try to kill an insect in the ear. Pull the ear up and back and point it toward the sun or a bright light. Insects are attracted to light and it may crawl out.

- If the insect doesn't crawl out, fill the ear canal with mineral, olive, or baby oil. The insect may float out.

- To remove other objects in the ear, tilt the head to the side and shake it. Gently pulling the ear up and back may straighten the ear canal and help dislodge the object.

- If the object is soft and can be easily seen, try *carefully* to remove it with tweezers. Do not try this if the person will not hold very still or if the object is in the ear so far that you can't see the tips of the tweezers. Use care not to push the object further in.

- Call a health professional if you cannot remove the insect or object.

Objects in the Eye

A speck of dirt or small object in the eye will often wash out with your tears. If the object is not removed, it may scratch the covering of the eye (cornea). Most corneal scratches are minor and heal on their own in a day or two.

Home Treatment

- Don't rub the eye, which could scratch the cornea. You may have to restrain small children from rubbing.

- Do not try to remove an object that is on the pupil, or that is stuck in the white of the eye. Cover both eyes and call a health professional.

- Wash your hands before touching the eye.

- If the object is at the side of the eye or on the lower lid, moisten a cotton swab or the tip of a twisted piece of tissue and touch the end to the speck. The object should cling to the swab or tissue. Some minor irritation is common after you have removed the object.

- Gently wash the eye with cool water. An eyedropper helps.

- Never use tweezers, toothpicks, or other hard items to remove any object. Eye damage may result.

When to Call a Health Professional

- If the object is on the pupil or is embedded in the eye. Do not pull out an object that is stuck in the eye.

- If you cannot remove the object.

- If pain is severe or persists, if it feels like there is still something in the eye, or if vision is blurred after the object is removed. The cornea may be scratched. Keep the eye closed.

Objects in the Nose

Children sometimes put small objects, like beads or popcorn, up their noses. If the child doesn't tell you about it, your first clue may be a foul-smelling green or yellow discharge from just one nostril. The nose may also be tender and swollen.

Home Treatment

- Spray a nasal decongestant (see page 292) in the affected nostril to reduce the swelling.

- Have the child pinch the other nostril closed and try to blow the object out.

- If you can see the object, try to remove it with blunt-nosed tweezers. Hold the child's head still and use care not to push the object in further. If the child resists, do not try tweezers. Some minor bleeding from the nostril is not serious.

When to Call a Health Professional

- If you are unable to remove the object after several tries.

Poisoning

FOR ANY POISONING: Call 911 or your local poison control number immediately.

Children will swallow just about anything, including poisons. When in doubt, assume the worst. Always believe a child who indicates that some poison has been swallowed, no matter how unappetizing the substance is. Following the steps below will not harm anyone who has *not* swallowed poison.

If you suspect food poisoning, see page 41.

Prevention

About 80 percent of poisonings occur in children age one to four. Develop poison prevention habits before your child is born, and certainly before she is crawling. Infants grow so fast that sometimes they are crawling and walking before you have time to protect them.

- Never leave a poisonous product unattended, even for a moment.

Lead Poisoning

Infants and young children exposed to lead are at risk of developing learning disabilities and growth problems.

Lead is present in old paint, water pipes, and other substances. Lead-based paint may be a hazard in older homes, especially if it is flaking and peeling.

To reduce the risk of lead poisoning:

- Keep painted surfaces in good repair, and clean paint flakes and chips from older painted surfaces such as floors and windowsills carefully. The dirt next to a house painted with lead-based paint can become very contaminated.

- Keep young children away from home remodeling and refinishing projects.

- If your home has lead or lead-soldered water pipes, let the water run for a few minutes before using it for cooking or formula.

- Have your child's blood lead level tested at about age one year.

Call your local health unit/public health office for more information on preventing lead poisoning.

- Lock all drugs and vitamins away from children. Aspirin is the most common source of childhood poisoning, especially flavored baby aspirin. Lock up drugs between doses.

- Do not keep poisons such as drain opener, dishwasher detergent, oven cleaner, or plant food under your kitchen sink. Keep them completely out of reach of children. Dishwasher detergent is especially dangerous.

- Keep products in their original containers. Never store poisonous products in food containers.

- Use childproof latches on your cupboards.

- Use "Mr. Yuk" stickers and teach your children to recognize them.

Home Treatment

- Call a poison control centre, hospital, or health professional *immediately.* Have the poison container with you so you can tell them what it is.

- If vomiting begins, place the head lower than the chest to prevent vomited material from entering the lungs.

Puncture Wounds

Puncture wounds are caused by sharp, pointed objects that penetrate the skin. Nails, tacks, ice picks, knives, needles, and animal bites can all cause puncture wounds. Puncture wounds are easily infected because they are difficult to clean and provide a warm, moist place for bacteria to grow.

Home Treatment

- For minor puncture wounds caused by small objects of familiar shape, make sure that nothing is left in the wound, such as the tip of a needle. Check to see if the object is intact.

- Allow the wound to bleed freely to clean itself out unless there has been a large loss of blood or the blood is squirting out. If bleeding is heavy, see page 216.

- Clean the wound thoroughly with soap and water.

- For the next four to five days, soak the wound in warm water several times a day. This will clean the wound from the inside out. If the wound is closed, an infection under the skin may not be detected for several days.

When to Call a Health Professional

- If the wound is in the head, chest, or abdomen, unless it is minor.

- If there is blue, white, or cold skin, numbness, tingling, loss of feeling, or the person is unable to move a limb below the wound.

- If your tetanus shots are not up to date (see page 18), especially if the object that caused the puncture wound was dirty, such as a rusty nail, or a farm implement.

- If a deep wound to the foot occurred through a shoe.

- If an animal bite is severe and may need stitches, or if it is on the hand or face.

- If you are unable to remove an object from the wound.

- If signs of infection develop:

  ○ Increased pain, swelling, redness, or tenderness

  ○ Heat or red streaks extending from the wound

  ○ Discharge of pus

  ○ Fever of 37.8°C (100°F) with no other cause

| Scrapes |

Scrapes or abrasions happen so often that they seem unimportant. Good home treatment will reduce scarring and prevent infection.

Home Treatment

- Scrapes are usually very dirty. Remove large pieces of debris with tweezers, then scrub vigorously with soap and water and a wash-cloth. The injured person will probably complain loudly, but cleaning is necessary to prevent infection and scarring. If you have a water sprayer in your kitchen sink, try using that on the scrape with additional scrubbing.

- Apply steady pressure with a clean bandage or cloth to stop bleeding.

- Ice may help reduce swelling and bruising.

- If the scrape is large or in an area rubbed by clothing, apply an anti-biotic ointment and cover it with a non-stick (Telfa) bandage. This type of bandage won't stick and is held in place by adhesive around the edges. Putting the ointment on the bandage first will be less painful.

When to Call a Health Professional

- If your tetanus shots are not up to date. See page 18.

- If the scrape is very large and dirty.

- If you cannot remove dirt and debris embedded under the skin. They may cause tattooing or infection if not removed.

- If signs of infection develop:

  ○ Increased pain, swelling, redness, or tenderness

  ○ Heat or red streaks extending from the scrape

  ○ Discharge of pus

  ○ Fever of 37.8°C (100°F) or higher with no other cause

Removing Splinters

If you can grasp the end of the splinter with tweezers, gently pull it out. If the splinter is embedded in the skin, clean a needle with alcohol and make a small hole in the skin over the end of the splinter. Then lift the splinter with the tip of the needle until it can be grasped with the tweezers and pulled out.

After the splinter has been removed, wash the area with soap and water. Apply a bandage if needed to keep the wound clean; otherwise, leave it open to the air. Watch for signs of infection (see left).

Call a health professional if the splinter is very large or deeply embedded and cannot be easily removed, or if the splinter is in the eye.

Shock

Shock may occur due to sudden illness or injury. When the circulatory system is unable to get enough blood to the vital organs, the body goes into shock. Sometimes, even a mild injury will lead to shock.

The signs of shock include:

- Cool, pale, clammy skin

- Dilated pupils

- Weak, rapid pulse

- Shallow, rapid breathing

- Low blood pressure

- Thirst, nausea, or vomiting

- Confusion or anxiety

- Faintness, weakness, dizziness, or loss of consciousness

Shock is a life-threatening condition. Prompt home treatment can save lives.

Home Treatment

- Have the person lie down and elevate his legs 12 inches or more. If the injury is to the head, neck, or chest, keep the legs flat. If the person vomits, roll him to one side to let fluids drain from the mouth. Use care if there could be a spinal injury (see right).

- Control any bleeding (see page 216) and splint any fractures (see page 75).

- Keep the person warm, but not hot. Place a blanket underneath him and cover him with a sheet or blanket, depending on the weather. If the person is in a hot place, try to keep him cool.

- Take and record the person's pulse every five minutes.

- Comfort and reassure him to relieve anxiety.

When to Call a Health Professional

- Call for help if signs of shock develop and do not go away completely within a few minutes of laying the person down, elevating his or her feet, and covering the person with a warm blanket.

Spinal Injuries

Any accident involving the neck or back must be considered a possible spinal injury. Permanent paralysis may be avoided if the injured person is immobilized and transported correctly.

Signs of a spinal injury include:

- Severe pain in neck or back

- Bruises on head, neck, shoulders, or back

- Weakness, tingling, or numbness in the arms or legs

- Loss of bowel or bladder control

- Bleeding or clear fluid discharge from ears or nose

- Unconsciousness

Home Treatment

- If you suspect a spinal injury, do not move the person unless there is an immediate threat to life, such as fire. Don't drag victims from automobile accidents.

- If the person is in immediate danger, keep the head and neck supported and aligned while you move him to safety.

- If it was a diving accident, don't pull the injured person from the water as you may cause permanent damage. Float the person face up in the water until help arrives. The water will act as a splint and keep the spine immobile.

- If you suspect a spinal injury, call a health professional to transport the injured person.

Unconsciousness

An **unconscious** person is completely unaware of what is going on and is unable to make purposeful movements. Fainting is a form of brief unconsciousness; a coma is a deep, prolonged state of unconsciousness.

Causes of unconsciousness include stroke, epilepsy, heat exhaustion, diabetic coma, insulin shock, head or spinal injury, suffocation, drunkenness, shock, bleeding, and heart attack.

Fainting is usually a short loss of consciousness most often due to a momentary drop in blood flow to the brain. When you fall or lie down, blood flow is improved and you regain consciousness. This lightheadedness is a mild form of shock, and is usually not serious. If it happens often, there may be a more serious problem. Dizziness and fainting can also be brought on by sudden emotional stress or injury. See page 112.

Home Treatment

- Make sure the unconscious person can breathe. Check for breathing and, if necessary, open the airway and begin rescue breathing. See page 204.

- Check the pulse. If there is none, call for help and start cardiopulmonary resuscitation (CPR). See page 204.

- Keep the person lying down.

- Look for a medical identification bracelet, necklace, or card that identifies a medical problem such as epilepsy, diabetes, or drug allergy.

- Treat any injuries.

- Do not give the person anything to eat or drink.

When to Call a Health Professional

- If someone has completely lost consciousness.

- If unconsciousness follows a head injury. A head injury victim needs to be carefully observed. See page 221.

- If a person with diabetes loses consciousness. He or she may have **insulin shock** (low blood sugar) or be in a **diabetic coma** (too much sugar in the blood).

Be true to your teeth or your teeth will be false to you.
Dental Proverb

Chapter 15

Mouth and Dental Problems

Your teeth will last a lifetime if you care for them properly. Regular brushing, flossing, and visits to a dentist will help keep your teeth healthy.

Choose a dentist as carefully as you choose any other doctor. See page 5 for tips on finding a dentist who meets your needs and is concerned about preventive care.

Canker Sores

Canker sores are painful open sores on the inner membranes of the mouth and cheek. Possible causes of canker sores include injury to the inside of the mouth, infection, stress, genetic predisposition, and female hormones. The sores usually heal in 7 to 10 days.

Prevention
• Avoid injury to the inside of your mouth:

  ○ Chew food slowly and carefully.

  ○ Use a soft-bristle toothbrush and brush your teeth thoroughly but gently.

• Avoid foods that seem to cause sores.

Home Treatment
• Avoid coffee, spicy and salty foods, and citrus fruits.

• Apply an oral paste, like Orabase, to the canker sore. It will protect the sore, ease pain, and speed healing. Amosan is another over-the-counter canker sore medication. Anbesol may help relieve pain.

Mouth and Dental Problems

Problem	Possible Causes
White spots, sores, or bleeding in mouth	See Canker Sores, p. 233; see thrush, p. 135. If unexplained sores last longer than 14 days, call a health professional.
Bleeding gums	Gum disease. See Dental Problems, p. 235.
Toothache	See p. 239.
Sores on the lips	See Cold Sores below.
Bad breath	May be a sign of dental problems, indigestion, or upper respiratory infection.
Pain and stiffness in jaw, with headache	See TMJ, p. 239; Tension Headaches, p. 125.

• Rinse your mouth with a mixture of 15 ml of hydrogen peroxide in a half-litre of water.

• A thin paste of baking soda and water applied to the sore may bring relief.

When to Call a Health Professional

• If mouth sores develop after starting a medication.

• If a canker sore, or any sore, does not heal in 14 days.

• If a sore is very painful or recurs frequently.

• If white spots that are not canker sores appear in the mouth and are not improving in one to two weeks.

Cold Sores

Cold sores (fever blisters) are small red blisters that usually appear on the lip and outer edge of the mouth. They often weep a clear fluid and form scabs after a few days. They are sometimes confused with impetigo (see page 137), which usually develops between the nose and upper lip. The fluid that weeps from impetigo is cloudy and honey-colored, not clear.

Cold sores are caused by a herpes virus. Herpes viruses (chickenpox is another kind) stay in the body after the first infection. Later, something that triggers the virus causes it to become active again. Cold sores may appear after colds, fevers, exposure to the sun, stressful times, or during menstruation. Sometimes, they appear for no apparent reason.

Prevention

- Avoid kissing someone who has a cold sore and avoid direct skin contact with genital herpes sores (see page 198). Both types of herpes can affect either the mouth or genitals. Condoms help reduce the risk.

- Use a sunscreen on your lips and wear a hat if exposure to the sun seems to trigger cold sores.

- Reducing stress may help in some cases. Practise relaxation exercises often. See page 248.

Home Treatment

- At the first sign of a cold sore (tingling or prickling at the site where the sore will appear), apply ice to the area. This may help reduce the severity of the sore.

- Apply petroleum jelly (Vaseline) to ease cracking and dryness.

- Apply a paste made of cornstarch and a little water.

- Blistex or Lipactin may ease the pain. Don't share them with others.

- Be patient. Cold sores usually go away in 7 to 10 days.

When to Call a Health Professional

- If sores last longer than two weeks, or occur frequently.

- If you have many or frequent cold sores. A prescription medication may reduce the frequency and severity of outbreaks.

Dental Problems

Dental disease is preventable. You can keep all of your teeth by practicing good home care and having regular professional checkups. Brush and floss regularly. Both tooth decay and gum disease are the result of bacterial plaque.

Plaque and Tooth Decay

Bacteria are always present in the mouth. When they are not removed by brushing and flossing, bacteria stick to the teeth and multiply into larger and larger colonies called plaque. Plaque forms as a sticky, colorless film on your teeth.

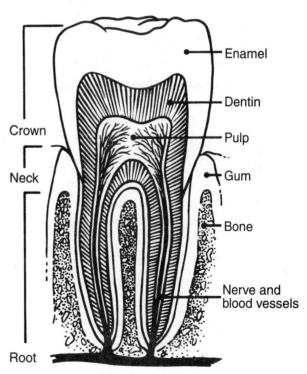

Crown

Neck

Root

Enamel

Dentin

Pulp

Gum

Bone

Nerve and blood vessels

The tooth

This sticky plaque damages teeth in two ways. First, food particles, especially refined sugars, stick to it. The plaque uses that food to grow more bacteria and to produce acid. Second, the plaque holds the acid against the tooth surface. If not removed, the acid will eventually eat through the tooth enamel, causing tooth decay.

If you eat only at mealtimes, it takes about 24 hours for bacteria and acid to harm your teeth. This is enough time for you to brush the plaque off and wash away the acid. If you eat a lot of between-meal snacks, plaque builds up faster and you need to brush more often.

Plaque and Gum (Periodontal) Disease

Periodontal disease, an inflammation of the gums and in the bone supporting them, is a major cause of tooth loss. It is caused by bacterial plaque that builds up and sticks to the teeth.

The first stage of the disease, called **gingivitis**, is marked by swollen, bleeding gums and bad breath. This stage is painless and, unfortunately, many people do not seek treatment.

As the disease progresses, the supporting bones and ligaments are affected. The gums recede, creating gaps between the teeth, which eventually fall out.

People with diabetes and those who smoke or chew tobacco are at increased risk of gum disease.

However, everyone is at risk; an estimated 75 to 80 percent of North Americans have some form of gum disease.

Occasional bleeding when you brush or floss is an early sign of gum disease. However, with good care, it won't take long to get your gums back to normal. Brush and floss your teeth every day, and follow the prevention guidelines.

Prevention

- Have your teeth checked and cleaned at least once a year by a dentist or dental hygienist.

- Eat crunchy foods that naturally clean the teeth (apples, carrots, and other raw vegetables), and foods with ample vitamin C, like citrus fruits and broccoli.

Brushing

Brush and floss properly to remove plaque. Brush at least twice a day for three to five minutes each time. Clean every surface of every tooth.

1. Use a toothbrush with soft, rounded-end bristles and a head that allows you to reach all parts of your mouth. Replace your toothbrush every three to four months.

2. Use a fluoride toothpaste and use only a small dab (pea-sized or smaller). Tartar-control toothpastes may help slow the formation of hard plaque buildup (tartar) on the teeth, but daily brushing with any toothpaste and flossing are the best tartar-control methods.

3. Place the brush at a 45° angle where the teeth meet the gums. Press firmly, and gently rock the brush back and forth using small circular movements. Do not scrub if you have a stiff-bristled brush. Vigorous brushing can make the gums recede and scratch your tooth enamel.

4. Brush all surfaces of the teeth, tongue side and cheek side. Pay special attention to the front teeth and behind the back teeth.

5. Brush the chewing surfaces vigorously with short back-and-forth strokes.

6. Brush the tongue. Plaque on the tongue can cause bad breath and is an ideal environment for bacteria to grow.

7. Use disclosing tablets periodically to see if any plaque is left on the teeth. Disclosing tablets are chewable tablets that will color any plaque left on the teeth after brushing. They are available at most drugstores.

Flossing

Brushing properly can remove most dental plaque. Regular flossing is the best way to remove plaque that forms between the teeth and below the gum line. Floss once a day using one of the following methods:

1. The finger-wrap method: Cut off a piece of floss 18 to 20 inches long. Wrap one end around the left middle finger and the other end around the right middle finger, until your hands are about two to three inches apart.

2. The circle method: Use a piece of floss about 12 inches long. Tie the ends together, forming a loop. If the loop is too large, wrap the floss around the middle fingers to make it smaller.

Finger-wrap method

To floss the upper teeth, use the thumb of one hand and forefinger of the other as shown in the illustration.

Flossing upper teeth

To floss the lower teeth, use both forefingers to guide the floss as in the illustration. The fingers should be about ½ inch apart.

Flossing lower teeth

Curve the floss around each tooth and gently slide it under the gum line. Move the floss firmly up and down several times to scrape off the plaque. Popping the floss in and out without scraping will not remove much plaque.

Flossing tools may be especially helpful for adults who are flossing a child's teeth. Use the same scraping motion to remove plaque.

With practice, flossing will become easy. Any bleeding should subside as gums become healthy.

Flossing tools

Dental Care for Children

Children should have their first dental visit before the age of three; anytime between 18 and 24 months is a good time for this visit. Establish a regular pattern of visits to the dentist for your child.

- Start caring for your children's teeth early, before permanent teeth have come in. Clean your child's mouth every day. Start soon after birth by wiping all around your baby's mouth with a clean, dampened face cloth or gauze pad. This will get the child used to regular cleaning and can also ease teething discomfort. Once teeth appear (at about six months), smear a little fluoride toothpaste on a dampened face cloth, gauze pad, or baby toothbrush and gently clean your baby's teeth. It is important to do this every day.

- Do not put an infant or small child to bed with a bottle of juice or milk. Prolonged contact with the sugar in these liquids can cause tooth decay. Nursing an infant to sleep is fine, however.

- Start toothbrushing as soon as the teeth come in. Brush your children's teeth for the first four to five years, until they have enough dexterity to take over the job. A good teaching method is to have your child brush in the morning and you brush at night until they master the skill. Use disclosing tablets to see if the child is removing all the plaque.

- Start flossing as soon as the child has teeth that touch each other. As with brushing, you will have to help with flossing until the child is old enough to manage it. Flossing tools can help.

Sealants and Fluoride

Sealants are a plastic coating applied to the chewing surfaces of the back teeth to protect them from developing cavities. Sealants are especially good for the permanent molars when they first emerge in the mouth, usually between age 6 and age 11. Even with sealants, regular brushing and flossing are essential.

Fluoride is a mineral that strengthens tooth enamel and reduces the harmful effects of plaque. Children and adults need fluoride to build and keep strong teeth. Talk with your dentist about the amount of fluoride in your area's drinking water, and discuss fluoride treatments if needed.

When to Call a Health Professional

- See your dentist for regular cleanings and exams.

- If your gums bleed when you press on them or bleed often when you brush your teeth.

- If teeth are loose or moving apart or if there are changes in the way your teeth fit together when you bite.

- If gums are very red, swollen, or tender, or if pus is present.

- If you have a toothache. Toothaches are caused when the inside of the tooth (dentin) is exposed. The pain may go away temporarily, but the problem will not. Take aspirin, ibuprofen, or acetaminophen for pain relief until you can get an appointment. A cold pack on your jaw may also help.

TMJ Syndrome

The olive-sized joint in front of your ear that connects your jawbone to your skull is called the temporomandibular joint (TMJ). TMJ syndrome is a set of symptoms that relate to damage, wear and tear, or unusual stress to the joint. The symptoms can include:

- Pain in and around the joint

- Noises such as clicking, popping, or snapping in the joint

- Inability to "open wide"

- Muscle pain and spasms where the jaw muscles attach to the bone

- Headache, neck and shoulder pain, ear or eye pain, and difficulty swallowing

The cause of TMJ syndrome is difficult to determine. The most likely causes include:

- Injury, such as a direct blow to the jaw, whiplash, or forceful stretching of the jaw during dental work

- Chronic tooth grinding, clenching, or gum chewing

- Arthritis in the joint

- Chronic muscle tension due to stress, anxiety, depression, or poor posture (usually affects the jaw muscles more than the joint)

- Teeth that do not fit together when you bite (malocclusion)

Home treatment and nonsurgical treatments will successfully relieve most TMJ symptoms. Your doctor may recommend use of a plastic mouth plate (splint), physical therapy, or prescription pain relievers. Surgery is needed for a very small percentage of TMJ problems.

Prevention

- Regularly practise progressive muscle relaxation, particularly before going to sleep. See page 248.

- Stop chewing gum or tough foods at the first sign of pain or discomfort in your jaw muscles.

- Avoid biting your nails and nibbling on pencils or other objects, which forces your jaw into an awkward position and may cause pain.

- Maintain good posture with your ear, shoulder, and hip in a straight line. See page 49.

Home Treatment

- Continue the prevention tips.

- Avoid chewing gum and hard or chewy foods.

- Avoid opening your mouth too wide.

- Avoid cradling a telephone receiver between your shoulder and jaw.

- Rest your jaw, keeping your teeth apart and your lips closed. (Keep your tongue on the roof of your mouth, not between your teeth.)

- Put an ice pack on the joint for eight minutes, three times a day. Gently open and close your mouth while the ice pack is on. If the jaw muscle is swollen, apply ice six times a day.

- Take aspirin or ibuprofen to reduce swelling and pain.

- If there is no swelling, use moist heat on the jaw muscle three times a day. Gently open and close your mouth while the heat is on. Alternate with the cold pack treatments.

- If you are under severe stress or suffer from anxiety or depression, see Chapter 18.

When to Call a Health Professional

- If the pain is severe.

- If TMJ symptoms occur after an injury to the jaw.

- If your jaw locks in certain positions.

- If any jaw problem or pain continues more than two weeks without improvement.

- If other mild TMJ symptoms do not improve after four weeks of home treatment.

If exercise could be packed into a pill, it would be the single most widely prescribed, and beneficial, medicine in the nation.
Robert Butler, M.D.

Chapter 16

Fitness and Relaxation

Staying fit and relaxed is not only good for your health, it is good for you. If you want to enjoy life more, the tips in this chapter can help.

The Benefits of Exercise

No amount of exercise can guarantee a long life. However, even moderate amounts of exercise can improve the likelihood of a healthy life. Even 30 minutes a day, every other day, of moderate physical activity can improve your health. Along with a positive attitude and a healthy diet, your fitness level plays a major role in how well you feel, what illnesses you avoid, and how much you enjoy life.

Consider the benefits of fitness presented here and find one or more reasons to commit to your own fitness program.

Benefits of Exercise
• Relieves tension and stress
• Provides enjoyment and fun
• Stimulates the mind
• Helps maintain stable weight
• Controls appetite
• Boosts self-image
• Improves muscle tone and strength
• Improves flexibility
• Lowers blood pressure
• Relieves insomnia
• Increases "good" (HDL) cholesterol
• Reduces risk of diabetes

Your Personal Fitness Plan

No one can prescribe the perfect fitness plan for you. You have to figure it out based on what you enjoy doing and what you will continue to do. The next few pages can be a big help.

Consistency is the most important, the most basic, and the most often neglected part of fitness. Consistency in regular exercise or moderate activity delivers all of the fitness benefits.

A good fitness plan has three parts: aerobic fitness, muscle strengthening, and flexibility. Read the section on each part. Then, see "Setting Your Fitness Goals" on page 245.

Aerobic Fitness

Aerobic conditioning strengthens your heart and lungs. Good aerobic exercises include brisk walking, running, stair climbing, biking, swimming, aerobic dance, or anything else that raises your heart rate and keeps it up for a while.

How Hard Should I Exercise?

Nice and easy does it. Exercise does not have to be intense to be of value. In fact, if you exercise too hard, you get less benefit than if you go at a moderate pace.

Above all, listen to your body. If the exercise feels too hard, slow down. You will reduce your risk of injury and enjoy the exercise much more.

Try the "talk-sing test" to determine your ideal exercise pace:

- If you can't talk and exercise at the same time, you are going too fast.

- If you can talk while you exercise, you are doing fine.

- If you can sing while you exercise, it would be safe to exercise a little faster.

Your exercise is most effective when you can talk, but not sing, while doing it.

Target Heart Rate

Another way to see how hard you are exercising is to check your heart rate. You gain the most aerobic benefits when your exercise heart rate is 60 percent to 80 percent of your maximum heart rate. After exercising for about 10 minutes, stop and take your pulse for 10 seconds (see page 23). Compare the number to the chart below. Adjust the intensity of your exercise so that your heart rate stays between the two numbers. However, the target heart rate is only a guide. Each individual is different, so pay attention to how you feel.

Target Heart Rate	
Age	10-second heart rate
20	20 - 27
25	20 - 26
30	19 - 25
35	19 - 25
40	18 - 24
45	18 - 23
50	17 - 23
55	17 - 23
60	16 - 22
65	16 - 21
70	15 - 20

Target heart rate is 60 percent to 80 percent of maximum heart rate (maximum heart rate = 220 minus your age).

How Often and How Long Should I Exercise?

Most studies show that exercising for 30 minutes three times a week is enough to improve fitness. However, sometimes it's easier to make exercise a habit if you do it every day.

With exercise, harder is not better, but longer is. Although you can get good fitness benefits from as little as 10 minutes of exercise per day, extending your exercise time will increase your rewards. This is true for up to one hour of exercise per day. Beyond that, there may be diminishing health returns and increasing risk of injuries.

Warm Up and Cool Down

For the first five minutes of your exercise routine, start out slowly and easily so your muscles have a chance to warm up.

End your exercise with a little cool-down period. Gradually slow your pace, then do a few light stretches to improve flexibility. See page 244.

Drink some extra water before and after exercising.

Muscle Strengthening

Strengthening your muscles improves your work and athletic performance and prevents fatigue. Muscle-strengthening exercises will also improve your posture and help you feel more energetic.

Resistance training, with free weights, weight-training equipment, or inexpensive rubber tubing, can quickly increase your muscle strength.

Other simple, safe, and effective strengthening exercises include bent-knee curl-ups, chin-ups, push-ups, side leg-lifts, and other calisthenics to improve abdominal, neck, arm, shoulder, and leg strength.

Flexibility

Stretching can increase your range of motion and reduce stiffness and pain. Stretching is particularly important during the cool-down phase when your muscles are warm. See the stretches on page 244 and Resource 66 on page 306.

- Stretch slowly and gradually. Don't bounce. Maintain a continuous tension on the muscle.

- Relax and hold each stretch for a count of 20.

- Exhale as you stretch, to further relax your muscles. If stretching hurts, you have gone too far or you are doing something incorrectly.

Try to stretch a little every day. Take a stretch break instead of a coffee break.

Overcome Barriers to Exercise

There are six barriers to exercise that are all easy to overcome.

1. No time? Try shorter periods of activity spread throughout the day, such as three 10-minute walks.

2. Too tired? It's often lack of exercise that makes you tired. Exercise gives you energy. Try it.

3. Embarrassed? Many people are, especially at first. Be proud that you're taking care of your body.

Calf stretch   Triceps stretch   Latissimus stretch   Curl-ups
(abdominal muscles)

Hamstring stretch   Groin stretch   Quadriceps stretch

Hip flexor stretch

Stretching exercises

Exercise Caution

Moderate exercise is safe for most people. To be safe, start slowly and gradually increase the intensity of your exercise. However, if you can answer yes to any of the following questions, talk with your doctor before beginning an exercise program.

- Do you have heart trouble?

- Do you have undiagnosed chest pains?

- Do you have high blood pressure?

- Do you often feel faint or dizzy?

- Do you have arthritis or other bone or joint problems that might be aggravated by improper exercise?

- Do you have diabetes? You may want to talk with your doctor about how increased exercise affects your insulin needs.

Men over age 40 who have been inactive *or* who have two or more risk factors for heart disease* *and* who plan to start a *vigorous* exercise program (running or fast bicycling or swimming) may wish to talk with their doctors about any possible risks.

*Cholesterol over 200, blood pressure over 140/90, smoking, diabetes, or family history of heart disease before age 45.

4. No partner? Yes, it's more fun to exercise with a friend. If your regular exercise partner quits, find another one.

5. Bad weather? Too hot, too cold, too wet, too windy—it never seems right for exercise. Lots of people exercise come rain or shine. Try a variety of indoor and outdoor activities.

6. Too costly? You had to let the fitness club membership expire. You can't afford a mountain bike. You panic at the price of running shoes. It all costs money. But can you afford not to exercise? Try a low-cost option, such as walking instead of driving.

Setting Your Fitness Goals

Are you as strong, flexible, and physically fit as you would like to be? If you are, good for you. We hope this chapter has helped you reaffirm the exercises you are already doing. However, if you want to make some improvements, here's one piece of advice: try to improve a little bit at a time.

The only way to walk a mile is to take one step at a time. The only way to improve your fitness level is to take it one step at a time.

- Pick one aspect of fitness (aerobic, strength, flexibility) you want to improve first.

- Pick an activity that you enjoy. You're more likely to keep doing something you like.

- Set a one-month goal that you think you can reach. For example, plan to walk for 10 minutes at lunch three days a week, or stretch for five minutes each morning.

- Start today. Keep a record of what you do.

- When you reach your first goal, reward yourself! Then set a new one.

Consistency brings success. Each success may be a small one, but small successes can quickly add up to physical fitness that will make a big difference in your life.

Stress and Distress

Stress is the physical, mental, and emotional reactions you experience as the result of changes and demands in your life.

Stress is part and parcel of common life events, both large and small. It comes with all of life's daily hassles, traffic jams, long lines, petty arguments, and other relatively small irritations. Stress also comes with crises and life-changing events, such as illness, death of a loved one, marriage problems or divorce, losing a job, getting a new job, or children leaving home.

All these events may force you to adjust, whether you are ready to or not. Unless you can regularly release the tension that comes with stress, it can greatly increase your risks of physical and mental illness.

Because many major life events are beyond your control, take charge of those aspects of your life that you can

manage. One major change doesn't mean that all areas of your life must change. Continue to participate in the same activities you did before the event happened.

Not all stress is bad. Positive stress (eustress) is a motivator, challenging you to act in creative and resourceful ways. When changes and demands overwhelm you, negative stress (distress) sets in. This section has specific techniques you can use to cope with stress in your life.

What Stress Does to the Body

At the first sign of alarm, chemicals released by the pituitary and adrenal glands and the nerve endings automatically trigger these physical reactions. The reactions to stress are universal:

- Heart rate increases to move blood to the muscles and brain.

- Blood pressure goes up.

- Breathing rate increases.

- Digestion slows down.

- Perspiration increases.

- Pupils dilate.

- You feel a rush of strength.

Your body is tense, alert, and ready for action. For primitive people, these reactions were an advantage in the face of sudden danger, preparing them for survival by either "fight or flight." Today, our bodies still react the same way but it is not as acceptable to either fight or run away (although we often wish we could).

After the natural "alarm" reaction to a real or perceived threat, our bodies stay on alert until we feel the danger has passed. When the stressor is gone, the brain signals an "all clear" sign to the pituitary and adrenal glands. They stop producing the chemicals that caused the physical reaction, and the body returns to normal.

Problems with stress occur when the brain fails to give the "all clear" signal. If the alarm state lasts too long, you begin to suffer from the consequences of constant stress. Unrelieved stress can lead to many health problems.

Recognizing Stress

Sometimes it's difficult to recognize or admit that stress is affecting your health. If you can learn to watch for its effects and take corrective action quickly, you will be able to cope with your stress.

The signs of stress are classic. You may get a headache, stiff neck, nagging backache, rapid breathing, sweaty palms, or an upset stomach. You may become irritable and intolerant of even minor disturbances. You may lose your temper more often and yell at your family for no good reason. Your pulse rate may increase and you may feel jumpy or exhausted all the time. You may find it hard to concentrate.

When these symptoms appear, recognize them as signs of stress and find a way to deal with them. Just knowing why you're crabby may be the first step in coping with the problem. It is your attitude toward stress, not the stress itself, that affects your health the most.

Managing Stress

Some people try to relieve stress by smoking, drinking, overeating, or taking pills. There is a better way. Avoid the dangerous side effects of tobacco, alcohol, and drugs by learning to control your stress level. You can do this by using your body to soothe your mind and using your mind to soothe your body.

Stress and tension affect our emotions and feelings. By expressing those feelings to others, we are able to better understand and cope with them. Talking about a problem with a spouse or a good friend is a valuable way to reduce tension and stress.

Crying can also relieve tension. It's part of our emotional healing process. Expressing yourself through writing, crafts, or art may also be a good tension reliever.

Exercise is a natural response to stress; it is the normal reaction to the fight-or-flight urge. Walking briskly will take advantage of the rapid pulse and tensed muscles caused by stress and release your pent-up energy. After a long walk, your stress level is lower and more manageable.

The rest of this chapter is devoted to other skills and techniques that will help you increase your resistance to stress and better cope with those stressors you choose to accept.

Relaxation Skills

Whatever you do to manage stress, you can benefit from the regular use of relaxation skills. Relaxation is the exact opposite to the fight-or-flight response.

When learning relaxation skills, you must remove yourself from all outside distractions. It may take some practice to become comfortable with these techniques. Once you've trained your body and mind to relax (two to three weeks), you'll be able to produce the same relaxed state whenever you want.

The following three methods of relaxation and meditation are among the simplest and most effective. They should be done twice a day for about 20 minutes. Pick a time and place where you won't be disturbed or distracted.

Roll Breathing

The object of roll breathing is to develop full use of your lungs and get in touch with the rhythm of your breathing. It can be practised in any position, but it is best to learn it lying on your back, with your knees bent.

1. Place your left hand on your abdomen and your right hand on your chest. Notice how your hands move as you breathe in and out.

2. Practise filling your lower lungs by breathing so that your left hand goes up when you inhale and your right hand remains still. Always inhale through your nose and exhale through your mouth.

3. When you have filled and emptied your lower lungs 8 to 10 times, add the second step to your breathing: inhale first into your lower lungs as before, and then continue inhaling into your upper chest. As you do so, your right hand will rise and your left hand will fall a little as your abdomen falls.

4. As you exhale slowly through your mouth, make a quiet, whooshing sound as first your left hand and then your right hand falls. As you exhale, feel the tension leaving your body as you become more and more relaxed.

5. Practise breathing in and out in this manner for three to five minutes. Notice that the movement of your abdomen and chest is like rolling waves rising and falling in a rhythmic motion.

Practise roll breathing daily for several weeks until you can do it almost anywhere, providing you with an instant relaxation tool any time you need one.

CAUTION: Some people get dizzy the first few times they try roll breathing. If you begin to hyperventilate or become lightheaded, slow your breathing. Get up slowly.

Progressive Muscle Relaxation

The body responds to tense thoughts or situations with muscle tension, which can cause pain or discomfort. Deep muscle relaxation reduces the muscle tension as well as general mental anxiety. You can use an audio tape to help you go through all the muscle groups or you can do it by just tensing and relaxing each muscle group. Deep muscle relaxation is effective in combatting stress-related health problems and often helps people get to sleep.

Muscle Groups and Procedure

Pick a place where you can lie down on your back and stretch out comfortably, such as a carpeted floor.

Tense each muscle group for 4 to 10 seconds (hard but not to the point of cramping), then give yourself 10 to 20 seconds to release it and relax. At various points, review the various muscle groups and relax each one a little more each time.

How to Tense Muscle Groups

Hands: Clench them.

Wrists and forearms: Extend them and bend the hands back at the wrist.

Biceps and upper arms: Clench your hands into fists, bend your arms at the elbows, and flex your biceps.

Shoulders: Shrug them. (Review the arms and shoulders area.)

Forehead: Wrinkle it into a deep frown.

Around the eyes and bridge of the nose: Close your eyes as tightly as possible. (Remove contact lenses before beginning the exercise.)

Cheeks and jaws: Grin from ear to ear.

Around the mouth: Press your lips together tightly. (Review the face area.)

Back of the neck: Press your head back hard.

Front of the neck: Touch your chin to your chest. (Review the neck and head area.)

Chest: Take a deep breath and hold it, then exhale.

Back: Arch your back up and away from the floor.

Stomach: Suck it into a tight knot. (Review the chest and stomach area.)

Hips and buttocks: Press the buttocks together tightly.

Thighs: Clench them hard.

Lower legs: Point your toes toward your face, as if trying to bring the toes up to touch your head.

Lower legs: Point your toes away and curl them downward at the same time. (Review the area from the waist down.)

When you are finished, arouse yourself thoroughly by counting backwards from five to one.

Relaxation Response

The relaxation response is the exact opposite of a stress response. It slows heart rate and breathing, lowers blood pressure, and helps relieve muscle tension.

Technique (adapted from Herbert Benson, MD):

1. Sit quietly in a comfortable position with your eyes closed.

2. Begin progressive muscle relaxation. See page 248.

3. Become aware of your breathing. Each time you exhale, say the word "one" (or any other word or phrase) silently or aloud. Concentrate on breathing from your abdomen and not your chest.

Instead of focusing on a repeated word, you can fix your gaze on a stationary object. Any mental stimulus will help you to clear your mind.

Continue this for 10 to 20 minutes. As distracting thoughts enter your mind, don't dwell on them, just allow them to drift away.

4. Sit quietly for several minutes, until you are ready to open your eyes.

5. Notice the difference in your breathing and your pulse rate.

Don't worry about becoming deeply relaxed. The key to this exercise is to remain passive, to let distracting thoughts slip away like waves on the beach.

Practise for 10 to 20 minutes once or twice a day, but not within two hours after a meal. When you have set up a routine, you can achieve the relaxation response with little effort.

For a more complete description of the relaxation response, see Resource 113 on page 308.

Never eat more than you can lift.
Miss Piggy

Chapter 17

Nutrition

This chapter gives some guidelines for good eating and some hints on how to help your children establish healthy eating habits. Children learn best by example, so practise good eating habits along with them. For more information, see the resources under "Nutrition" on page 308.

Seven Simple Guidelines for Eating Well

1. Eat a variety of foods. Include a daily selection of:

• Whole-grain and enriched breads, cereals, and grain products

• Vegetables

• Fruits

• Milk, cheese, and yogurt

• Meats, poultry, fish, eggs, dried beans and peas, tofu

2. Maintain a healthy weight. See page 264.

3. Choose a diet low in fat, saturated fat, and cholesterol. Fats have twice as many calories per gram as any other food. A high-fat diet increases your risk of heart disease and some cancers. See page 256.

4. Eat plenty of vegetables, fruits, and grain products. Complex carbohydrates (grains, vegetables, and starches) and fruits pack the most nutrients per calorie. See page 252.

5. Use sugars only in moderation. Sugars have little, if any, vitamins, minerals, or fiber. See page 256.

6. Use salt and sodium only in moderation. For some people, sodium increases blood pressure. See page 262.

7. If you drink alcohol, do so only in moderation. Alcohol is high in calories and has no nutrients. For men, this means not more than two drinks

per day; for women, not more than one. A drink is equal to 360 ml (12 ounces) of beer, 150 ml (5 ounces) of wine, or 45 ml (1½ ounces) of hard liquor (vodka, gin, etc.).

Eating Well: A Basic Plan

Eat a variety of foods from Canada's Food Guide to Healthy Eating every day. Eat more from the bread and cereal and fruit and vegetable groups than from the other groups. Most people who follow this plan will get all the vitamins, minerals, and other nutrients their bodies need and will have little trouble controlling their weight.

Grain Products
(Breads, Cereals, and Starches)

Starches are carbohydrates, which have less than half the calories per gram than fat. Unprocessed starches (whole grains, vegetables) also contain large amounts of vitamins, minerals, fibre, and water.

Contrary to popular belief, bread, potatoes, rice, and pasta are not fattening! Starchy foods are fattening only when you add fat to them. Try nonfat yogurt or salsa instead of butter and sour cream on baked potatoes. Use fresh vegetable and tomato sauces instead of creamy sauces on pasta.

Fruits and Vegetables

Fresh fruits and vegetables provide vitamins, minerals, and fibre and are naturally low in fat. Many fruits and vegetables contain a lot of vitamins A (beta carotene) and C, especially

oranges and other citrus fruits, broccoli, sweet potatoes, winter squash, carrots, spinach, and other leafy greens. A diet that includes lots of fruits and vegetables helps protect you against heart disease and cancer.

Fruits and vegetables are most nutritious when eaten fresh and raw or lightly cooked. Steam or microwave vegetables to retain more vitamins.

**Fruits and Vegetables
Against Cancer**

Fruits and vegetables are key elements of good basic nutrition. They contain lots of fibre, especially when eaten raw. A diet high in fibre may protect you against colon cancer. Many vegetables and fruits contain the two antioxidant vitamins, A (beta carotene) and C, which protect against some cancers. Beta carotene is found in carrots, apricots, winter squash, sweet potatoes, cantaloupe, and broccoli. Vitamin C is found in citrus fruits such as oranges and in cantaloupe, strawberries, peppers, broccoli, and tomatoes.

Vegetables in the cabbage family, including broccoli and cauliflower, appear to protect against several types of cancer.

Health Canada recommends that you eat at least five servings per day of fruits and vegetables to lower your risk of cancer.

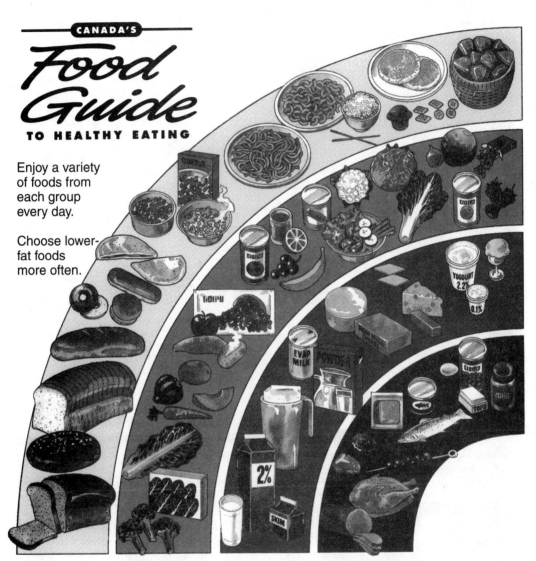

Health   Santé
Canada   Canada

CANADA'S

Food Guide

TO HEALTHY EATING

Enjoy a variety
of foods from
each group
every day.

Choose lower-
fat foods
more often.

Grain Products
Choose whole
grain and enriched
products more
often.

Vegetables & Fruit
Choose dark
green and orange
vegetables and
orange fruit more
often.

Milk Products
Choose lower-fat
milk products
more often.

Meat & Alternatives
Choose leaner meats,
poultry and fish, as
well as dried peas,
beans and lentils
more often.

Canada

CANADA'S
Food Guide
TO HEALTHY EATING
FOR PEOPLE FOUR YEARS AND OVER

Different People Need Different Amounts of Food

The amount of food you need every day from the 4 food groups and other foods depends on your age, body size, activity level, whether you are male or female and if you are pregnant or breast-feeding. That's why the Food Guide gives a lower and higher number of servings for each food group. For example, young children can choose the lower number of servings, while male teenagers can go to the higher number. Most other people can choose servings somewhere in between.

Grain Products

5-12

SERVINGS PER DAY

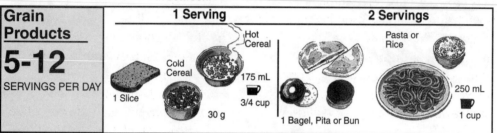

1 Serving	2 Servings
Hot Cereal	Pasta or Rice
Cold Cereal	
1 Slice	175 mL 3/4 cup	250 mL 1 cup
30 g	1 Bagel, Pita or Bun

Vegetables & Fruit

5-10

SERVINGS PER DAY

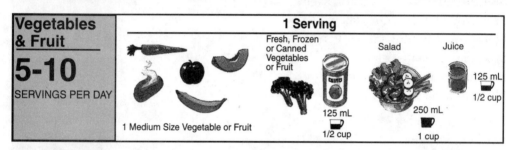

1 Serving

Fresh, Frozen or Canned Vegetables or Fruit   Salad   Juice

1 Medium Size Vegetable or Fruit   125 mL 1/2 cup   250 mL 1 cup   125 mL 1/2 cup

Milk Products

SERVINGS PER DAY
Children 4–9 years: 2-3
Youth 10–16 years: 3-4
Adults: 2-4
Pregnant & Breast-feeding Women: 3-4

1 Serving

Cheese

MILK   3"x1"x1" 50 g   2 Slices 50 g   175 g 3/4 cup

250 mL 1 cup

Other Foods

Taste and enjoyment can also come from other foods and beverages that are not part of the 4 food groups. Some of these foods are higher in fat or Calories, so use these foods in moderation.

Meat & Alternatives

2-3

SERVINGS PER DAY

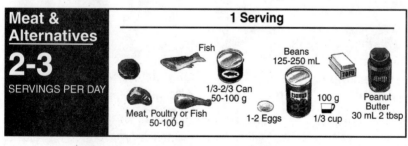

1 Serving

Fish   Beans 125-250 mL   TOFU

1/3-2/3 Can 50-100 g

Meat, Poultry or Fish 50-100 g   1-2 Eggs   100 g 1/3 cup   Peanut Butter 30 mL 2 tbsp

Enjoy eating well, being active and feeling good about yourself. That's VITALITY

Fibre

Fibre has no vitamins or minerals, yet it is important to good health. There are two types of fibre.

Insoluble fibre in whole-grain products provides bulk for your diet. Together with fluids, insoluble fibre stimulates the colon to keep waste moving out of the bowels. Without fibre, waste moves too slowly, increasing your risk for constipation, colon and bowel cancer, and diverticulosis.

Soluble fibre found in fruit, beans, peas and other legumes, and oats helps lower cholesterol, reducing your risk of heart disease. The fibre in legumes can also help regulate blood glucose and cholesterol levels.

Do you need more fibre? If your bowel movements are soft and easy to pass, you probably get plenty of fibre. If they are hard and difficult to pass, more fibre and water may help. See page 32 for more information on constipation.

Small Changes Can Make a Big Difference

You don't have to change your whole diet at once. Pick one easy change and stick with it. Add others once you've had success with the first change.

- Buy only whole-grain bread.
- Buy only skim or 1% milk.
- Use less oil for cooking.
- Eat fish at least twice a week.
- Eat a raw vegetable at lunch.
- Drink an extra glass of water when you wake each morning.

To increase fibre in your diet:

- Eat at least five servings of fruits and vegetables a day. Eat fruits with edible skins and seeds: kiwis, figs, blueberries, apples, and raspberries. Eat more of the stems of broccoli and asparagus.

- Switch to whole-grain and whole-wheat breads, pasta, tortillas, and cereals. The first ingredient listed should be whole-wheat flour. If it just says wheat flour, it means white flour, from which much of the fibre has been removed.

- Eat more cooked dried beans, peas, and lentils.

- Popcorn is a good high-fibre snack. However, avoid added oil, butter, and salt.

Water

One easy way to improve your diet is to drink more water. Active people need two quarts of water a day, and people who exercise regularly need even more. If you drink other fluids, you can get by with less, but plain water is best.

Caffeine

There is no convincing evidence that a moderate amount of caffeine (two to three cups of coffee or cola per day) will do you any harm if you are healthy.

Caffeine is mildly addictive, and cutting back too quickly may cause a headache. Gradual reductions will prevent headaches.

Sugar

What's wrong with sugar? It comes from a vegetable (sugar beets or sugar cane), is relatively cheap, tastes good, is fat-free, and is even a carbohydrate. Can sugar be all that bad?

From a health point of view, the biggest problem with sugar is that it is stripped of all vitamins, minerals, and fibre. What is left are crystals of pure calories.

In moderation, sugar does little harm. However, if too many of your calories come from sugar, you will either gain weight or not get enough of the other nutrients you need. Sugar also contributes to cavities.

- All sugars are basically alike. Honey and brown or raw sugar have no advantage over other sugars.

- Be aware of hidden sugars in flavored yogurt, canned, and processed foods. Check the label for words that end in "-ose," like dextrose, fructose, sucrose, lactose, and maltose, which are forms of sugar. Corn syrup is another common form of sugar.

- Limit foods that list sugar among the first few ingredients.

- Look for breakfast cereals that have six grams or less of added sugar per serving.

- You can reduce the sugar in some homemade baked goods provided you are familiar with the recipe results.

- Choose fresh fruit more often instead of prepared desserts, which may be high in sugar as well as fat.

Artificial Sweeteners

Although artificial sweeteners do help you avoid sugar, losing weight depends more on reducing calories from fat. Avoid using artificially sweetened foods to justify eating more high-fat food.

Aspartame (NutraSweet) and saccharin are considered safe, but the effects of long-term use are not known. Use them in moderation.

Fats

Fat (butter, lard, cream, oil, margarine, mayonnaise, and grease in food) accounts for 37 percent of the calories in the average Canadian diet. Fat has more than twice as many calories per gram as carbohydrates or protein.

How much fat is too much? The Nutrition Recommendations for Canadians recommend that less than 30 percent of total calories come from fat. Reducing dietary fat from 37 percent to 30 percent may slow the development of heart disease, reduce cancer risk, and improve your overall diet. But is it enough?

Many scientists think a diet with 30 percent fat is still too high for a healthy heart. A diet of 20 percent fat will reduce the risk of heart disease even more. There is some evidence that a 10-percent fat diet, along with other lifestyle changes, can even reverse narrowing of the arteries (arteriosclerosis). However, a 10-percent fat diet is challenging to maintain.

Based on your heart disease risks, you may wish to set a goal for how much fat to include in your diet. A nutritionist or registered dietitian can help you with a menu plan to meet your goal.

15 Simple Ways to Reduce Fat

When eating meat:

1. Eat more poultry and fish. Choose lean cuts of beef, pork, or veal.

2. Remove all visible fat before cooking. Poultry skin may be removed either before or after cooking.

3. Broil, bake, or poach instead of frying.

4. Reduce serving sizes to 50 g to 100 g (about two to three ounces) and don't take seconds.

5. Replace some meat with cooked dry beans and grains.

When using dairy products:

6. Use skim or 1 percent milk.

7. Choose low-fat, part skim milk cheeses like gruyere, Farmer's, Jarlsberg Swiss, mozzarella, or ricotta. Look for low-fat or nonfat Cheddar and Monterey Jack cheeses.

8. Substitute low-fat or nonfat cottage cheese and yogurt for cream and sour cream, or use fat-free sour cream and cream cheese.

In cooking:

9. Steam vegetables, saute with one teaspoon of oil or less, or cook with wine or defatted broth.

10. Use non-stick pans or add oil to a preheated pan (less oil goes further this way).

11. Season vegetables with herbs and spices instead of butter and sauces.

12. Experiment using less oil than is called for in recipes. You may need to increase other liquids. Use applesauce to replace some or all of the fat in some baked goods.

In general:

13. Avoid crackers, chips, cookies, margarine, and peanut butter made with hydrogenated oil, palm oil, coconut oil, or cocoa butter.

14. Eat plenty of carbohydrates to fill you up (fruits, vegetables, grains, bread, pasta, etc.).

15. Let salads go naked, modestly dressed with lemon juice, or use fat-free mayonnaise or dressings.

Cholesterol

Cholesterol is a waxy substance that is produced by the human body and is also found in animal products. Cells need cholesterol to function. Unfortunately, any excess cholesterol builds up inside the arteries. Cholesterol deposits (arteriosclerosis) are the major cause of heart attacks and strokes.

The 80-20 Rule

If you are generally healthy, you don't need to worry about maintaining a perfect diet. If you make healthy eating choices 80 percent of the time, occasional high-fat or high-calorie foods the other 20 percent of the time won't be a problem.

A high cholesterol level in your blood is a risk factor for heart disease and stroke. The higher your cholesterol level, the higher the risk. However, not all cholesterol is bad.

Good Cholesterol

Fat travels through your bloodstream attached to protein in a combination called a lipoprotein. Two lipoproteins are the main carriers of cholesterol: low-density lipoprotein (LDL) and high-density lipoprotein (HDL).

LDL acts like a fat delivery truck. It picks up cholesterol from the liver and delivers it to the cells. When

---

Calculating Percent Fat

Each gram (g) of fat has 9 calories. To calculate the percent of a food's total calories that come from fat, multiply the grams of fat times 9 and then divide by the total number of calories. Multiply your result by 100 to get the percent.

For example, an 8-ounce serving of 2% milk has 5 grams of fat and 130 total calories:

$$\frac{5 \text{ g fat x 9 calories/g x 100}}{130 \text{ calories}} =$$

$$= 34.6\% \text{ calories from fat}$$

The new food labels contain information about the percentage of your daily fat allotment in a serving of food.

For example, a food that has six grams of fat per serving provides 10 percent of the daily fat allotment in a 2,000 calorie diet.

Balance higher-fat foods with lower-fat vegetables, fruits, and grains.

---

more cholesterol is ready for delivery than the cells can take, LDL cholesterol deposits the extra cholesterol on the artery walls. A lot of LDL cholesterol in your blood *increases* your risk of heart disease and stroke.

HDL works like a garbage truck. It removes excess cholesterol from the bloodstream and takes it to the liver. A lot of HDL cholesterol *decreases* your risk of heart disease and stroke.

Cholesterol Screening

Not everyone needs to have their cholesterol level checked. If you are a man over 45 or a woman over 55 years of age, cholesterol testing may be beneficial.

Normally, testing is not necessary unless you have one of the following risk factors for coronary artery disease (heart disease):

• Family history of premature coronary artery disease (before age 55 in father or brother; before age 65 in mother or sister)

• Smoking

• High blood pressure (over 140/90) or taking high blood pressure medication

• Diabetes

• Abdominal obesity

It's a good idea to have your cholesterol checked if you have:

• Physical signs of high blood cholesterol or family members (mother, father, sister, brother, child) with high blood cholesterol

• Coronary artery disease (heart disease)

However, experts don't agree on the best schedule for cholesterol testing. Discuss with your doctor the schedule that is best for you, based on your risk factors.

High cholesterol is one of many risk factors that increase your risk of heart disease. Smoking, high blood pressure, and lack of exercise may be more important than your cholesterol level in increasing your risk of heart disease.

Whether or not your total cholesterol, HDL, and LDL are in the desirable range, you may wish to consult with a health professional to plan diet and lifestyle changes.

You can also follow the recommendations listed on page 257 under "15 Simple Ways to Reduce Fat" and refer to Chapter 16 for fitness and exercise tips. (See table at right for an explanation of HDL, LDL, and total cholesterol levels).

For most people, a low-fat diet (see page 257) and exercise are all they need to lower cholesterol. People who have heart disease (or who are at very high risk) may need medication as well as exercise and a low-fat diet to lower their cholesterol.

How to Reduce Your Cholesterol

- Eat less total fat. Because a high-fat diet increases cholesterol, just cutting back on cholesterol is not enough. You must cut back on total fats as well. See page 257.

- Buy a cooking oil that is liquid at room temperature (such as canola, corn, olive, soybean, sunflower, or cottonseed oil) and use less of it.

What Do the Numbers Mean?

The most commonly used cholesterol numbers for determining your risk of heart disease are listed here.

Desirable: All of the following:

- Total cholesterol below 5.2 mmol/l

- HDL cholesterol above 0.9 mmol/l for men or above 1.1 mmol/l for women

- LDL cholesterol below 3.4 mmol/l

- Total to HDL ratio below 3.5

- LDL to HDL ratio lower than 3

Borderline high-risk: One or more of the following:

- Total cholesterol between 5.2 and 6.2 mmol/l

- LDL cholesterol between 3.4 and 4.1 mmol/l

- Total to HDL ratio 3.5 to 4.5

High-risk: One or more of the following:

- Total cholesterol above 6.2 mmol/l

- HDL cholesterol below 0.9 mmol/l for men or below 1.1 mmol/l for women

- Total to HDL ratio 4.5 or higher

- LDL to HDL ratio 3 or higher

- Eat two to three servings (50 g to 100 g or three to four ounces) of baked or broiled fish per week. Most fish contain omega-3 fatty acids that help lower blood cholesterol and triglycerides. In general, fish with darker flesh, such as mackerel, lake trout, herring, salmon, and halibut, have more omega-3 oils. The safety and value of fish-oil supplements is not yet known.

• Exercise more. Exercise increases your protective HDL cholesterol level.

• Quit smoking to increase your HDL levels and reduce your risk of heart disease.

• Lose weight. Losing even 5 to 10 pounds can increase HDL levels and lower your total cholesterol.

• Eat more soluble fibre, which lowers overall cholesterol. See page 255.

Reversing Heart Disease

A low-fat diet and lifestyle changes may actually reverse the process of heart disease and help reopen arteries that are clogged by plaque.

Participants in the Lifestyle Heart Trial followed a vegetarian diet containing less than 10 percent of calories from fat and no caffeine. They also stopped smoking, got 30 minutes of exercise at least six days a week, and practised a relaxation technique (deep breathing, stretching, progressive muscle relaxation, etc.) for one hour each day. After a year, over 80 percent of the participants had lost weight, reduced their cholesterol, and most importantly, reduced the amount of blockage in their coronary arteries.

For more information, see Resource 74 on page 306.

• Attend a low-fat diet workshop, consult a registered dietitian, or read Resource 97 on page 308 to learn ways to lower your fat intake to 30 percent, 20 percent, or less of total calories, based on your goal.

Protein

Protein is important for maintaining healthy muscles, tendons, bones, skin, hair, blood, and internal organs. Most adults get all the protein they need.

Protein deficiencies are rare. If you eat animal products (milk, cheese, eggs, fish, meat), your diet will contain plenty of protein. Even if you don't eat animal products (vegans), if your diet includes a wide variety of vegetables, legumes, fruits, breads and cereals, you will get all the protein you need.

Vitamins

Vitamins are exciting! These 13 tiny, unseen elements of food have no calories, yet are essential to good health.

Vitamins A, D, E, and K are fat-soluble and can be stored in the liver or fat tissue for a relatively long time. The other nine vitamins are water-soluble and can be retained by the body for only short periods. They include:

• Thiamine

• Riboflavin

• Niacin

• Pantothenic acid

• Biotin

• Folate (folic acid)

• Vitamin B_6

• Vitamin B_{12}

• Vitamin C

For most people, a diet that contains a variety of foods from Canada's Food Guide to Healthy Eating (pages 253 and 254) provides all the vitamins needed for good health.

If you eat less than 1500 calories per day, consider a low-dose vitamin-mineral supplement (see page 263).

Minerals

Minerals help regulate the body's water balance, hormones, enzymes, vitamins, and fluids. Minerals must be maintained in a delicate balance to ensure proper functioning of the systems they serve. Eating a variety of foods is the best way to get all the minerals you need.

A total of 60 minerals have been discovered in the body, and 22 are essential to health. We know the most about calcium, sodium, and iron.

The Recommended Daily Intakes for Calcium	
Age	**Calcium (mg/day)**
1-2 years	500
2-3 years	550
4-6 years	600
7-9 years	700
10-12 years	male 900 female 1100
13-15 years	male 1100 female 1000
16-18 years	male 900 female 700
19-49 years	male 800 female 700
50+	male 800 female 800

Calcium

Calcium is the primary mineral needed for building and maintaining strong bones. Calcium is especially important to growing children and women, especially in the peak bone-building years between the teens

---

Lactose Intolerance

People whose bodies produce too little of the enzyme lactase have trouble digesting the lactose sugar in milk. Symptoms of lactose intolerance include gas, bloating, cramps, and diarrhea after drinking milk or eating dairy products.

Tips for dealing with lactose intolerance include:

- Eat small amounts of dairy products at any one time.

- Drink milk only with snacks or meals.

- Try cheese, which usually does not cause symptoms. Most of the lactose is removed during processing.

- Yogurts made with active cultures provide their own enzymes and cause fewer tolerance problems.

- Pretreated milk, enzyme treatments, and enzyme tablets (LactAid) are available in most stores.

- If you cannot tolerate milk in any form, include other calcium-rich foods in your diet. See left.

- Severe lactose intolerance may increase your need for calcium supplements. Ask your doctor.

and early 30s. Calcium also helps women prevent osteoporosis, which can occur after menopause. See page 71.

A cup of skim milk has about 313 mg of calcium. Nonfat and low-fat yogurt has 442 mg per cup. Other good sources of dietary calcium include broccoli, greens, kidney beans, and low-fat cheese.

While dietary calcium is preferred, low-dose calcium supplements can also help keep bones strong. One 500-mg TUMS (calcium carbonate) tablet provides about 200 mg of calcium. A few TUMS tablets per day can help adults meet their calcium needs, but should not replace natural forms of calcium such as milk and other dairy products, tofu, soy milk, broccoli, or greens.

Sodium

Salt is the most familiar source of sodium. About 40 percent of salt is pure sodium. Sodium is also hidden in foods that don't taste salty, such as cheddar cheese and processed foods. Sodium is also a major ingredient of monosodium glutamate (MSG), disodium phosphate, and baking powder.

Most people get far more sodium than they need. Our bodies need only 500 mg of sodium per day. Anything over 2500 mg of sodium per day is probably too much.

For some people, excess sodium causes high blood pressure. If you are not sodium-sensitive, salt may not be a problem for you. See page 26.

Creative Salt Substitute

Mix together and put in a shaker:

2.5 ml (½ teaspoon) cayenne pepper

2.5 ml (½ teaspoon) garlic powder

5 ml (1 teaspoon) each:

Basil	Onion Powder
Black pepper	Parsley
Mace	Sage
Marjoram	Savory
Thyme	

If you want to cut back on the sodium in your diet:

• Limit ready-mixed sauces and seasonings, frozen dinners, canned soups, and salad dressings, which are usually packed with sodium. Low-sodium products contain 50 percent less sodium than regular products.

• Eat lots of fresh or frozen fruits and vegetables. These foods have very little sodium.

• Don't put the salt shaker on the table or get a shaker that lets very little salt come out. Or, use salt substitute sparingly.

• Always measure the salt in recipes and use half of what is called for.

Iron

The body needs small amounts of iron to make hemoglobin, which carries oxygen in the blood. Adults need about 10 to 15 mg of iron per day. People who have increased blood loss

Vitamin-Mineral Supplement Buyer's Guide

Research shows that vitamins from food may prevent some diseases, but it remains unproven whether supplements do the same. However, if you choose to take vitamin and mineral supplements, the following guidelines may be helpful:

• Choose a balanced, multiple vitamin-mineral supplement rather than a specific vitamin or mineral, unless it has been prescribed by a doctor. Too much of any one vitamin or mineral might be toxic and can interfere with the body's ability to use other vitamins and minerals.

• Choose a supplement that provides about 100 percent of the RNI (Canadian Recommended Nutrient Intakes) for vitamins and minerals.

• Avoid taking much more than 100 percent of the RNI for any vitamin or mineral. This is particularly important for the fat-soluble vitamins A, D, E, and K and for minerals. Because they are stored in the body, large doses can build up to toxic levels.

• Don't use a supplement to make up for a poor diet.

• High-priced brand-name vitamins are no better than store or generic brands.

• Check expiration dates.

from ulcers or heavy menstrual periods, or who regularly take aspirin, blood thinners (anticoagulants), or arthritis medications, may need more iron. An inexpensive blood test can determine if you need additional iron.

To get more iron in your blood:

• Vitamin C helps you absorb more iron from food. Drink a glass of orange or other citrus juice and eat a bowl of iron-enriched cereal. High-iron cereals have at least 25 percent of the Canadian Recommended Nutrient Intakes.

• Increase absorption of vegetable iron by eating meat, poultry, or fish along with the vegetables. The iron in animal tissue improves the absorption of the iron in vegetables.

Iron Supplements

Women who menstruate and who eat less than 1500 calories per day may wish to consider a multivitamin-mineral supplement that contains iron. (Men are much less likely to need iron supplements.) A low-dose ferrous-form iron supplement containing no more than 20 mg is safe for most women. However, too much iron can cause a number of serious medical problems or mask the development of others. Do not take more than 20 mg without consulting your doctor. Take the supplement with orange or other citrus juice. Keep iron supplements away from children.

Iron Deficiency Anemia

Chronic blood loss of any kind depletes the body's store of iron. Symptoms of iron deficiency anemia include paleness and fatigue. A blood test is needed to confirm the diagnosis because anemia has many causes.

A Healthy Weight

People come in all shapes and sizes. Genetics, exercise, and the food you eat all play a role in determining your body's shape and size.

Focus on Health, Not Weight

Eating well, enjoying physical activity, and accepting your body size are the keys to good health. Although excess body fat does increase your risks of heart disease, diabetes, and stroke, it is more important to focus on healthy habits rather than trying to achieve a certain body size or shape.

Eating healthy, lower-fat foods and adding regular physical activity to your life can help you lose weight and establish some good health habits that you can maintain for life.

Exercise Makes It Easier

Regular exercise makes you feel stronger, more energetic, and in better overall health. As a bonus, regular exercise makes maintaining a healthy weight a little easier.

Even small amounts of exercise, done every day or every other day, can make a big difference. Pick an exercise you enjoy enough to stick with for a long time. Even a five-minute walk every day is a good start. Add more exercise when you can.

Exercise Keeps You Strong

Exercise helps build your lean muscle mass when you are losing weight. One of the biggest problems with diets is that if you don't exercise while you diet, you will lose both fat and lean muscle mass. Dieters often suffer from weakness and low energy. If you are trying to lose weight, include a regular exercise program.

Never Go Hungry

Skipping meals is not a good way to lose weight. Going hungry, even for a few hours, can cause your metabolic rate to drop and make you more likely to overeat later. Take time to savor your food and relax during meals.

Focus on Reducing Fat, Not Calories

Eat a variety of nutritious, low-fat foods. Rather than counting calories, focus on eating more fruits and vegetables and less fat. See the ways to reduce fat on page 257.

Get Help From Your Friends

The food customs and habits of friends and family affect what you eat. Ask friends and family to:

- Encourage you to respect yourself regardless of what you weigh.

- Celebrate events with a variety of nutritious foods and activities that everyone can enjoy.

- Serve low-fat options with meals, and make water and low-fat snacks available.

- Offer small servings, and don't insist on second helpings.

- Join you in a walk, swim, or other enjoyable activity.

Help Yourself to Good Thoughts

Develop a positive attitude about your-self. Think of yourself as healthy, and take pride in making positive nutrition and exercise choices. Focus on living a healthy life regardless of your weight.

Nutrition for Children

Focus your whole family's diet on whole grains, fruits, vegetables, low-fat dairy products, and lean meats. Offer a wide variety of choices, but don't force a child to eat an unwanted food. Respect your child's ability to decide how much food to eat.

- Limit the amount of sugar in infants' and toddlers' diets. Your children can learn to enjoy healthy sweets, such as fruits.

- Avoid using food as a reward or punishment.

Child-Sized Environment

Imagine yourself eating at a giant's table. That's how a child can feel eating at an adult-sized table in an adult-sized chair.

- Provide a booster seat and child-sized utensils. However, fingers are fine until a child can hold utensils easily.

- Give children smaller plates and smaller servings (one tablespoon per year of age is a good serving size guide). Let the child ask for seconds.

Food Allergies

Less than one percent of adults have true food allergies. Most adverse reactions to foods are due to food intolerances, reactions to food additives, or food poisoning. Most true food allergies are to legumes, nuts, shellfish, eggs, wheat, and milk. An allergic reaction to a food can result in ana-phylactic shock. See page 83.

Consider breast-feeding your child for at least the first six months if either parent has a history of any allergy, including hay fever. Children who are breast-fed develop fewer food allergies than those who are not. By gradually introducing simple solid foods into your child's diet, any allergy will be more easily found. Children often outgrow food allergies by age six. If your child was allergic to a food when younger, try rein-troducing it as he gets older (unless the reaction was severe).

Healthy Snacks

Young children have small stomachs and high energy needs, so they need frequent snacks to supplement meals. Plan between-meal snacks as part of the day's total food intake. They should provide good nutrition, not just empty calories.

- Fruits and fruit juices are good snacks. Other good choices are raw vegetable sticks with fat-free dress-ing, cereal, yogurt, cheese, or soup.

- Serve meals and snacks on a regular schedule. Do not serve snacks so close to a meal that they interfere with the child's appetite.

- Choose cookies and other desserts that are low in fat and high in nutrients. Fig bars or oatmeal raisin cookies are good choices.

- For more information on feeding children, see Resource 43 on page 305.

Diabetes

The starches, sugars, fats, and protein in the food you eat are converted to glucose, a sugar that your body uses for fuel. Insulin is a hormone produced by the pancreas to control the amount of glucose in the blood. Without insulin, the body cannot use or store glucose, so too much glucose stays in the blood.

Type I, or insulin-dependent diabetes mellitus (IDDM), occurs when the pancreas fails to make enough insulin. It usually occurs in childhood or adolescence, but can develop at any age. People with type I diabetes must inject insulin every day.

Type II, or non-insulin-dependent diabetes mellitus (NIDDM), occurs when body cells become resistant to insulin. This reduces the amount of glucose that can be used by the cells at any one time. Type II diabetes is more common among adults, especially those who are overweight and over age 40.

Many people with type II diabetes are able to control their blood sugar through weight control, regular exercise, and a sensible diet. Some may need insulin injections and/or oral medications to lower blood sugar.

Risk factors for type II diabetes include:

- Age 40 or over

- Overweight (20 percent more than ideal weight)

- Family history of diabetes

- African-American, Hispanic, or Aboriginal origin

The symptoms of diabetes are vague, and by themselves, seldom lead to a doctor visit. They include:

- Increased thirst

- Frequent urination (especially at night)

- Increased appetite

- Unexplained weight loss

- Fatigue

- Skin infections

- Slow-healing wounds

- Recurrent vaginitis

- Difficulty with erections

- Blurred vision

- Tingling or numbness in hands or feet

A blood test is needed to accurately diagnose diabetes. Blood glucose tests are inexpensive and very low risk. Ask your doctor if you should eat or fast before the test.

Prevention

At this time, there is no known way to prevent type I diabetes.

In most cases, the risk of type II diabetes can be reduced by regular exercise (see Chapter 16) and by maintaining a healthy body weight.

Home Treatment

- Believe that you can control diabetes. Diabetes requires making significant, long-term lifestyle changes, and can be overwhelming at first. Focus on making one change at a time, and soon you will have good control over your life and your diabetes.

- Take good care of your feet. Diabetes impairs nerve function and blood flow to the feet, increasing your risk of infection. Take care to avoid cuts and sores, and promptly treat any injuries to your feet.

- Get regular eye exams. Eye changes caused by diabetes often have no symptoms until they are quite advanced. Early treatment may slow their progress and save your sight.

- Eat a healthful diet to help keep your blood sugar in control and maintain a healthy weight. Pay special attention to eating low-fat foods and to the other eating recommendations in this chapter.

- Get regular aerobic exercise to help regulate your blood sugar, reduce your risk of heart disease, and control your weight. Work closely with your doctor to determine how your activity level affects your blood glucose levels and medication needs.

- Depending on how strictly you are controlling your blood sugar levels and how difficult they are to control, you may wish to track the following daily:

  ○ The time and content of each meal.

  ○ The kind and amount of exercise you get.

  ○ How tired or energetic you feel.

  ○ If you have a home glucose monitor, check your blood sugar level as directed by your doctor.

This record will help you understand how your body reacts to different foods and exercise, so you can correct glucose imbalances before they get out of control.

- If drugs are prescribed to control your blood sugar, take them as directed. Too little medication will make your blood sugar higher than normal; too much will make it lower than normal. As you improve your diet and exercise, you may need less medicine. Check with your doctor.

- The Canadian Diabetes Society is a good resource for more information on diabetes.

When to Call a Health Professional

- If a person with diabetes loses consciousness.

- If signs of high blood sugar develop in a person who has diabetes:

  ○ Frequent urination

  ○ Intense thirst

  ○ Dim vision

  ○ Rapid breathing

  ○ Fruity smelling breath

- If signs of low blood sugar persist longer than 15 minutes after a person who has diabetes has eaten something containing sugar:

  - Fatigue, weakness, nausea

  - Hunger

  - Double or blurred vision

  - Pounding heart

  - Confusion, irritability, appearance of drunkenness

- If your blood sugar levels fall outside the range your doctor has recommended.

- For a blood glucose test, if you suspect diabetes but have not been diagnosed.

He who laughs, lasts.
Mary Pettibone Poole

Chapter 18

Mental Self-Care and Mental Wellness

Mental health problems are similar to other health problems: some can be prevented; others will go away on their own with a little care and home treatment; and some need professional attention.

This chapter is organized in two sections. The first section, Mental Self-Care, covers some common mental and emotional health problems and describes what you can do at home and when you should seek professional help.

The second section, Mental Wellness, describes how you can use your mind and emotions to boost your immune system and improve your health.

Mental Self-Care

Medical science is discovering that mental health problems often have a physical cause. Psychological

problems are no longer thought of as character weaknesses or flaws.

We now know that mental health problems can begin when psychological or emotional stress (such as the loss of a loved one) triggers chemical imbalances in the brain. While some people can withstand more stress than others, nobody is immune to mental illness.

Because mental health problems have both physical and psychological causes, both self-care and professional care are often needed. The goal is to reduce stress and to restore the normal chemical balance in the brain.

Seeking Professional Help

This chapter does not cover all mental health problems. If you have mental or emotional symptoms that are not addressed here, contact your health professional. In general, it is a good idea to seek professional help when:

- A symptom becomes severe or disruptive.

- A disruptive symptom becomes a continuous or permanent pattern of behaviour and does not respond to self-care efforts.

- Symptoms become numerous and affect all areas of your life and do not respond to self-care or communication efforts.

- You are thinking of suicide.

There is a wide range of professional and lay resources to choose from for mental health problems.

Family doctors: Mental health problems may have physical causes. Your doctor can review your medical history and medications for clues, provide some counseling, prescribe medications, or refer you to other resources.

Psychiatrists: Psychiatrists are medical doctors who specialize in mental disorders. They counsel patients, prescribe medications, and order medical treatments.

Psychologists, social workers, and counselors: These professionals receive special training in helping people deal with mental health problems. They help patients identify, understand, and work through disturbing thoughts and emotions.

Therapist Selection Tips

Here are some ways to improve your likelihood of finding the therapy that's right for you.

- Ask people you trust for a good referral.

- Ask mental health professionals to help you identify the real problem and develop a self-management plan to resolve it.

- Emphasize the importance of self-care in your treatment plan.

- Ask about group therapy options.

- Cultivate special friends, join support groups, or look for peer counseling opportunities. Understanding and acceptance can help you resolve the problem.

- Check out 12-step programs such as Alcoholics Anonymous, Overeaters Anonymous, and other groups that can help you deal with addiction problems. Such programs are usually free, effective, and available in most communities.

Pastors: People often turn to their clergy for counseling and advice in times of emotional distress. Many pastors have formal training in counseling, and many do not.

Support groups: Talking with others who are coping with the same problem is often helpful. See Resource 108 on page 308.

Alcohol and Drug Problems

The overuse or abuse of alcohol or other drugs is called substance abuse. It is common, costly, and associated with many medical problems.

Alcohol Problems

A person has an **alcohol problem** if his use of alcohol interferes with health or daily living. A person develops **alcoholism** if he or she becomes physically or psychologically dependent on alcohol.

Long-term heavy drinking causes liver, nerve, heart and brain damage, high blood pressure, stomach problems, sexual problems, and cancer. Alcohol abuse can also lead to violence, accidents, social isolation, and difficulties at work and home or with the law.

Symptoms of an alcohol problem include personality changes, blackouts, drinking more and more for the same "high," and denial of the problem. A person with alcoholism may gulp or sneak drinks, drink alone or early in the morning, and suffer from the shakes. He may also have family or work problems, or get in trouble with the law due to his drinking.

Alcohol abuse patterns vary. Some people get drunk every day. Some drink large amounts of alcohol at specific times, such as weekends. Others may be sober for long periods and then go on a drinking binge that lasts for weeks or months.

Someone with alcoholism may suffer serious withdrawal symptoms (such as trembling, delusions, hallucinations, sweating, and seizures) if he or she stops drinking suddenly ("cold turkey"). Once alcohol dependency develops, it becomes very difficult to abstain without outside help. Medical detoxification may be needed.

Drug Problems

Drug abuse includes the use of marijuana, cocaine, heroin, or other "street drugs," and the abuse of legal prescription drugs. Some people turn to drugs as a way to get a "high" or to deal with stress and emotional problems.

Tranquilizers, sedatives, painkillers, and amphetamines are misused most often, sometimes unintentionally.

Signs of Drug Use

- Chronic red eyes, sore throat, dry cough, and fatigue (in the absence of allergies).

- Major changes in sleeping or eating habits.

- Moodiness, hostility, or abusive behavior.

- Work or school problems, absenteeism.

- Loss of interest in favourite activities.

- Social withdrawal or changes in friends.

- Stealing, lying, and poor family relationships.

Drug dependence or addiction occurs when you develop a physical or psychological "need" for a drug. You may not be aware that you have become dependent on a drug until you try to stop taking it suddenly. Withdrawing from the drug can cause uncomfortable symptoms such as muscle aches, diarrhea, or depression. The usual treatment is to gradually reduce the dose of the drug until it can be stopped completely.

Screening Test

Many people will deny that they have a problem with alcohol or other drugs. The questions in the "Are You a Problem User?" chart on page 273 may help you, or others, recognize a problem.

Answering yes to two or more questions raises the possibility of an alcohol or drug problem and the need to seek help.

Prevention

- Look for signs of mental stress. Try to understand and resolve sources of depression, anxiety, or loneliness. Don't use alcohol or drugs to deal with these problems.

- If you drink, do so in moderation: less than two drinks a day for men and one drink a day for women. One drink is 360 ml (12 ounces) of beer, 150 ml (5 ounces) of wine, or 45 ml (1½ ounces) of hard liquor.

- Provide nonalcoholic beverages at parties and meals.

- Ask your pharmacist or doctor if any of your current medications could potentially lead to overuse or dependency. Be especially cautious of painkillers, tranquilizers, sedatives, and sleeping pills. Follow the instructions carefully, and do not exceed the recommended dose.

- Do not regularly use medications to sleep, lose weight, or relax without careful supervision by your doctor. Seek non-drug solutions.

- Do not suddenly stop taking any medication without your doctor's supervision. Serious symptoms can result if some medications are abruptly withdrawn.

- Avoid alcohol when you are taking medications. Alcohol can react with many drugs and cause serious complications.

Home Treatment

- Recognize early signs that alcohol or drug use is becoming a problem. See page 273.

- Attend an Alcoholics Anonymous meeting (a self-help group devoted to helping members get sober and stay sober).

- If you are concerned about another person's alcohol or drug use:

  ○ Never ignore the problem. Discuss it as a medical problem.

  ○ Build up his self-esteem and reaffirm his value as a person. Help him see that his life can be successful without alcohol or drugs. Let him know you will support his efforts to change.

◦ Ask if he would accept help. Don't give up after the first no; keep asking. When he agrees, act that very day to arrange for help. Call a health professional or Alcoholics Anonymous for an immediate appointment.

◦ Attend a few meetings of Al-Anon, a support group for family members and friends of alcoholics. Read some 12-step program information.

When to Call a Health Professional

• If you answer yes to two or more questions on the "Are You a Problem User?" chart below.

• If you recognize an alcohol or drug problem and are ready to accept help. Both outpatient and inpatient treatment programs are available.

Are You a Problem User?

Answer the questions honestly. Answer "yes" if the statement is true for alcohol or drugs (including prescribed, recreational, or illegal substances that can be described as mood-altering).

1. Have you ever tried to stop using alcohol or drugs for a week or so but could stop for only a couple of days?

2. Do you resent the advice of others who try to get you to stop or cut down your use of alcohol or drugs?

3. Have you tried to control your use of alcohol or drugs by changing from one type of drink or drug to another?

4. Do you envy people who can use alcohol or drugs without getting into trouble?

5. Has your use of alcohol or drugs impaired your family relationships, your work, your driving safety, or any other aspect of your life?

6. During the past year, have you missed days of work because of your use of alcohol or drugs?

7. Do you tell yourself you can stop using alcohol or drugs any time you want?

8. Do you sometimes go on binges with alcohol or drugs?

9. Do you ever have blackouts related to your alcohol or drug use?

10. Have you ever felt that your life would be better if you did not use alcohol or drugs?

If you answer "yes" to two or more questions, you may have a problem with alcohol or drugs. If so, talk with a health professional.

Anger and Hostility

Anger signals your body to prepare for a fight. When you get angry, adrenalin and other hormones are released into the blood stream. Blood pressure goes up.

Hostility is being ready for a fight all the time. Continual hostility keeps your blood pressure high and may increase your risk for heart attack and other illnesses. Being hostile also isolates you from other people.

Home Treatment

- Notice when you start getting angry. Don't ignore anger until it erupts.

- Identify the cause of the anger.

- Express anger in a healthy way:

  ○ Count to 10. Give your adrenalin level a little time to go down.

  ○ Try screaming or yelling in a private place, not at others.

  ○ Go for a short walk or jog.

  ○ Talk about it with a friend.

  ○ Draw or paint to release the anger.

  ○ Write in a daily journal.

- Use "I" statements, not "you" statements, to discuss your anger. Say "I feel angry when my needs are not being met," instead of "You make me mad when you are so inconsiderate."

- Forgive and forget. Forgiving helps lower blood pressure and ease muscle tension so you can feel more relaxed.

- Read books on anger and how to handle it. See Resources 18 to 20 on page 303.

- See page 282 for additional information on anger and violent behavior.

When to Call a Health Professional

- If anger has led or could lead to violence or harm to you or someone else.

- If anger or hostility interferes with your work, family, or friends.

Anxiety

Feeling worried, anxious, and nervous is a normal part of everyday life. Everyone frets or feels anxious from time to time. However, when anxiety becomes overwhelming and interferes with daily life, it is not normal.

Anxiety can cause both physical and emotional symptoms:

Physical Symptoms

- Trembling, twitching, or shaking

- Muscle tension, aches, or soreness

- Restlessness

- Fatigue

- Insomnia

- Breathlessness or rapid heartbeat

- Sweating or cold, clammy hands

Emotional Symptoms

- Feeling keyed up and on edge

- Excessive worrying

- Fearing that something bad is going to happen

- Poor concentration

- Excessive startle response

- Irritability or agitation

- Constant sadness

Anxiety from a specific situation or fear can cause some or all of these symptoms for a short time. When the situation passes, the symptoms subside.

Many people, including children and adolescents, develop anxiety disorders in which many of these symptoms occur when there is no identifiable cause.

Phobias and panic disorder are two common anxiety-related disorders. **Phobias** are irrational, involuntary fears of common places, objects, or situations. **Panic disorder** is characterized by distinct periods of intense fear and anxiety that occur when there is no clear cause or danger. Physical symptoms that may occur during a panic attack include hyperventilation, shaking, pounding of the heart, and feeling faint. Self-care, often combined with professional treatment, can be effective in managing these disorders.

Home Treatment

The following home treatment tips can relieve simple anxiety and also help in combination with medical care.

- Recognize and accept your anxiety about specific fears or situations. Then say to yourself, "Okay, I see the problem. Now I'll start to deal with it."

- Be kind to your body:

  ○ Relieve tension with vigorous exercise or massage.

  ○ Practise relaxation techniques. See page 248.

  ○ Get enough rest. If you have trouble sleeping, see Sleep Problems on page 280.

  ○ Avoid alcohol, caffeine, chocolate, and nicotine. They increase your anxiety level.

- Engage your mind:

  ○ Get out and do something you enjoy, such as going to a funny movie or taking a walk or a hike.

  ○ Plan your day. Having too much or too little to do can make you more anxious.

- Keep a record of your symptoms. Discuss your fears with a good friend. Confiding with others sometimes relieves stress.

- Get involved in social groups or volunteer to help others. Being alone makes things seem worse than they are.

- Learn more about anxiety. See Resources 21 to 23 on pages 303 and 304.

When to Call a Health Professional

- If anxiety interferes with your daily activities.

- If symptoms are severe and one week of home treatment has not helped.

- If you have sudden, severe attacks of fear or anxiety with intense physical symptoms (shaking, sweating) when there is no apparent reason to be afraid.

- If intense, irrational fears of common places, objects, or situations interfere with your daily life.

- If you suffer from nightmares or flashbacks to traumatic events.

- If you are unable to feel certain about things (e.g., whether you unplugged the iron) no matter how many times you check, or if repetitive, compulsive behaviors interfere with your daily activities.

Depression

Most people experience some form of depression at some point in their lives. Depression can range from a minor problem to a major life-threatening illness. Depression is treatable. For many people, treatment can mean a whole new life.

Medical science is getting closer to understanding depression. Most major depressions involve an imbalance of chemical messengers (neurotransmitters) in the brain. Many things can trigger these imbalances:

- Loss of a loved one or something that is highly valued

- Chronic stress or a stressful event

- Major illness

- Reaction to medications

- Alcoholism, drug abuse, dementia, and other mental health problems

---

Sadness or Depression?

If you have experienced four or more of the following symptoms nearly every day for more than two weeks, you may be suffering from depression:

- Feelings of sadness, anxiety, or hopelessness

- Lack of interest or pleasure in usual activities or pastimes

- Increase or decrease in appetite or unexplained gain or loss of weight

- Frequent backaches, headaches, stomach problems, or other aches that don't respond to treatment

- Insomnia or excessive sleepiness

- Low energy, fatigue, tiredness

- Feeling restless or irritable

- Feeling worthless or guilty

- Inability to concentrate, remember, or make decisions

- Frequent thoughts of suicide or death

Home treatment (see page 277) may be all that is needed for mild depression. However, if you are feeling suicidal or if home treatment doesn't help lift your mood within two weeks, contact a health professional. With counseling and medication, and continued home treatment, you can overcome most cases of depression.

- Reduced daylight during the winter seems to cause a form of depression called seasonal affective disorder in some people. See page 277.

Some people are genetically suscept-ible to chemical imbalances in the brain. Fortunately, effective treat-ments are available for them and others at high risk of depression.

Everyone gets sad. Gauging how deep and pervasive your sad feelings are can help you decide what to do. See "Sadness or Depression?" on page 276 to help determine if you are suf-fering from depression.

Feeling sad doesn't always mean you are heading for a major depression. Bad news or a disappointment can make you feel sad, perhaps for several days. This is normal and healthy as long as those sad feelings don't con-tinue indefinitely. Grief can also cause a normal sadness. See page 278.

Home Treatment

Most people will improve or recover from depression. Self-care may be enough to pull you out of a mild depression. For more serious depres-sion, self-care can add to the benefits of professional treatment.

- At the first sign of depression, ask a friend for some extra attention. You can lose objectivity about yourself when you feel blue.

- Consider what might be causing or adding to your depression:

  ○ Are medications causing it? Review your prescription and over-the-counter medications with a pharmacist or doctor.

  ○ If it's wintertime or you haven't been out in the sun for a while, read the information about sea-sonal affective disorder at right.

Seasonal Affective Disorder (Winter Depression)

There is increasing evidence (not yet conclusive) that a lack of sun-light during winter months can cause depression in some people. Symptoms include melancholy moods, changes in sleeping habits, cravings for sweets and starchy foods, and chronic fatigue. If you notice such a pattern developing during the winter, consider the following:

- When the sun does shine, go outside and soak it up. Protect your skin—it is the eye's expo-sure to sunlight that makes the difference.

- Go south for a sunny vacation, if you can.

- Some people may benefit from some form of light therapy (phototherapy). This may include sitting in front of bright, full-spectrum fluorescent lights for one to five hours a day or other approaches. Depression often improves by the end of the first week of daily treatments.

Light therapy should be super-vised by a health professional.

- Stay active. It is easier to *do* yourself into *feeling* better than to *feel* yourself into *doing* better.

- Get regular exercise. If nothing else, go for long walks. They help to clear the mind.

- Look for a laugh. Laughter, like exercise, can help restore balance to your system.

- Boost your self-esteem. Read the Mental Wellness section of this chapter.

Grief

Grief is a natural healing process that allows you to adjust to a significant change or loss. Grief may be expressed physically or emotionally, and may have some of the same symptoms as depression. The following tips may help ease the grieving process.

- Take as much time as you need to grieve. Review mementos, play nostalgic music, and read old letters.

- Let yourself cry. If you can let go and sob, do it.

- Talk about your grief with a friend. If your friend tells you to "snap out of it," find a more sympathetic listener. Your clergy may also help you understand and deal with your loss.

- Friends may feel awkward about mentioning your loss. Let them know it is alright to talk about it.

- See Resources 70 to 72 on page 306.

- Believe that this mood will pass. Then, look for signs that it is ending.

- Surround yourself with happy, upbeat people.

- Books can help. See Resource 86 on page 307.

When to Call a Health Professional

Because many things can contribute to depression, combining self-care and professional treatment is often most effective. The most common form of treatment combines counseling (psychotherapy) with medication. Inpatient treatment is sometimes needed in severe cases. Call for help:

- If you are feeling suicidal.

- If you suspect you are very depressed. See "Sadness or Depression?" on page 276.

- If you suspect you are depressed and two weeks of home treatment has not helped.

Eating Disorders

In a society where "thin is in," many of us have tried skipping meals or going on diets to lose weight. Unlike dieting, eating disorders are medical problems that cause disturbances in eating behavior.

Anorexia nervosa is a disorder of severe self-imposed dieting. It affects teenage girls most often. Symptoms include refusing to eat, extreme weight loss, a distorted body image (thinking she's fat when she is actually very thin), a preoccupation with food, low self-esteem, and excessive physical exercise.

Bulimia nervosa is an eating disorder characterized by binge eating and purging (forced vomiting or abuse of laxatives and diuretics). The binges are usually triggered by emotional upset, not hunger. Other symptoms include dry skin and brittle hair, swollen glands under the jaw from vomiting, depression and mood swings, a distorted body image, and secrecy to keep others from discovering their abnormal behavior.

People who have anorexia usually look starved, but most people who have bulimia maintain a normal weight and look healthy. Most people with anorexia deny they have a problem; people with bulimia know that they do, but keep it a secret.

Compulsive overeating is characterized by binging on food. An overeater will consume thousands of calories at a time, quickly and without pleasure. Because there is no purging, a compulsive overeater becomes obese.

Eating disorders appear to be caused by emotional and psychological factors. They tend to run in families, so there may be a genetic link.

Eating disorders require professional treatment. If untreated, they can lead to major health problems or even death. Treatment usually involves nutritional counseling, individual psychotherapy, and family therapy. A hospital stay may be required in extreme cases.

Prevention

- Teach and model healthy eating and exercise habits at home and at school.

- Help young people develop confidence and self-esteem. Accept them for who they are.

- Be careful about encouraging a young person to lose weight. Communicate that you love and care for her, regardless of how much she weighs.

- Don't set unrealistic expectations for your child. Striving to live up to them may lead to an eating disorder.

- Be alert to the stress in your child's life. Be available to talk over any problems.

When to Call a Health Professional

If you recognize any of these warning signs of an eating disorder:

- Body weight is a primary measure of self-worth.

- Having an unrealistic body image and an unrealistic fear of gaining weight.

- Significant unexplained weight loss or gain.

- Constant dieting on highly restricted diets.

- Obsessive exercise routines, especially leading to injury.

- Withdrawal from family and friends.

Sleep Problems

The term insomnia can mean:

• Trouble getting to sleep (taking more than 45 minutes to fall asleep).

• Frequent wakenings with inability to fall back to sleep.

• Early morning awakening.

However, none of these are problems unless they make you feel chronically tired. If you are less sleepy at night or wake up early, but still feel rested and alert, there is little need to worry.

Short-term insomnia, lasting from a few nights to a few weeks, is usually caused by worry over a stressful situation. Long-term insomnia, which can last months or even years, is often caused by general anxiety, medications, chronic pain, depression, or other physical disorders.

Sleep apnea is a sleep disorder usually caused by blockage in the upper airways. When airflow through the nose and mouth is blocked, breathing may stop for 10 seconds or longer. People who have sleep apnea usually snore loudly and are very tired during the day. It can affect children and adults.

Prevention

• Get regular exercise but avoid strenuous exercise within two hours before bedtime.

• Avoid alcohol and smoking before bedtime. Drink caffeine in moderation and not after noon.

• Drink a glass of warm milk at bedtime.

• Avoid drinking more than a glass of fluid before bedtime.

Home Treatment

• Don't take sleeping pills. They can cause daytime confusion, memory loss, and dizziness. Continued use of sleeping pills actually increases sleeplessness in many people.

• Try the following six-step formula for two weeks:

1. Use your bed for sleeping. Don't eat, watch TV, or even read in it.

2. Sleep only at bedtime. Don't take naps. (However, naps are fine if you don't have sleep problems.)

3. Forget "bedtime." Go to bed only when you feel sleepy.

4. If you lie awake for more than 15 minutes, get up and leave the bedroom.

5. Repeat steps 3 and 4 until it is time to get up.

6. Get up at the same time each day, no matter how sleepy you are.

• Review all of your prescription and over-the-counter medications with a pharmacist to rule out drug-related sleep problems.

• Read about anxiety on page 274.

When to Call a Health Professional

- If you suspect medications are causing sleep problems.
- If you or your partner snores loudly and heavily, and feels excessively sleepy during the day.
- If someone has an episode of sleep apnea (stops breathing, gasps, and chokes) during sleep.
- If your child snores, has difficulty breathing while asleep, sleeps restlessly and awakens frequently, or is very sleepy during the day.
- If a month of self-care doesn't solve the problem.

Suicide

If you are very depressed or feel overwhelmed, you may sometimes think of taking your own life. Occasional thoughts of suicide are not a problem. However, if thoughts of suicide continue, or if you have made suicide plans, it becomes a very serious matter.

People who are considering suicide are often undecided about choosing life or death. With compassionate help, they may choose to live.

Prevention

When you are depressed or when someone you know is depressed, be alert to the warning signs:

- Verbal warning. Up to 80 percent of people who commit suicide mention their intentions to someone.
- Preoccupation with death. A suicidal person may talk, read, draw, and write about death.
- Previous suicide attempt. Failed attempts are often followed by a successful attempt.
- Giving away prized possessions.
- Depression and social isolation. See page 276.

Home Treatment

- Use your common sense and a direct approach to determine if the suicide risk is high. Ask yourself or the person who you feel is at risk:
  - Do you feel there is no other way?
  - Do you have a suicide plan?
  - How and when do you plan to do it?
- Ask someone you trust to stay with you or the suicidal person until the crisis has passed.
- Encourage the person to seek professional help.
- Don't argue with ("It's not as bad as that") or challenge ("You're not the type") someone who is thinking of suicide.
- Don't ignore warning signs, thinking that you or another person will "snap out of it."
- Talk about the situation as openly as possible. Show understanding and compassion.

When to Call a Health Professional

- For urgent, life-threatening situations, call 911 or other emergency services.

- Call your doctor or your local Suicide Prevention hotline (look in the Yellow Pages):

  ○ If you are considering suicide.

  ○ If you suspect someone has made suicide plans.

Violent Behavior

Anger and arguments are normal parts of healthy relationships. However, anger that leads to threats or violence, such as hitting or hurting, is not normal or healthy. Physical, verbal, or sexual abuse is not an acceptable part of any relationship.

Violent behavior often begins with verbal threats or relatively minor incidents, but over time can become more serious, involving physical harm. Violent behavior seems to be mostly learned, so it is especially important to help your children learn that violence is not a healthy solution to conflict.

Prevention

- Seek nonviolent ways to resolve conflicts. Arguing is fine, even healthy, so long as it does not turn violent. See page 274 for more on controlling anger.

- Avoid using physical discipline so that your children will learn that violence is not a solution. If you need help with discipline, consider taking a course on parenting skills.

The best way to prevent violence with a firearm is not to keep firearms at home.

If you keep firearms at home:

- Make sure that no one in the home will have access to firearms or weapons unless they know how to use them safely.

- Lock up firearms unloaded. Lock ammunition in a separate place.

- Do not keep loaded firearms in a home where there are children or where there is someone who has a drug or alcohol problem, who is prone to violent behavior, or who has threatened suicide.

If a family member or someone else has threatened to harm you or your child:

- Tell someone: a trusted friend, clergy, or health professional.

- Identify local resources that can help in a crisis. Your local crisis line, health unit/public health office, women's centre or transition house, police department, or hospital has information on shelters and safe homes.

- Be alert to warning signs, such as threats or drunkenness, so that you can avoid a dangerous situation. If you can't predict when violence may occur, have an "exit plan" for use in an emergency.

When to Call a Health Professional

• If you or someone in your family is physically abused or the victim of violence. Physical abuse is a crime, no matter who does it.

• If you are concerned about violent behavior in yourself, a family member, or friend.

Check the Yellow Pages for hotlines and other resources for victims of abuse.

Mental Wellness

Mental wellness means thinking and feeling positive about yourself. You may have heard of psychosomatic illness, when a person "thinks" himself into being sick. Evidence now supports the idea of psychosomatic wellness. For sickness and for health, what you think has some influence on your health and well-being.

The Mind-Body Connection

Medical science is making remarkable discoveries about how expectations, emotions, and thoughts affect our health. This science is called psychoneuroimmunology, or PNI. It studies how the brain communicates with the rest of the body by sending chemical messengers into the blood.

Researchers have found that one function of the brain is to produce substances that can improve your health. Your brain can create natural painkillers called endorphins, gammaglobulin for fortifying your immune system, and interferon for combatting infections, viruses, and even cancer.

Your brain can combine these and other substances into a vast number of tailor-made prescriptions for what ails you. The substances that your brain produces depend in part on your thoughts and feelings.

In other words, your immune system's ability to heal the body is linked to your state of mind and your state of mental wellness. Your level of optimism and your expectations of what could happen can affect what goes on inside your whole body.

Positive Thinking

People with positive attitudes generally enjoy life more, but are they any healthier? The answer is often yes.

Optimism is a resource for healing. Optimists are more likely to overcome pain and adversity in their efforts to improve their medical treatment outcomes. For example, optimistic coronary bypass patients generally recover more quickly and have fewer postoperative complications than people who are less hopeful.

Conversely, pessimism seems to aggravate ill health. One long-term study showed that people who were pessimistic in college had significantly higher rates of illness through age 60.

We seem to develop a tendency toward either optimism or pessimism at an early age. However, even if your outlook on life tends to be gloomy, you can enjoy psychosomatic wellness by using your brain to support your immune system.

Boosting Your Immune System

Your immune system responds to your thoughts, emotions, and actions. In addition to staying fit, eating right, and managing stress, the following three strategies will help your immune system function better:

1. Create positive expectations for health and healing.

2. Open yourself to humor, friendship, and love.

3. Appeal to the Spirit.

1. Create positive expectations for health and healing.

Mental and emotional expectations can influence medical outcomes. The effectiveness of any medical treatment depends in part on how useful you *expect* it to be.

The "placebo effect" proves that expectations affect health. A placebo is a drug or treatment that provides no medical benefit except for the patient's belief that it will help. On the average, 35 percent of patients who receive placebos report satisfactory relief from their medical problem, even though they received no actual medication.

Changing your expectations from negative to positive may give your immune system a boost. Here's how:

• Stop all negative self-talk. Make positive statements that promote your recovery.

• Write your illness a letter. Tell it that you don't need it anymore and that your immune system is now ready to finish it off.

• Send yourself a steady stream of affirmations. An affirmation is a phrase or sentence that sends strong, positive statements to you about yourself, such as "I am a capable person," or "My joints are strong and flexible."

• Visualize health and healing. Add mental pictures that support your positive affirmations.

• Become a cheerleader for your immune system. Talk to it and encourage it to be strong and keep fighting.

2. Open yourself to humor, friendship, and love.

Positive emotions strengthen the immune system. Fortunately, almost anything that makes you feel good about yourself helps you stay healthy.

• Laugh. A little humor makes life richer and healthier. Laughter increases creativity, reduces pain, and speeds healing. Keep an emergency laughter kit of funny videotapes, jokes, cartoons, and photographs. Put it with your first-aid supplies and keep it well stocked.

• Seek out friends. Friendships are vital to good health. Close social ties help you recover more quickly from illness and reduce your risk of developing diseases ranging from arthritis to depression.

• Volunteer. People who volunteer live longer and enjoy life more than those who do not. By helping others, we help ourselves.

• Plant a plant and pet a pet. Plants and pets can be highly therapeutic. When you stroke an animal, blood pressure goes down and your heart rate slows. Animals and plants help us feel needed.

3. Appeal to the Spirit.

If you believe in a higher power, ask for support in your pursuit of healing and health. Faith, prayer, and spiritual beliefs can play an important role in recovering from an illness.

Your sense of spiritual wellness can help you overcome personal trials and things you cannot change. If it suits you, use spiritual images in visualizations, affirmations, and expectations about your health and your life.

Hardiness

Some people seem to have more protection from disease than others. Their immune systems appear to be more efficient. Researchers studying these hardy people have identified three personality factors that stand out:

1. Hardy people have a strong commitment to self, work, family, and other values.

2. Hardy people have a sense of control over their lives.

3. Hardy people generally see change in their lives as a challenge rather than a threat.

Developing a Hardy Personality

Can you develop more commitment, control, and acceptance of life's challenges? Apparently so, particularly if you start at an early age.

You can help your children become hardy by encouraging them in the following ways:

• Commitment: Be a role model for your children by your commitment to them, to your work, and to the community. The more accepted a child feels, the more he will be able to commit himself to others.

• Control: Provide a variety of tasks that are neither too difficult nor too simple. Experience with both success and failure followed by success helps children build a sense of control.

• The challenge of change: Encourage children to see changes as opportunities to try new things. Accentuate the positive and teach them that life is continually changing.

Adults can also develop hardiness. Training to develop more commitment, control, and challenge has proven to be effective.

Avoiding Guilt

There is no value in feeling guilty about health problems. While there is a lot we can do to reduce our risk of health problems and improve our chances of recovery, some illnesses develop and persist no matter what we do. Try to avoid feeling guilty, especially in applying the mental self-care suggestions in this chapter. If what you do helps, terrific. However, if your illness persists despite your best efforts, don't blame yourself. Some things just are. Do the best you can.

Be prepared.
Boy Scout Motto

Chapter 19

Your Home Health Centre

More health care takes place in your home than anywhere else. Having the right tools, medicines, supplies, and information on hand will improve its quality.

Store all your self-care resources in one central location, such as a large drawer in the bedroom or family room. Use the charts on tools and supplies and the list of resources in this chapter as checklists for keeping your home health centre well stocked.

Note: If small children are around, keep your supplies out of reach or protected by childproof safety latches.

Be familiar with the disaster preparation and response plan for your area. Keep the appropriate supplies on hand.

Self-Care Tools

Self-care tools are the basic equipment of your home health centre.

Cold Pack

A cold pack is a plastic envelope filled with gel that remains flexible at very cold temperatures. Buy two cold packs and keep them in the freezer. Use them for bumps, bruises, back sprains, turned ankles, sore joints, or any other health problem that calls for ice. A cold pack is more convenient than ice and may become the self-care tool you use the most.

You can make your own cold pack:

• Put one pint of rubbing alcohol and three pints of water in a one-gallon heavy duty plastic freezer bag.

• Seal the bag and then seal it in a second bag. Mark it "Cold pack: Do not eat," and place it in the freezer.

A bag of frozen vegetables will also work as a cold pack.

Humidifier and Vaporizer

Humidifiers and vaporizers add moisture to the air, making it less drying to your mouth, throat, and nose. A humidifier produces a cool mist and a vaporizer puts out hot steam.

A humidifier makes tinier particles of water that get into your respiratory system better, and the cool mist is more comfortable than hot steam.

However, humidifiers are noisy, produce particles that may be irritating to some people, and they need to be cleaned and disinfected regularly. This is especially important for people who have mold allergies.

A vaporizer's hot steam does not contain any irritating particles. Steam may feel good when you have a cold, but the hot water can burn anyone who overturns it or gets too close.

Humidity in the air can help to soothe a scratchy throat, ease a dry, hacking cough, and make it easier for someone with a stuffy nose to breathe. Added humidity will make your home more comfortable, especially in the winter when dry air is a problem.

Medicine Spoon

Medicine spoons are transparent tubes with marks for typical dosage amounts. A medicine spoon makes it easy to give the right dose of liquid medicine. While the spoons are convenient for anyone, they are a particular blessing for young children. The tube shape and large lip get most

---

Self-Care Tools

For every household:

- Blood pressure cuff*
- Cold pack*
- Dental mirror
- Eyedropper
- Heating pad
- Humidifier or vaporizer*
- Medicine spoon*
- Nail clippers
- Penlight*
- Scissors
- Stethoscope*
- Thermometer*
- Tweezers

For children under six, add:

- Bulb aspirator/syringe
- Rectal thermometer*
- Otoscope*

*Described in text

---

of the medication into a child's mouth without spilling. Buy one at your local pharmacy.

Otoscope

An otoscope is a flashlight with a special attachment for looking into the ear. With training, using an otoscope can help you decide if an ear infection is present. Inexpensive consumer model otoscopes are available but do not illuminate the ear canal and eardrum as well as the one your doctor uses. They can also be used as high-intensity penlights.

Penlight

A penlight has a small intense light that can be easily directed. It is useful for giving a physical exam and is easier to handle than a flashlight.

Stethoscope and Blood Pressure Cuff

If you have high blood pressure, it's a good idea to have both a stethoscope and a blood pressure cuff (sphygmo-manometer) to monitor your blood pressure regularly.

Purchase a flat diaphragm model stethoscope rather than a bell-shaped one. The flat surface makes it easier for you to hear.

Blood pressure cuffs come in many models. If you have difficulty reading the gauge on a regular cuff, look for one attached to an upright mercury column, or an electronic digital

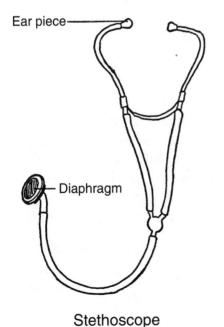

Ear piece

Diaphragm

Stethoscope

model. Ask your pharmacist to recommend a blood pressure kit and show you how to use it.

Thermometer

Buy a thermometer with easy-to-read markings. Digital electronic thermometers are accurate and easy to read. Temperature strips are very convenient and safe, but are not as accurate as mercury or electronic thermometers and should only be used to measure axillary (armpit) temperature. Thermometers that measure the temperature in the ear are fast, easy to use, and can be quite accurate, but are expensive.

Self-Care Supplies

See the Self-Care Supplies chart (next page) for a list of supplies that are useful to keep on hand in your home health centre. These products are inexpensive, easy to use, and generally available at any drugstore or pharmacy.

Over-the-Counter (OTC) Medications and Products

An over-the-counter (OTC) medication is any drug that you can buy without a doctor's prescription. However, don't assume that all OTC drugs are safe for you. These drugs can interact with other medications and can sometimes create serious health problems.

Carefully read the label of any over-the-counter drug you use, especially if you also take prescription medications for other health problems. Ask your pharmacist for help in finding the one best suited to your needs.

Some common OTCs include:

- Antacids
- Antidiarrheals
- Cold and allergy remedies
- Bulking agents and laxatives
- Pain relievers

These drugs can be very helpful when used properly, but can also create serious problems if used incorrectly. The following tips will help you use these common OTC drugs wisely and safely. In some cases, you may find that you don't need to take them at all. The chart on page 291 lists common health problems and suggestions for OTC products to treat them.

Antacids

Antacids are taken to relieve heartburn or indigestion caused by excess stomach acid. While they are safe if used occasionally, antacids may cause problems if taken regularly. There are several kinds of antacids. Learn what ingredients are in each type so that you can avoid any adverse effects.

- Sodium bicarbonate antacids (Alka-Seltzer, Bromo Seltzer) contain baking soda. If you have high blood pressure, or if you are on a salt-restricted diet, avoid these antacids because of their high sodium content. If used too frequently, they may interfere with kidney or heart function.

- Calcium carbonate antacids (TUMS, Caltrate) are sometimes used as calcium supplements (see page 261). However, these products may cause constipation.

Self-Care Supplies

Keep these on hand:

- Adhesive strips ("Band-aids") in assorted sizes
- Adhesive tape, one inch wide
- Butterfly bandages
- Sterile gauze pads, two inches square
- Elastic ("Ace") bandage, three inches wide
- Roll of gauze bandage, two inches wide
- Cotton balls
- Safety pins
- Tweezers
- Dental disclosing tablets and dental floss

- Aluminum-based antacids (Amphojel) are less potent and work slower than other products. They may also cause constipation. Some may cause calcium depletion and should not be taken by postmenopausal women. Check with your doctor before using aluminum antacids if you have kidney problems.

- Magnesium compounds (Phillip's Milk of Magnesia) may cause diarrhea.

- Aluminum-magnesium antacids (Maalox, Di-Gel, Mylanta, Riopan) are less likely to cause constipation or diarrhea than aluminum-only or magnesium-only antacids.

Antacid Precautions

- Try to eliminate the cause of frequent heartburn instead of taking antacids regularly. See Heartburn on page 36.

OTC Products for Home Use

Problem	OTC Product (example)	Comments
Allergies	Antihistamine (Chlor-Tripolon, Benadryl)	Useful for allergies and itching. See page 294.
Colds	Decongestant	See page 293 for precautions.
Constipation	Laxative or bulking agent (Metamucil)	Avoid long-term or regular use of laxatives. See page 295.
Cough, non-productive	Suppressant (Vicks Formula 44)	Ease a dry, hacking cough. See pages 95 and 293.
Cough, productive	Expectorant (Vicks Formula 44E)	Thin and help clear the mucus. See page 293 for precautions.
Diaper rash	Protectant (A&D Ointment, Desitin)	Protects skin from urine and stool. See page 158.
Diarrhea	Antidiarrheal (Pepto-Bismol)	Avoid long-term use. See page 35.
Dry skin	Lubricating cream (Vaseline Intensive Care)	Also see page 132.
Heartburn	Antacid (TUMS, Maalox), acid controller (Pepcid-AC)	Avoid long-term use. See page 36.
Itching	Hydrocortisone cream (Cortate)	Antihistamines are also helpful. See page 132.
Pain, fever, inflammation	Aspirin, ibuprofen	Help relieve swelling and pain. May cause stomach upset. See page 295.
Pain, fever	Acetaminophen (Tylenol)	Less stomach irritation. Safe for children. See page 296.
Scrapes, skin infections	Antibiotic ointment (Baciguent, Polysporin)	May cause local allergic reaction. Keep creams cool and dry. Discard if out of date.

• Consult your doctor or pharmacist before taking an antacid if you take other medications. Antacids may interfere with the absorption and action of some drugs, such as antibiotics, digitalis, and anticoagulants. Also consult your doctor if you have ulcers or kidney problems.

Antidiarrheals

There are two types of antidiarrheal drugs: those that thicken the stool and those that slow intestinal spasms.

The **thickening** mixtures (Kaopectate) contain clay or fruit pectin and absorb the bacteria and toxins in the intestine. They are safe because they do not go into the system, but these products also absorb the bacteria needed for digestion. Long-term use is not advised.

Antispasmodic antidiarrheal products slow the spasms of the intestine. Loperamide (Imodium A-D) is an example of this type of preparation. Donnagel contains both thickening and antispasmodic ingredients.

Antidiarrheal Precautions

• Diarrhea helps rid your body of an infection, so try to avoid using antidiarrheal medications for the first six hours. After that, use them only if there are no other signs of illness, such as fever, and if cramping and pain continues.

• Be sure to take a large enough dose. Take antidiarrheal preparations until the stool thickens, then stop immediately to avoid constipation.

• Replace depleted body fluids. Dehydration can develop when someone has diarrhea, especially an infant, child, or older adult. See page 34 for a rehydration drink you can make at home to prevent dehydration.

Cold and Allergy Remedies

In general, if you take drugs for your cold, you'll get better in about a week. If you take nothing, you'll get better in about seven days. Rest and liquids are probably the best treatment for a cold (see page 93). Antibiotics will not help. However, medications help relieve some cold symptoms, such as nasal congestion and cough.

Allergy symptoms, especially runny nose, often respond to antihistamines. Antihistamines are also found in many cold medications, often together with a decongestant. However, the value of antihistamines in treating cold symptoms is under debate.

Decongestants

Decongestants make breathing easier by shrinking swollen mucous membranes in the nose, allowing air to pass through. They also help relieve runny nose and postnasal drip, which can cause a sore throat.

Decongestants can be taken orally or used as nose drops or sprays. Oral decongestants (pills) are probably more effective and provide longer relief, but cause more side effects. Sudafed (pseudoephedrine) is an oral decongestant.

Sprays and drops provide rapid but temporary relief. Neo-synephrine (phenylephrine) is an effective nasal spray. Sprays and drops are less likely to interact with other drugs than oral decongestants.

Decongestant Precautions

• Do not give cold medicines or oral decongestants to infants under age six months. Over-the-counter cold medicines have not been proven effective for preschool children.

• *Do not* use medicated nasal sprays or drops more than three times a day, or for more than three days. Continued use will cause a "rebound effect": the mucous membranes swell up more than before using the spray.

• Drink extra fluids when taking cold medications.

• Decongestants can cause problems for people with certain health problems, such as heart disease, high blood pressure, glaucoma, diabetes, and overactive thyroid. They may also interact with some drugs, such as certain antidepressants and high blood pressure medications. Read the package carefully and ask your pharmacist or doctor to help you choose one.

Cough Preparations

Coughing is your body's way of getting foreign substances and mucus out of your respiratory tract. Coughs are often useful and you don't want to eliminate them. Sometimes, though, coughs are severe enough to impair breathing or prevent rest.

Water and other liquids, such as fruit juices, are probably the best cough syrups. They help soothe the throat, and also moisten and thin mucus so that it can be coughed up more easily.

You can make a simple and soothing cough syrup at home by mixing one part lemon juice with two parts honey. Use as often as needed. This can be given to children over one year old. Also see page 94.

There are two kinds of cough medicines. **Expectorants** help thin the mucus, making it easier to "bring up" when you have a productive cough. Look for expectorants containing guaifenesin, such as Robitussin and Vicks Formula 44E.

Suppressants control or suppress the cough reflex and work best for a dry, hacking cough that keeps you awake. Look for suppressant medications containing dextromethorphan, such as Robitussin-DM or Vicks Formula 44.

Saline Nose Drops

Saline nasal drops for a stuffy nose are easy to make at home. They will keep nasal tissues moist so they can filter the air and will not cause a rebound effect.

Mix 1.5 ml (¼ teaspoon) salt in ¼ litre (1 cup) of body temperature water (too much salt will dry nasal membranes).

Place the solution in a clean bottle with a dropper (available at drugstores). Use as necessary. Make a fresh solution every three days.

To insert drops, lie on your back with your head hanging over the side of the bed. This helps the drops get farther back. Try to prevent the dropper from touching your nose.

Over-the-counter saline sprays (Salinex) are convenient, inexpensive, and sterile.

Don't suppress a productive cough too much (unless it is keeping you from getting enough rest).

Cough Preparation Precautions

• Cough preparations can cause problems for people with certain health problems, such as asthma, heart disease, high blood pressure, and enlarged prostate. They may also interact with some drugs, such as sedatives and certain antidepressants. Read the package carefully and ask your pharmacist or doctor to help you choose one.

• Cough suppressants can stifle breathing. Use them with caution if you have chronic respiratory problems and when giving them to someone who is very old or frail.

• Read the label so you know what the ingredients are. Some cough preparations contain a large percentage of alcohol; others contain codeine. There are many choices. Ask your pharmacist to advise you.

Antihistamines

Antihistamines dry up nasal secretions, and are commonly used to treat allergy symptoms and itching.

If your runny nose is due to allergies, an antihistamine will help. For cold symptoms, home treatment and perhaps a decongestant (see page 292) will probably be more helpful. It is usually best to take only single-ingredient allergy or cold preparations, instead of those containing many active ingredients.

Chlor-Tripolon (chlorpheniramine) and Benadryl (diphenhydramine) are single-ingredient antihistamine products.

Dristan, Coricidin, and Triaminic contain both a decongestant and an antihistamine.

Antihistamine Precautions

• Do not give antihistamines to infants under age four months. For children between four months and one year, ask your doctor first.

• Drink extra fluids when taking allergy medications.

• Antihistamines can cause problems for people with certain health problems, such as asthma, glaucoma, epilepsy, and enlarged prostate. They may also interact with some drugs, such as certain antidepressants, sedatives, and tranquilizers. Read the package carefully and ask your pharmacist or doctor to help you choose one that will not cause problems.

• The drowsiness that antihistamines often cause usually diminishes with continued use. If it continues, or if the medication isn't helping your allergies after one week, call your doctor for advice.

Bulking Agents and Laxatives

There are two types of products to prevent or treat constipation.

Bulking agents such as bran or psyllium (Metamucil) are not laxatives, but ease constipation by increasing the volume of stool and making it easier to pass. Regular use of bulking agents is safe and helps make them more effective.

Laxatives (Correctol, Ex-Lax, Senokot, Dulcolax) speed up the passage of stool by irritating the lining of the intestines. Regular laxative use is not recommended.

There are many other ways to treat constipation, such as drinking more water. See page 32.

Laxative Precautions

• Take any laxative or bulking agent with plenty of water or other liquids.

• Do not take laxatives regularly. Overuse of laxatives decreases tone and sensation in the large intestine, causing laxative dependence.

• Regular use of some laxatives (Correctol, Ex-Lax, Feen-A-Mint) may interfere with your body's absorption of vitamin D and calcium, which can weaken your bones.

Pain Relievers

There are dozens of pain reliever products. Most contain either aspirin, ibuprofen, or acetaminophen. These three all relieve pain and reduce fever. Aspirin and ibuprofen also relieve inflammation. Generic products are chemically equivalent to more expensive brand-name products, are often less expensive, and will generally work equally well.

Aspirin is widely used for relieving pain and reducing fever in adults. It also relieves minor itching and reduces swelling and inflammation. Most tablets contain 325 mg. Although it seems familiar and safe, aspirin is a very powerful drug.

Aspirin Precautions

• Aspirin causes more childhood poisonings than any other drug. Keep all aspirin, especially baby aspirin, out of children's reach.

• Aspirin can irritate the stomach lining, causing bleeding or ulcers. If aspirin upsets your stomach, try a coated brand, such as Entrophen. Talk with your doctor or pharmacist to determine what will work best for you.

• Aspirin increases the risk of Reye's Syndrome in children. Do not give aspirin to children and teens under age 20 years unless recommended by a doctor.

• Some people are allergic to aspirin. (They may also be allergic to ibuprofen.)

• Throw aspirin away if it begins to smell like vinegar.

• If you are taking an anticoagulant, take aspirin only after consulting with your physician.

• Do not take aspirin for a hangover. Aspirin used with alcohol increases the risk of stomach irritation.

• High doses may result in aspirin poisoning (salicylism). Stop taking aspirin and call a health professional if any of these symptoms occur:

  ○ Ringing in the ears

  ○ Visual disturbances

  ○ Nausea

  ○ Dizziness

  ○ Rapid, deep breathing

Other Uses of Aspirin

In addition to relieving pain and inflammation, aspirin is effective against many other ailments. Because of the danger of side effects and the interactions aspirin may have with other treatment, **do not try these uses of aspirin without a doctor's supervision.**

Heart Attacks and Strokes

Aspirin in low but regular doses helps prevent heart attacks and strokes in certain people at high risk. Doses as low as 30 mg per day have helped. Aspirin may also help as a first-aid measure for heart attacks. Chewing half a tablet may be enough to help.

Stomach and Colon Cancer

Some studies have shown that one aspirin per day can reduce the risk of cancers in the digestive system.

Migraines

Regular, low-dose aspirin use may reduce the frequency of migraines.

Ibuprofen (Advil, Motrin) is another nonsteroidal anti-inflammatory drug (NSAID). Like aspirin, it relieves pain and reduces fever and inflammation. Also like aspirin, it can cause nausea, stomach irritation, and heartburn. Both drugs should be used with caution by people who take blood thinners (anticoagulants).

For liquid forms of ibuprofen, follow the dosage instructions on the label. For adults and children over age 12 years, take one to two 200-mg ibuprofen tablets three times a day.

Acetaminophen (Tylenol) reduces fever and relieves pain. It does not have the anti-inflammatory effect of NSAIDs, such as aspirin and ibuprofen, but also does not cause stomach upset and other side effects. For liquid forms, follow the dosage instructions on the label. Take every four hours, as needed:

Age	Single Dose
Newborn to under 4 months	40 mg
4 months to under 12 months	80 mg
12 months to under 2 years	120 mg
2 and 3 years	160 mg
4 and 5 years	240 mg
6, 7 and 8 years	320 mg
9 and 10 years	400 mg
11 and 12 years	480 mg
13 years and older	640 mg

Do not exceed dosage limits. People who drink more than three alcoholic beverages a day should discuss use with their doctors. Excess use of acetaminophen can contribute to alcohol-induced liver damage.

Prescription Medications

There are thousands of different prescription medications, used to treat hundreds of different medical conditions. Your doctor and your pharmacist are your best sources of information about your prescription medications. Good books are available that contain information on many different prescription drugs. See Resource 2 on page 302.

Guidelines for taking every kind of prescription medication could fill several books. Common types covered here include antibiotics, minor tranquilizers, and sleeping pills.

Antibiotics

Antibiotics are prescription drugs that kill bacteria. They are effective against bacteria only, and have no effect on viruses. Antibiotics will not cure the common cold, flu, or any other viral illness. Unless you have a bacterial infection, it's best to avoid the possible adverse effects of antibiotics, which may include:

• **Side effects**, including **allergic reactions**. Common side effects of antibiotics include nausea, diarrhea, and increased sensitivity to sunlight. Most side effects are mild, but some, especially allergic reactions, can be severe. An allergic reaction can be life-threatening. If you have any unexpected reaction to an antibiotic, tell your health professional before another antibiotic is prescribed.

• **Secondary infections**. Antibiotics kill most of the bacteria in your body that are sensitive to them, including those that help your body. They may destroy the bacterial balance in your body, leading to stomach upset, diarrhea, vaginal infections, or other problems.

• **Bacterial resistance**. Bacteria build resistance to antibiotics that are used frequently; and when only part of a prescription is taken, the stronger bacteria survive. Many common bacteria have developed antibiotic-resistant strains, which are very difficult to treat.

Medication Guidelines

Basic guidelines for taking prescription and over-the-counter medications include:

• Use medications only if non-drug approaches are not working.

• Know the benefits and side effects of a medication before taking it.

• Take the minimum effective dose.

• Never take a drug prescribed for someone else.

• Follow the prescription instructions exactly or let your doctor know why you didn't.

• Keep medications in their original containers with the caps on tightly and stored according to directions.

• Store all medications out of reach of children.

• Do not take medications in front of small children. They are great mimics. Don't oversell the "candy" taste of children's medicines or leave children's vitamins accessible to small children.

• Add a consumer's guide to medications to your home health library. See Resource 2 on page 302.

When you and your health professional have decided that an antibiotic is necessary, follow the instructions with the prescription carefully.

- Take the whole dose for as many days as prescribed, unless you have severe unexpected side effects. Antibiotics kill off many bacteria quite quickly, so you may feel better in a few days. If you stop taking it too soon, the weaker bacteria will have been eliminated, but the stronger ones may survive and flourish.

- Be sure you understand any special instructions about taking the medication. They should be printed on the label, but double check with your doctor and pharmacist.

- Store antibiotics in a dry, cool place. They will usually keep their potency for about a year. However, most antibiotics are prescribed for a specific illness in the amount needed to cure it. Liquid antibiotics are always dated. Check carefully to see if they need refrigeration.

- Never give an antibiotic prescribed for one person to someone else.

- Do not take an antibiotic prescribed for another illness without a health professional's approval.

Minor Tranquilizers and Sleeping Pills

Minor tranquilizers like Valium, Librium, Xanax, and Tranxene, and sleeping pills like Dalmane, Restoril, and Halcion are widely prescribed. However, these drugs can cause problems, including memory loss, addiction, and injuries from falls due to drug-induced unsteadiness.

Minor tranquilizers can be effective for short periods of time. However, long-term use is of limited value and introduces the risk of addiction and mental impairment.

Sleeping pills may help for a few days or a few weeks, but using them for more than a month generally causes more sleep problems than it solves. For other approaches, see page 280.

If you have been taking minor tranquilizers or sleeping pills for a while, talk with your doctor about re-evaluating your need for the medication or reducing your dosage. If you have experienced any unsteadiness, dizziness, or memory loss, tell your doctor.

Medication Problems

Several kinds of adverse medication reactions can occur:

Side effects: Predictable but unpleasant reactions to a drug. They are usually mild, but can be inconvenient. In some cases, they are more serious.

Allergies: Some people have severe, sometimes life-threatening reactions (called anaphylaxis) to certain medications. See page 83 for signs of an allergic reaction.

Drug-drug interactions: Occur when two or more prescription or over-the-counter drugs mix in the body and cause an adverse reaction. The symptoms can be severe and may be misdiagnosed as a new illness.

Adverse Drug Reactions

Side effects, drug-drug and food-drug interactions, over-medication, and addiction may cause:

- Nausea, indigestion, vomiting

- Constipation, diarrhea, incontinence, or difficulty urinating

- Dry mouth

- Headache, dizziness, ringing in the ears, or blurred vision

- Confusion, forgetfulness, disorientation, drowsiness, or depression

- Difficulty sleeping, irritability, or nervousness

- Difficulty breathing

- Rashes, bruising, and bleeding problems

Don't assume any symptom is a normal side effect that you have to suffer with. Call your doctor or pharmacist any time you suspect your medicines are making you sick.

Drug-food interactions: Occur when medications react with food. Some drugs work best when taken with food, but others should be taken on an empty stomach. Some drug-food reactions can cause serious symptoms.

Over-medication: Sometimes the full adult dose of a medication is too much for small people and those over age 60. Too much of a drug is very dangerous.

Addiction: Long-term use of some medications can lead to dependency and cause severe reactions if they are withdrawn suddenly. Narcotics, tranquilizers, and barbiturates must be taken very carefully to prevent addiction. See page 271.

Save Money on Medications

Over-the-counter and prescription medications can be very expensive. Here are some ways to cut your medication costs:

- Buy generic over-the-counter products. They are chemically equivalent to name-brand drugs, but are usually cheaper. Ask your pharmacist or doctor if generic forms of your prescription medications are available and appropriate for you.

- Shop around and compare prices between several pharmacies. Prices can vary widely. It may be worth paying a little more if you know and trust the pharmacist.

- Ask your doctor for samples of newly prescribed medications, or ask your pharmacist to fill only the first week's worth of pills. If the medication has to be changed later, you can save the price of the full prescription.

- Once you have found a pharmacy you like, stay with it. This way the pharmacist will get to know you and your health needs.

Home Medical Tests

Many common medical tests are now available in home kits. Combined with regular visits to your health professional, home tests can help you monitor your health and, in some cases, detect problems early.

Home medical tests must be very accurate (over 95 percent) to be approved by the Health Protection Branch, Health Canada. However, they must be used correctly to give such accurate results. Follow the package directions exactly. If you have questions, ask your pharmacist or check the label for the company's toll-free phone number to call.

Home medical tests are especially helpful if you have a chronic condition that requires frequent monitoring, such as diabetes, asthma, or high blood pressure. Ask your doctor which home medical tests would be appropriate for you. Descriptions of some common tests follow.

Urinalysis

Some of the more common medical lab tests on urine can be done at home. Home urinalysis can help you monitor diabetes. It is also useful if you have frequent bladder infections.

Blood Glucose Monitoring

If you have diabetes, you may already monitor your blood sugar levels (glucose) using a finger prick and a test strip or an electronic monitor.

This test should always be used under a doctor's supervision. Never adjust your insulin dose based on a single abnormal test, unless your doctor has specifically instructed you to do so.

Check with your doctor if you have symptoms of abnormal blood sugar levels, even if the test is normal. See page 266.

Blood Pressure Monitoring

If you have high blood pressure, it is important to monitor your blood pressure frequently. With a little instruction, you can easily monitor your blood pressure at home.

By checking your blood pressure at home, when you are relaxed, you will be able to track changes due to your home treatment and medications.

• Do not make any changes to your medications based on your home blood pressure readings without consulting your doctor.

• Check your blood pressure at different times of day to see how rest and activities affect it. For regular readings, check it at the same time of day. Blood pressure is usually lowest in the morning and rises during the day.

• For the most accurate reading, sit still for five minutes before taking your blood pressure.

• Calibrate (adjust) the blood pressure device yearly.

Tests for Blood in Stool

The fecal occult blood test can detect hidden blood in the stool, which may indicate colon cancer or other problems. However, the ability of this test and another test called flexible sigmoid-oscopy to detect colon cancer is controversial.

Home Pregnancy Tests

Home pregnancy tests are reliable and require only a few steps. Follow the package instructions and report all positive results to your doctor. See page 173.

Home Medical Records

Your home health centre is a good place to keep your family's medical records, too. A three-ring binder or wire-bound notebook with dividers for each member of the family is helpful. Each person should have a cover sheet listing:

• Diagnosed chronic conditions: arthritis, asthma, diabetes, high blood pressure, etc.

• Any known allergies to drugs, foods, or insects.

• Information that would be vital in an emergency; such as a pacemaker, a hearing aid, diabetes, epilepsy, or if someone is deaf or blind.

• Name and phone number of primary doctor.

Other important information that should be included:

• An up-to-date list of medications. Include name of drug, purpose, dose, instructions, doctor and date prescribed.

• Immunization records: Childhood immunizations, tetanus, influenza, pneumonia.

• Health screening results: Blood pressure, cholesterol, vision, hearing.

• Records of major illnesses and injuries, such as pneumonia, bronchitis, broken bones, or major infections.

• Records of any major surgical procedures and hospitalizations.

• Records listing major diseases in members of your family: heart disease, stroke, cancer, diabetes.

Home Health Library: Self-Care Resources

Good information is the most important self-care resource for the home. Many of the resources listed below are available at your local bookstore or public library. If not, ask the bookstore to order the ones you want.

Other sources of health information may be available in your community. Check the phone book for your local chapter of the Canadian Cancer Society, Canadian Heart and Stroke Foundation of Canada, Canadian Arthritis and Rheumatism Society, Canadian Diabetes Association, Canadian Lung Association, and other organizations.

If you subscribe to an on-line service such as Prodigy, AOL Canada, or CompuServe, check for health databases, electronic bulletin boards and discussion groups, and other services. You may be able to access medical journal articles, textbooks, and other publications on-line.

There are many electronic health information sources available through national and provincial governments, health ministries, and regional health authorities. Try some of the following:

- British Columbia Ministry of Health at http://www.hlth.gov.bc.ca/

- The Calgary Regional Health Authority at http://www.crha-health.ab.ca/

- Health Canada at http://www.hwc.ca/

Other sites containing general health and self-care information that you may wish to access are:

- Health Information Research Unit, McMaster University at http://www-hsl.mcmaster.ca/tomflem/top.html/

- Mayo Foundation for Medical Education and Research at http://www.mayo.ivi.com/

- Medical Self-Care Archives at http://healthy.net/library/journals/self-carearchives/

- Healthyway at http://bc.sympatico.ca/healthyway

- United States Department of Health Healthfinder at http://www.healthfinder.gov/search.htm/

General Purpose Resources

1. D. W. Kemper et al., *Healthwise Handbook* (12th ed.), Healthwise, 1995. Available from Healthwise, Inc., P.O. 1989, Boise, ID 83701, (208) 345-1161.

2. J. W. Long, MD, *The Essential Guide to Prescription Drugs 1992: Everything You Need to Know for Safe Drug Use,* Harper-Collins, 1992.

3. E. Pinkney and C. Pinkney, *Patient's Guide to Medical Tests,* Facts on File.

4. Canadian Medical Association, *Complete Guide to Medical Symptoms* (1st ed.), Reader's Digest Association (Canada), 1994.

5. *Canadian Medical Association Home Medical Encyclopedia*, Reader's Digest Association (Canada), 1992.

6. C. Carver, MD, *S.O.S. Medicare*, Medica Publishing, RR. 2, Lanark, Ontario, 1994.

7. J. Engel, *The Complete Canadian Health Guide*, Key Porter Books, 1993.

8. B. L. Harden and C. R. Harden, *Alternative Health Care: The Canadian Directory* (1st ed.), Noble Ages Publishing, 1996.

9. D. W. Kemper and M. Mettler, *Healthwise for Life: Medical Self-Care for Healthy Aging* (2nd ed.), 1996. Available from Healthwise, Inc., P.O. Box 1989, Boise, ID 83701, (208) 345-1161.

10. S. Kirchheimer. *The Doctors Book of Home Remedies II*. Bantam Books, 1995.

11. D. M. Vickery, MD, and J. F. Fries, MD, *Take Care of Yourself* (6th ed.), Addison-Wesley, 1996.

Special Concerns Resources

AIDS

12. *Managing Your Health: A Guide for People Living With HIV or AIDS* (Canadian Edition), Community AIDS Treatment Information Exchange (CATIE) & Toronto People with AIDS Foundation, 1996. Available from the National AIDS Clearinghouse, 400 - 1565 Carling Avenue, Ottawa, Ontario K1Z 8R1. Tel: (613) 725-3434 Fax: (513) 725-1205.

Alcohol Problems

13. *Alcoholics Anonymous: The Story of How Thousands of Men and Women Have Recovered From Alcoholism* (3rd ed.), Alcoholics Anonymous World Services, Inc., 1976.

14. *The Twelve Steps of Alcoholics Anonymous,* interpreted by The Hazelden Foundation, Harper and Row, 1987.

Alzheimer's Disease/Dementia

15. N. L. Mace and P. V. Rabins, MD, *The 36-Hour Day: A Family Guide to Caring for Persons With Alzheimer's Disease, Related Dementing Illnesses, and Memory Loss in Late Life,* The John Hopkins University Press, 1991. Also available from the Alzheimer's Association, (800) 272-3900.

16. M. Larkin, *When Someone You Love Has Alzheimer's,* Dell, 1995.

17. F. G. Davidson, *The Alzheimer Sourcebook for Caregivers*, Lowell House, 1994.

Anger

18. R. Williams, MD, and V. Williams, *Anger Kills: 17 Strategies for Controlling the Hostility That Can Harm Your Health,* Random House, 1993.

19. A. Ellis, *Anger,* Carol Publishing Group, 1985.

20. H. G. Lerner, PhD, *The Dance of Anger,* Harper & Row, 1989.

Anxiety

21. E. Bourne, *The Anxiety and Phobia Workbook,* New Harbinger, 1990.

22. R. Z. Peurifoy, *Anxiety, Phobias, and Panic: Taking Charge and Conquering Fear,* Life Skills, 1992.

23. A. Seagrave and F. Covington, *Free From Fears,* Poseidon Press, 1989.

Arthritis
24. K. Lorig and J. Fries, MD, *The Arthritis Helpbook,* Addison-Wesley, 1991.

Also see Resource 49.

Asthma
25. Canadian Lung Association, *Help Yourself to Better Breathing,* 1991. Available from your local chapter of the Canadian Lung Association.

26. A. Weinstein, MD, *Asthma: The Complete Guide to Self-Management of Asthma for Patients and Their Families,* McGraw-Hill, 1987.

27. B. Zimmerman et al., *The Canadian Allergy and Asthma Handbook* (revis. ed.), Random House Canada, 1996.

Also see Resource 49.

Back Pain
28. R. McKenzie, *Treat Your Own Back,* Spinal Publications, 1989.

29. R. Cailliet, MD, *Low Back Pain Syndrome,* Davis Co., 1988.

30. M. E. Allen and B. Pothier, *Take Charge of Your Back: The Exercise Guide to a Healthy Back*, University Back Centre, Simon Fraser University, Burnaby, British Columbia, 1990.

Cancer
31. R. Buckman, *What You Really Need to Know About Cancer: A Comprehensive Guide for Patients and Their Families*, Key Porter Books, 1996.

32. Dollinger et al., *Everyone's Guide to Cancer Therapy*, 2nd ed., Somerville House Publishing, 1995 (adapted by the Canadian Medical Association).

33. J. Engel, *The Complete Breast Book*, Key Porter Books, 1996.

34. L. S. Goldenberg, *Prostate Cancer: All You Need to Know to Take an Active Part in Your Treatment,* Intelligent Patient Guide, 1995.

35. I. Olivotto et al., *Breast Cancer: All You Need to Know to Take an Active Part in Your Treatment,* Intelligent Patient Guide, 1995.

36. M. E. Pezim, *Colon and Rectal Cancer: All You Need to Know to Take an Active Part in Your Treatment*, Intelligent Patient Guide, 1995.

37. D. Spiegel, *Living Beyond Limits: New Hope and Help for Facing Life-Threatening Illness,* Times Books, 1993.

38. M. Stoppard, *The Breast Book: The Essential Guide to Breast Care and Breast Health for Women of All Ages*, Random House Canada, 1996.

Child Health
39. S. P. Shelov, MD, ed., *Caring for Your Baby and Young Child,* Bantam Books, 1991.

40. B. Schmitt, MD, *Your Child's Health,* Bantam, 1991.

41. A. Eisenberg et al., *What to Expect the First Year,* Workman Publishing, 1989.

42. R. Pantell et al., *Taking Care of Your Child,* Addison-Wesley, 1990.

43. E. Satter, *How to Get Your Child to Eat … But Not Too Much,* Bull Publishing, 1991.

44. R. Ferber, *Solve Your Child's Sleep Problem,* Simon & Schuster, 1986.

45. D. E. Greydanus, ed., *Caring for Your Adolescent*, American Academy of Pediatrics, 1991.

46. D. Dinkmeyer, Sr., G. D. McKay, J. S. Dinkmeyer, *Parenting Young Children*, American Guidance Service, 1989.

47. *Canadian Medical Association Complete Book of Mother and Baby Care*, Reader's Digest Association (Canada), 1996.

48. J. L. Wykoff, PhD, and B. C. Unell, *How to Discipline Your Six- to Twelve-Year-Old Without Losing Your Mind*, Doubleday Books, 1991.

Chronic Illnesses

49. K. Lorig et al., *Living a Healthy Life With Chronic Conditions: Self-Management of Heart Disease, Arthritis, Stroke, Diabetes, Asthma, Bronchitis, Emphysema, and Others*, Bull Publishing, 1993.

Depression

50. M. Seligman, *Learned Optimism,* Random House, 1991.

Also see Resources under Mental Self-Care.

Diabetes

51. L. Jovanovic-Peterson, MD, C. M. Peterson, MD, and M. B. Stone, *A Touch of Diabetes: A Guide for People Who Have Type II, Non-Insulin Dependent Diabetes,* DCI Publishing, 1991.

52. D.W. Guthrie, RN, PhD, and R. N. Guthrie, MD, *The Diabetes Sourcebook,* Lowell House, 1995.

53. *Equilibrium: A Treatment and Lifestyle Guide for Persons With Type 2 Diabetes*, Canadian Diabetes Association, 1996.

54. *In Sync: Understanding and Dealing With Type 1 Diabetes,* Canadian Diabetes Association, 1996.

55. D. Hatton, *Diabetes & You: A Manual for Children, Parents and Caregivers*, B.C. Children's Hospital, 1-A46, 4480 Oak Street, Vancouver, B.C. V6H 3V4. Tel: (604) 875-2345, Fax: (604) 875-3231, 1996.

Also see Resource 49.

Drugs

56. B. Berube, *Understanding Canadian Non-Prescription Drugs: A Consumer's Guide to Safe Use*, Key Porter Books, 1994.

57. *Canadian Medical Association New Guide to Prescription and Over-the-Counter Drugs.* Reader's Digest Association (Canada), 1996.

58. D. L. Smith, *Understanding Canadian Prescription Drugs: A Consumer's Guide to Correct Use*, Key Porter Books, 1992.

Elder Care

59. M. Mettler and D. W. Kemper, *Healthwise for Life: Medical Self-Care for Healthy Aging,* Healthwise, 1992.

60. D. W. Kemper et al., *Growing Wiser: The Older Person's Guide to Mental Wellness,* Healthwise, 1986.

Both available from Healthwise, P.O. Box 1989, Boise, ID, 83701, (208) 345-1161.

61. J. Fries, MD, *Aging Well,* Addison Wesley, 1989.

First Aid

62. *First on the Scene: The Complete Guide to First Aid and CPR*, St. John Ambulance, Ottawa, 1995.

63. *Cardiopulmonary Resuscitation - Heart Saver*, Heart and Stroke Foundation of Canada, 1994.

64. *First Aid - The Vital Link,* Canadian Red Cross Society, Mosby Lifeline, Toronto, 1994.

Fitness

65. P. Lyons and D. Burgard, *Great Shape: The First Fitness Guide for Large Women*, Bull Publishing, 1990.

66. B. Anderson, *Stretching,* Shelter Publications, 1992.

67. *Active Living*, Human Kinetics Canada, 475 Devonshire Road, Suite 100, Windsor, Ontario N8Y 2L5, 1-800-465-7301 or E-mail: HKCAN@MNSI.NET

68. *Fitness Walking*, Human Kinetics Canada, 475 Devonshire Road, Suite 100, Windsor, Ontario N8Y 2L5, 1-800-465-7301 or E-mail: HKCAN@MNSI.NET

69. *Full Life Fitness*, Human Kinetics Canada, 475 Devonshire Road, Suite 100, Windsor, Ontario N8Y 2L5, 1-800-465-7301 or E-mail: HKCAN@MNSI.NET

Grief

70. M. Colgrove, H. Bloomfield, P. McWilliams, *How to Survive the Loss of a Love*, Bantam, 1991.

71. E. Neeld, *Seven Choices,* Crown, 1990.

72. H. S. Schiff, *Living Through Mourning: Finding Comfort and Hope When a Loved One Has Died,* Penguin Books, 1986.

Health Law

73. L. E. Rozovsky, *Canadian Patient's Book of Rights: A Consumer's Guide to Canadian Health Law* (rev. ed.), Doubleday Canada, 1994.

Heart Disease

74. D. Ornish, MD, *Dean Ornish's Program for Reversing Heart Disease,* Ballantine, 1992.

75. G. C. Griffin, MD, and W. P. Castelli, MD, *How to Lower Your Cholesterol and Beat the Odds of a Heart Attack,* Fisher Books, 1993.

Also see Resource 49.

Incontinence

76. K. L. Burgio, MD, K. L. Pearce, and A. J. Lucco, MD, *Staying Dry: A Practical Guide to Bladder Control,* The Johns Hopkins University Press, 1991.

Inflammatory Bowel Disease

77. F. G. Saibil, *Crohn's Disease and Ulcerative Colitis*, Key Porter Books, 1996.

Irritable Bowel Syndrome

78. E. F. Shimberg, *Relief From Irritable Bowel Syndrome*, Ballantine, 1988.

Medical Consumerism

79. D. W. Kemper et al., *It's About Time: Better Health Care in a Minute (or two),* Healthwise, 1993. Available from Healthwise, P.O. Box 1989, Boise, ID 83701, (208) 345-1161.

80. C. Inlander and E. Weiner, *Take This Book to the Hospital With You,* Pantheon, 1991.

81. D. R. Stutz, MD, and B. Feder, *The Savvy Patient: How to Be an Active Participant in Your Medical Care,* Consumers Union, 1990.

82. R. Arnot, MD, *The Best Medicine,* Addison-Wesley, 1992.

Medical Tests

83. P. Shtasel, *Medical Tests and Diagnostic Procedures,* Harper/Collins, 1991.

Men's Health

84. *Staying Strong For Men Over 50: A Common Sense Health Guide.* Available from AARP, Stock no. D15296, 601 E Street NW, Washington, DC 20049.

85. Y. Taguchi, *Private Parts: An Owner's Guide to the Male Anatomy* (2nd ed.), McClelland & Stewart, 1996.

Mental Self-Care

86. D. Burns, MD, *The Feeling Good Handbook,* New American Library/Dutton, 1990.

87. D. Sobel, MD, and R. Ornstein, *The Healing Brain,* Simon and Schuster, 1988.

88. S. Locke, MD, and D. Colligan, *The Healer Within,* New American Library, 1986.

89. D. Goleman and J. Gurin, eds., *Mind/Body Medicine: How to Use Your Mind for Better Health*, Consumer Reports Books, 1993.

90. G. Emery and J. Campbell, *Rapid Relief From Emotional Distress,* Fawcett, 1987.

91. F. I. Kass, *The Columbia University College of Physicians and Surgeons Complete Guide to Mental and Emotional Health,* Henry Holt & Company, 1992.

92. B. Moyers, *Healing and the Mind,* Doubleday, 1993.

93. P. Zimbardo, *Shyness,* Addison-Wesley, 1990.

Migraine

94. V. South, *Migraine*, Key Porter Books, 1994.

Neck Pain

95. R. McKenzie, *Treat Your Own Neck,* Spinal Publications Ltd. (New Zealand), 1989.

96. M. E. Allen and B. Pothier, *Take Charge of Your Neck: The Exercise Guide to a Healthy Neck,* University Back Centre, Simon Fraser University, 1990.

Nutrition

97. *Health Counts,* John Wiley and Sons, Inc., 1991.

98. E. R. Blonz, *The Really Simple, No-Nonsense Nutrition Guide,* Conari Press, 1993.

99. *Canada's Food Guide to Healthy Eating*, Health and Welfare Canada, 1992.

100. *Nutrient Value of Some Common Foods,* Health and Welfare Canada, 1988.

101. R. Swartz, *The Enlightened Eater*, MacMillan Canada, 1994.

Pain

102. E. M. Catalan, *The Chronic Pain Workbook: A Step-by-Step Guide for Coping With and Overcoming Your Pain,* New Harbinger Publications, 1987.

103. M. Caudill, *Managing Chronic Pain: A Behavioral Medicine Program Workbook*, Guilford, 1994.

Pregnancy

104. A. Eisenberg, *What to Expect When You're Expecting,* Workman Publishing, 1991.

105. P. Simkin et al., *Pregnancy, Childbirth, and the Newborn,* Meadowbrook, 1991.

106. C. Marshall, *From Here to Maternity: Your Guide for the Nine-Month Journey Toward Motherhood,* Prima Publishing, 1991.

107. *Baby's Best Chance: Parent's Handbook of Pregnancy and Baby Care* (4th ed.), British Columbia Ministry of Health, MacMillan Canada, 1994.

Self-Help Groups

108. B. White, E. Madara, *The Self-Help Sourcebook: Finding and Forming Mutual Aid Self-Help Groups*, Saint Clares-Riverside Medical Center, 1992, (201) 625-7101.

Sleep Problems

109. P. Hauri and S. Linde, *No More Sleepless Nights*, John Wiley & Sons, 1990.

110. J. P. Caldwell, *Sleep*, Key Porter Books, 1995.

Smoking

111. T. Ferguson, MD, *The No-Nag, No-Guilt, Do-It-Your-Own-Way Guide to Quitting Smoking,* Putnam, 1988.

112. *Fifty Most Often Asked Questions About Smoking and Health and the Answers* (2nd ed.), Canadian Cancer Society, 1991.

Stress

113. H. Benson and M. Klipper, *The Relaxation Response,* Avon Books, 1976.

114. M. Davis et al., *The Relaxation and Stress Reduction Workbook*, New Harbinger, 1994.

Stroke

115. *Canadian Family Guide to Stroke*, Heart and Stroke Foundation of Canada, 1996.

Surgery

116. C. B. Inlander, *Good Operations, Bad Operations: The People's Medical Society's Guide to Surgery*, Penguin Books, 1993.

117. A. Gross et al. *Surgery: A Complete Guide for Patients and Their Families*, Harper Collins, 1989.

118. J. R. Macho and G. Cable, *Everyone's Guide to Outpatient Surgery*, Somerville House Publishing, 1996.

Vision Problems

119. B. M. Kwitko and M. Ross, *Eyes*, Key Porter Books, 1996.

Wellness

120. H. Benson and E. M. Stuart, *The Wellness Book*, Carol Publishing Group, 1992.

121. D. W. Kemper et al., *Pathways: A Success Guide for a Healthy Life*, Healthwise, 1985. Available from Healthwise, P.O. Box 1989, Boise, ID 83701, (208) 345-1161.

122. R. Ornstein and D. Sobel, MD, *Healthy Pleasures*, Addison-Wesley, 1989.

Women's Health

123. The Boston Women's Health Collective, *The New Our Bodies, Ourselves, A Book By and For Women*, 1992.

124. K. Johnson, *Trusting Ourselves: The Complete Guide to Emotional Well-Being for Women*, Atlantic Monthly Press, 1991.

125. B. D. Shephard, MD, and C. A. Shephard, *The Complete Guide to Women's Health*, Penguin Books, 1990.

126. *The Womanly Art of Breast-Feeding*, La Leche League International, New American Library, 1991.

127. K. Huggins, *Nursing Mother's Companion*, Harvard Common Press, 1991.

128. *Canadian Medical Association, Woman's Body: A Manual for Life*, Reader's Digest Association (Canada), 1995.

129. C. DeMarco, *Take Charge of Your Body: A Woman's Health Advisor* (6th ed.), Well Woman Press, 1995.

130. J. Engel, *The Complete Breast Book*, Key Porter Books, 1996.

131. M. Stoppard, *The Breast Book: An Essential Guide to Breast Care and Breast Health for Women of All Ages*, Random House Canada, 1996.

Also see entries under Pregnancy.

Index

Cluster headaches, 125
Cold pack, 287
    guidelines for use, 77
Cold sores, 234
    increased frequency of, 201
Colds, 92
    dizziness and, 113
    medications for, 292
Colic, 155
Complete Canadian Health Guide, The, 303
Complete Guide to Medical Symptoms, 302
Complete Guide to Mental and Emotional
    Health, The, 307
Complete Guide to Women's Health, The,
    309
Compulsive overeating, 279
Concussion, see Head injuries, 221
Condoms, 196, 197
    sexually transmitted diseases and, 199
      201, 235
Confusion, following head injury, 222
    shock and, 231
Conjunctivitis (pinkeye), 109
Constipation, 32
    hemorrhoids and, 37
    irritable bowel syndrome and, 39
    laxatives, 295
    with abdominal pain and fever, 31
Consumer, medical, see Medical consumer
Contact dermatitis, 141
Contact lenses, 111
Contraception
    also see birth control
    morning-after, 197
Contraceptive Technology, 196
Contusions (bruises), 211
Convulsions, with fever, 163
COPD (chronic obstructive pulmonary
    disease), 89
Coricidin, 294
Corns and calluses, 147
Correctol, 295
Cortate, 291
Coughs, 94
    chart, 95
    dry and hacking, 95
    expectorants, 293
    productive, 88, 89, 94, 98
    suppressants, 293
    with asthma, 85
    with bronchitis, 89
    with chest pain, 89, 98
    with croup, 157

    with pneumonia, 98
    with tuberculosis, 107
CPR, 204
    ready reference chart, 207
Crabs, see Lice, 141
Cradle cap, 156
Cramps
    leg, 70
    menstrual, 179
    muscle, 70
    stomach, 35, 39, 42
    with exercise, 70
Cross-training, and sports injuries, 74
Croup, 157
Cuts, 217
Cystitis, 181

D

Dairy foods, 261, 262
Dance of Anger, The, 303
Dandruff, 132
Dean Ornish's Program for Reversing
    Heart Disease, 306
Decision-making, shared, 6
Decongestants, 292
    high blood pressure and, 26
DEET, 139, 145
Dehydration, 33
    rehydration drinks for, 34, 159
Dental care
    brushing, 236
    disclosing tablets, 237
    flossing, 237
    fluoride, 236, 239
    sealants, 239
Dental problems, also see Mouth
    problems
    accidental tooth loss, 208
    bleeding gums, 236
    chart, 234
    gingivitis, 236
    gum (periodontal) disease, 236
    jaw pain, 239
    plaque, 235
    TMJ (temporomandibular joint)
      syndrome, 239
    tooth decay, 235
    toothache, 239
Dental visits, frequency of, 239
Depo-provera, 196, 197
Depression, 276
Dermatitis, see Rashes, 141
Dermatologist, 11

G

Gallbladder, 91

Gallbladder disease, hormone therapy and, 178

Gas, with abdominal bloating, 39

Gastric ulcers, 43

Gastroenteritis, see Stomach flu, 41
  in children, 159

Gastroenterologist, 11

Gastroesophageal reflux disease (GERD), 36

Gastrolyte, 35

Gatorade, and dehydration, 34

Gelusil, 37, 44

Generic drugs, 295, 299

Genital herpes, 198

Genitals
  female, 171
  male, 188
  sores on, 198, 199
  warts, 198

GERD (gastroesophageal reflux disease), 36

Geriatrician, 11

German measles, see Rubella, 19, 165

Giardia lamblia, 35

Gingivitis, 236

Glands, swollen, 102, 104

Glaucoma, 119

Golfer's elbow, 66

Gonorrhea, 199

Good Operations, Bad Operations, 306

Good Samaritan law, 204

Gout, 62

Great Shape, 306

Grief, 278

Growing pains, 70

Growing Wiser, 306

Guilt, 285

Gum (periodontal) disease, 236

Gums, bleeding, 236

Gun safety, 282

Gynecological health, 171

Gynaecologist, 11

H

Haemophilus influenzae type b (Hib)
  vaccine, 19

Hair problems
  bald spots, 140
  cradle cap, 156
  dandruff, 132

lice, 141
  ringworm, 135

Hammertoes, 63

Hands, pain or tingling in, 59, 67, 266

Hardiness, 285

Hay fever, 81

HBV (hepatitis B virus), 19, 199

HDL cholesterol, 258, 259
  hormone therapy and, 178

Headache
  caffeine and, 125
  emergency symptoms, 121
  encephalitis and, 96
  facial pain and, 99
  fever, stiff neck, vomiting, and, 96
  head injuries and, 221
  in children, 123
  jaw pain and, 125, 239
  meningitis and, 96
  migraines, 124
  neck pain and, 57, 125
  one-sided, 124, 125
  possible causes (chart), 122
  recurring, 124, 125
  sudden and severe, 122, 124, 125
  tension, 125
  tracking symptoms, 126
  vascular, 124
  vomiting and, 96, 124
  with one-sided weakness, numbness, speech or vision problems, 121
  with visual disturbances, 121, 124

Head & Shoulders, 132

Head injuries, 221

Head lice, 141

Healer Within, The, 307

Healing and the Mind, 307

Healing Brain, The, 307

Health fraud, 13

Health habits, 17

Healthwise Approach, 1

Healthwise for Life, 305

Healthwise Handbook, 302

Healthy Pleasures, 309

Hearing loss, 114, 116, 117

Hearing test, frequency of, 21

Heart attack, 91
  aspirin and, 296
  see CPR, 204

Heartbeat, also see Pulse
  pounding or racing, 224, 275
  rapid or irregular, 91

N